C000113531

A Swag
of Memories

A Swag
of Memories

Brian Taylor

HACHETTE AUSTRALIA

HACHETTE AUSTRALIA

Previously published by Thomas C Lothian Pty Ltd
as *The Brumby Mare* (2005) and *The Moonlight Stallion* (2006)

Published in Australia and New Zealand in 2008
by Hachette Australia
(An imprint of Hachette Livre Australia Pty Limited)
Level 17, 207 Kent Street, Sydney NSW 2000
Website: www.hachette.com.au

Copyright © Brian Taylor 2008

This book is copyright. Apart from any fair dealing
for the purposes of private study, research, criticism
or review permitted under the *Copyright Act 1968*,
no part may be stored or reproduced by any process
without prior written permission. Enquiries should
be made to the publisher.

Cataloguing–in–Publication data is available
from the National Library of Australia

ISBN 978 0 7336 2325 7

Cover design by Grant Slaney, MAPG
Cover photo courtesy of Newspix
Author photo courtesy of the *Toowoomba Chronicle*
Originally designed and typeset by Jan Schmoeger, Designpoint
Digital production by Bookhouse, Sydney
Printed in Australia by Griffin Press, Adelaide

Hachette Livre Australia's policy is to use papers
that are natural, renewable and recyclable products
and made from wood grown in sustainable forests.
The logging and manufacturing processes are expected
to conform to the environmental regulations
of the country of origin.

CONTENTS

Author's Note

I read from an old diary, from times gone by, that was always in my swag:

> *With a plate of curried corned beef, a fistful of damper and a quart pot of black tea, I sat on the tailboard of the wagonette to enjoy my evening meal in the cattle camp.*
>
> *It is not only the beauty of the sun's effect on the towering crimsoned storm clouds that makes a sunset so glorious out in the bush. It is also the pulse effect of the animal and insect noises and the birds settling down for the night. These all blended together to make the last of the sun's shafted rays so becoming ...*

It is to my friends of the stock camps of long ago that I would like to dedicate these memories. Some are mentioned in these pages, many are not. Many have rolled their swags for the last time, and many have gone to their place in the dreamtime. I am grateful to them all for the knowledge I discovered under their wings, and I would be grateful to know that they reckoned I had come up to scratch.

It has been a great journey for me, to carry my swag and go bush through the years of recollection. I went back into those rollicking wagonette and packhourse mustering camps, and relived the wonderful friendships with bush mates along the way. The life we knew never really left us; it was who we became.

I hope this book will give others less fortunate the opportunity to absorb something of the Australian bush spirit as we knew it. Times have changed, but the bees still buzz in the bloodwood trees and the yellow bellies still bite in the Barcoo River, and most everything is within one's grasp, if you but try. This is a spiritual country; nurture it and be rewarded.

I would like to thank Carene and daughter Tania for preparing the manuscript, and sons Martin and Glenn for their wonderful support. I am grateful to Jean Dunn, my original editor, and especially to Matthew Kelly of Hachette Livre Australia, my publisher.

Brian Taylor

I WOULDN'T BE A BUSHMAN

I wouldn't be a bushman
If I didn't write some lines
And tell about the yarns we spun
And our hell-raisin' times;
The nights we spent together
Around the campfire glow
Quoting verse and singing songs
That only bushmen know.
Abou how we stuck together
When the going was getting rough
And showed those dashing pikers
That we were just as tough.
And how Jim Doolan saed the day
When his mare went crashing down;
He got her to her feet once more
And wheeled the lead around.
I cherish now the memories
Of those cool, still moonlight nights
As I sat for hours by waterholes
That reflected a thousand lights.
The munch of hobbled horses
And the song of the Condamine bells,
The thoughts that used to linger then
No words can quite retell.

BRIAN TAYLOR

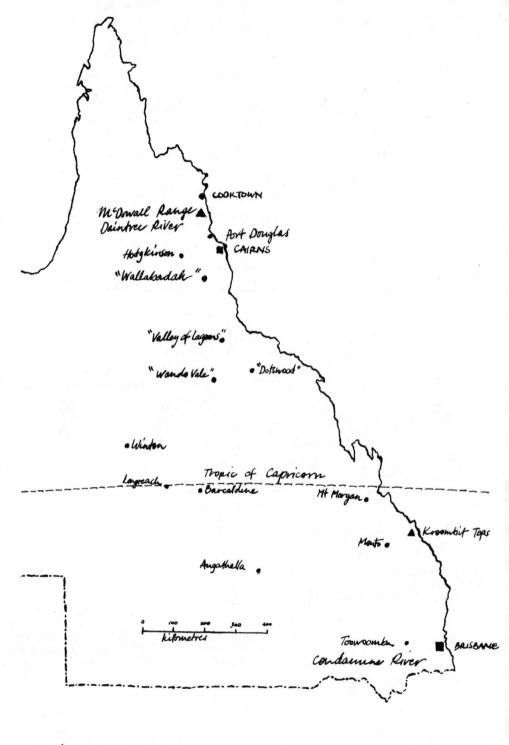

COOKTOWN

McDowall Range
Daintree River

Port Douglas
CAIRNS

Hodgkinson

"Wallabadah"

"Valley of Lagoons"

"Wando Vale"

"Dotswood"

Winton

Tropic of Capricorn

Longreach
Barcaldine

Mt Morgan

Kroombit Tops

Monto

Augathella

0   100   200   300   400
kilometres

Toowoomba   BRISBANE
Condamine River

Sketch map of Queensland

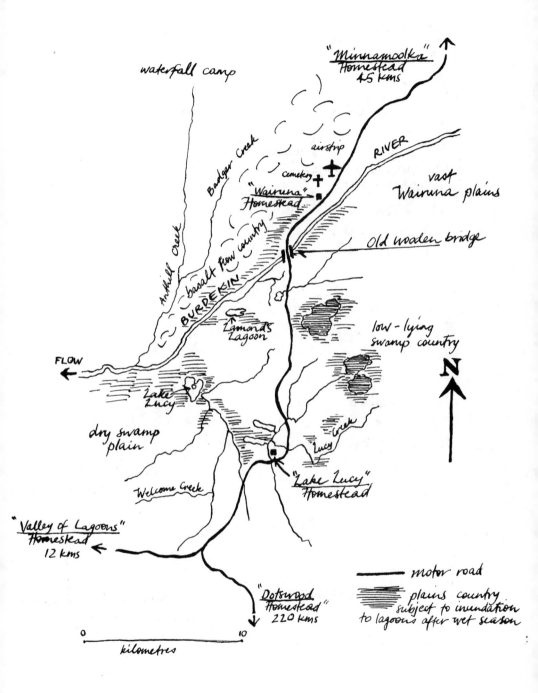

"Minnamoolka"
Homestead
45 kms

waterfall camp

Badger Creek

airstrip

RIVER

cemetery

vast
Wairuna plains

"Wairuna"
Homestead

Old wooden bridge

Anthill Creek

basalt flow country

BURDEKIN

Lamond's
Lagoon

low - lying
swamp country

FLOW

N

Lake
Lucy

Lucy Creek

dry swamp
plain

"Lake Lucy"
Homestead

Welcome Creek

"Valley of Lagoons"
Homestead
12 kms

———— motor road

————— plains country
subject to inundation
to lagoons after wet season

"Dotswood
Homestead"
220 kms

0   10

kilometres

Sketch map of the lower Valley of Lagoons

The Morning

Daylight dawning sends shadows sprawling;
Dewdrops dripping from green leaves hanging;
Jewelled webs waiting, in soft breeze wavering;
Shafted sunlight through dark shadows searching.
Solitary wedgetail, on corkscrew winding,
Higher and higher to watch over all.

The milkers are wending their way from the valley,
Nostrils are steaming with clover-sweet breath.
At the howl of the dingo, the mare's to her feet;
With plaited legs flailing, the foal's to her flank.
In an instant the geese by the creek are a gaggle,
And the curlew gives its last eerie night call.
The ravenous crow in jerky flight follows,
His echoing call of contempt, for all.

BRIAN TAYLOR

UP THE CREEK

'The Daintree' is a belt of coastal country in Far North Queensland that encompasses the Thornton Range and the McDowall Range catchments, and is thought to have been in perpetual rainforest for the last one hundred and ten, or so, million years. Thankfully, it is still in existence, having escaped the volcanic activity that wiped out many Queensland rainforests twenty million years ago and affected some areas on the Atherton Tablelands even more recently. The tremendous tropical rainfall over this large catchment area to the west feeds the Daintree River, which can be placid and beautiful, though at odd times I have heard it described in non-biblical terms.

My link with the Daintree began many years ago when I ventured up the river, to be stopped at the last gate on the gravel road by a sign which read, 'The Bible says we should forgive those that trespass—we don't, we shoot the Bastards'. How could I refuse such an invitation? There was no need of a further sign, 'Beware of the Dog'. Too late—a pack of ankle biters, and upwards to bull tossers, tore out to meet me as I neared the humble dwelling on foot.

This was my first encounter with the Harlow family. They were reputed to be a no-nonsense bunch, brought up 'pullin' tits' on the Daintree, so to speak, in the early days of dairying. The boys had learnt to pull their weight when their father went to war, so earning their place as landholders in this unforgiving but picturesque valley in the rainforest.

I later left in great spirits, with a mass of knowledge, but knowing full well that I had yet to come to terms with brother Bob—who lived over the other side of the McDowalls with his Aboriginal wife and a tidy bunch of 'billy lids'.

It was Bob who had first walked a crawler tractor across the tops, through the scrub to China Camp, paving the way for the power-line construction and a track later to be affectionately called the Creb track. It was literally a track, which twisted and turned over the contours in an agonising fashion, crossing gullies and onward through the scrub. Its four-wheel-drive wheel ruts had become like tram tracks for vehicles to follow. When dry, it was a pleasure trip; in the Wet, a quagmire, frightening and threatening beyond belief.

The first time I did meet Bob, he came out of his old home among the trees down on the Bloomfield River, all bristly, like a boar out from under a log with the dogs onto him. Have you at any price! Well, Bob's price was, has been and always will be, Fair and Square. That's all it has cost me for one of life's great friendships.

Over the years since, Bob and his wife, Vivien, have, until her untimely death, been so kind to me, helping me to under-stand the Daintree country, learn its ways, its history, and its significance to the Aboriginal people. What I learned from them complemented the knowledge passed on to me by another great bushman of the area, Charlie McCracken of Miallo.

I had become interested in the ancient walking track of the Wugil Wugil people, from Bloomfield River to the Daintree. This had become the overlanding stock route from Laura across to China Camp, Salt Box pocket, up to Gold Hill, across to Devil Devil creek, down the Zig Zag track, and onto the Whomp-hole and Baird's Crossing of the Daintree River. This was a tremendous undertaking for those early drovers.

The first time Bob and I did the journey, we too did it on foot, the track having long been overgrown since the cessation of the droving days. We left China Camp at a reasonably early hour and climbed right across the ranges and down the Zig Zag onto the rocky upper reaches of the Daintree River, arriving just on dusk. From then on, we went down the river in the dark, having to negotiate crossings. The only light we had was Bob's cigarette lighter and the evening star overhead, whose brilliance contrasted with the blackness of the river and the unfriendly rainforest that grew practically to the water's edge.

Passing broken water, it was hard to hear myself think. The air was fresh and heavy, and all the sounds seemed magnified. In long stretches of still water, the river just seemed to sit there, black and ominous in the starlight. The reflection of the stars on that soulless water could, to the faint-hearted, have been a host of crocodile eyes. Awesome, frightening yet beautiful, we were walking through the most pristine, organic place on earth.

Suddenly, there was a frightening crash. A wild pig, disturbed from its fossicking in the forest floor debris, bolted for somewhere within the forest, which was blacker than the night itself.

On edge now, we listened for the sound of crocodiles that Bob knew lurked in these big pools of the upper reaches. The constant sounds of frogs, insects and birds of the night, all the while signifying that all was normal, gave us a false sense of security. When there is silence in the night, there is trouble.

Near a pile of pulpy forest debris, left high and dry by an abated flood, Bob stopped, listening intently for some considerable time. Then, removing the ever-present cigarette, he got down on his haunches and eyeballed the water, to pick up any movement at all in the starlight. The moments seemed too intense even to breathe.

Then, he said, 'When I say go, you better hit your straps quick smart, and follow me. Don't stop till you hit the other side. I can't pick anything up in the water, but you never can tell. These crinkly-backed bastards are pretty cunnin'!'

And so, on down the river we went. Hearts were trumps and my eyesight become better by the minute! All the aches and pains from such an arduous day's travel, the persistent stinging of the nettles and the uncomfortable drag of wet clothes, were shed like a lizard's skin after the first crossing, and I became truly alert.

We made it down to Bob's brother's place at ten that night, where a great mate, Mike Gale, had lit a fire on the riverbed gravel and been patiently waiting for some considerable time. We arrived just as he was about to put out the fire and move on, having decided that we must indeed have fallen on bad times. In a huddle around that little fire, we shared a drink and shivered in our boots as we recalled, undramatically, the day's travel—glad to be alive; glad it was all behind us.

It was then that Bob told me of the horse taken up near Landers Creek, and a bullock at Baird's Crossing quite recently. 'Never crossed my mind to mention it before', or so he said. 'I always thought we'd be here well and truly before dark. Bet that's why the missus would have gone on down to the township. She musta reckoned, by now, we bin took, for sure. Aboriginals are funny like that, you know.'

The next time we came through over the same track from Bob's cattle property on the Ten Mile, we had saddle-horses and a packhorse plant, and it was an equally exciting adventure. I knew where I was going in the now familiar country, thoroughly enjoying the magnificence of the rainforest, the bird life and the magic little creeks that came out of story-book hideaways in the undergrowth. There were also magnificent views of this playground, which has been home to a people for longer than anyone will ever know.

We left the horses hobbled at the bottom of the Zig Zag, covered the packs and saddles with a tarp and came on down the 'goat track' onto the Daintree proper—then by boat, ultimately in the dark, for the eight miles down to the Daintree township. The river had a fair run on, and it was dirty, rolling and powerful. We had precious little freeboard to play with. The bloke we had in the bow with a spotlight took great delight in spotting crocodiles on the banks and was paying little heed to guiding us away from broken and surging water, which may have caused us to founder.

~

The first trip I did through the Daintree from the river crossing and over the top to China Camp in a four-wheel drive was also a heart stopper. There was one other bloke in the cab with me, and four at the back, on the deck of the flat top. I had learned to treat this country with respect, with no room ever to rip, tear and bust, for its sheer massiveness and isolation were daunting.

The dropaways on some of the inclines could put the fear of Hell into the uninitiated. I recall getting to the bottom of a bad slope in a hurry; it was too steep for the gears to hold us back, and to brake was out of the question. My cab companion, a grown man, was huddled in fear under the dash of the Toyota. Meanwhile, the ones on the back had bailed out on the way down to avoid an imminent disaster, or so they reckoned.

I have been over the Daintree and ridden the Track on horseback three times since, and feel completely comfortable with the country's many moods.

~

They really do happen—these phone calls requesting help in the middle of the night. It was my mate Gordon, who was employed by the federal Aboriginal Affairs department.

'You want a job?'

'Yeh, where is it?'

'Somewhere in the Daintree National Park.'

'When do I start?'

'Now!'

'What have we got?'

'Two no-hopers from Canberra; government blokes, who went in south of Ayton on the Bloomfield road, to come out on the Creb track, in a four-wheel drive, but no gear and, my guess, no brains either. They are well overdue and the weather has turned bad. I have got the old Land Rover and half a set of wheel chains down on the coast. You wanna be in it?'

'Yeah, boots and all. I'll meet you at Kuranda, quick as I can get there; be a couple of hours.'

The Land Rover was an old campaigner. It was neither weather-proof, warm, dry or comfortable, but it was practical, and it was all we had.

It was well into the night when we eventually headed out on the recovery, and we became aware of the sudden cold, as some tropical weather changes can become in the North. It would not be long before the first hurdle, our confrontation with the Daintree River. At this time of the night there was no one to contact as to the condition of the water. Gordon had said that the deteriorating weather had been mostly over the McDowalls during the day, which may not have affected the river yet.

The tiny Daintree township appeared, came and went in our watery headlights. It sat in the valley, lifeless, snuffed, like a drowned hurricane lamp in the gloom. Jim Bouleaux, one-time manager and top cattleman of Bluff Downs, would be sleeping the sleep of contentment in his house behind the humble Daintree store.

Rumbling across the wooden decked bridge and gravel road along the Daintree River flat, we became instantly aware that the rain had come over the McDowalls. It was not too long before the characteristic hum of the motor gave way to the screeching of perished wipers and the squelch and rattle of the rough gravel road. I could feel Gordon's anxiety building in the dark cabin. The damp cold was creeping up through my body, and I shivered at the thought of that ominous first river crossing. Would we be able to pick the shallows if it had already begun to rise? The river at the crossing is wide, and the gravel beds shifted from time to time.

We continued on up the valley and stopped at the first real vantage point where, on a clear day, old man crocs could often be seen basking, or just waiting! Nothing could have been further from my mind right then; all I wanted to see, if possible in the strong torchlight, was the river flow. The visibility was bad, but I couldn't hear the river, so at least that was a good sign.

'Too bad,' said Gordon, 'can't pick it in the beam. It's hard to tell from here, but we'll soon know.'

Off the road now, through the last gate and down across the grass terraces to the water's edge. Through the smeared windscreen I could make out the expanse of slow-moving black water, which seemed to swallow up our meagre headlights.

'Doesn't look too bad just yet, mate. What do you think?'

Overcoming a hollowness in my stomach I replied, 'Well, Gordon, I can see the sandbank below the gate over there, so if we take it easy and stay on the edge of the ripple-line all the way across; can you pick it? Where the water lifts up over the shallows.'

'OK, here we go, there's no stopping us now.'

It is always a concern, in deep water, when the water rolls away off the top of the mudguards and comes rushing in under the doors. The headlights reflecting off the bow wave play tricks with vision, and it's a relief to get safely to the other side and have all the water drain out of the vehicle.

Gordon hesitantly announced, 'That was pretty dumb mate—water that high—we should have taken the fan belt off.'

'Yeah,' I said, 'we're on a tough call, better sharpen ourselves up.'

Now the bush, and what lay ahead for us. What of the two blokes who were the cause of all this concern? Were they dead, alive, drowning, frozen, starving, or just hopelessly lost? We had to proceed cautiously and do our best in a practical manner, keeping within the bounds of safety. The McDowall Ranges are no place for heroes, least of all fools. We put the chains on the front tyres, and away we went.

The seldom-used track presented a curtain of foliage. On inclines the debris-littered clay track was running water in the wheel ruts, and the rain was intensifying with every incline we traversed. A shower of mud would occasionally come up over the front leaving us temporarily blinded and the windscreen wipers begging for mercy until the squally rain gave the vehicle a brisk sluicing. Progress was slow as we rocked, slid, waddled and ground our way forward. The old Land Rover seemed to know we were on a mission.

The dimly lit cabin was cold, and I could see Gordon's white knuckles bared as he wrestled with the steering wheel on yet another muddy incline. Hard to the left, pause—hard to the right, as he endeavoured to use the chains on the outside of the tyres to get the maximum grip. We zigzagged and practically clawed our way up the slopes.

I thumbed the torch on to check the time and, on looking across at my friend, I was shocked to see that his face was almost pallid and gaunt looking. He had been doing such a good job, it never occurred to me to take a turn. On the changeover I ran around the front of the vehicle, got a boot full of mud, and realised the temperature was plummeting.

'Pity the poor buggers out in this tonight.'

On and on through the night; dawn, and we were still going. A couple of major creek crossings to go, then over the top and down the dreaded red slope. If these city slickers were alive, not lost but just bogged down, we reckoned that would be where we'd find them. The red slope was renowned for its treachery when wet; nearly four hundred yards of volcanic red clay; it was like a slide going down, and almost impossible on the homeward run in the wet.

'There is a vehicle down there, mate', said Gordon. 'It's off the track and up along the creek a bit. Grey Toyota. Can't see any smoke—poor buggers must be frozen by now.'

As we pulled up alongside I noticed the remains of a small campfire on a mound in front of the vehicle. Half-burned sodden wood and an empty cigarette packet; it had been a pathetic effort that would not have survived even on a fine day.

The two would-be bushmen extracted themselves from the vehicle, almost in slow motion, like expressionless green tree-frogs climbing out of a pot of cold porridge—limbs quite dysfunctional and a ghost-like expression on their faces. They stood huddled before us in the rain, shoulders wrapped in sodden cotton bedsheets. 'This time of the year in the far north you don't need blankets', they'd been told down south.

'Are we glad to see you blokes'—shiver! shiver! shake! shake!—'got any smokes?'

'Nope—neither of us smoke.'

'Got any rum, you blokes?'

'Nope—neither of us drink.'

'Just our bloody luck—anyway can you get us out of here?'

'Too right mate, that's what we're here for.'

There was nothing wrong with their vehicle, a hired near-new four-wheel drive. It had plenty of rubber on the tyres, but no chains. They obviously had no experience in bush driving. Going by the tracks left at the base of the red slope, the vehicle had been driven without engaging four-wheel drive!

Gordon and I decided we would take one vehicle at a time up the slope. It seemed the best option, as we didn't have a winch. Then once on top we should be able to take a vehicle each all the way out. The old Land Rover had made it quite clear on the journey in that it could climb trees, swim and do anything but quack. However, on the way out it would have to pull out all stops. The prospect of failure was a possibility, but not an option.

The persistent rain had cleared the muddy slurry from our wheel tracks and, with everybody helping, we somehow managed to get the Land Rover to the top, but not without incident. Near the top the old track used to swing to the left, and it was here that there was a momentary falter.

The vehicle paused in its progress, lost all traction, and I feared that it would begin a backward slide. I ran to the front, jumped on the bumper bar, hanging on to whatever was available, and stacked out to the left like a trapeze on a yacht, putting all my weight over the wheel. Gordon seized the moment and swung the steering wheel; the chains on the outside of the front wheels grabbed and, in an instant, with a roar and a crash and a shower of mud and a 'Yackai!', we disappeared over the top and into the scrub.

That could have been dangerous but, as it turned out, loss of skin and wait-a-while rips around the ears were compensated by the elation of our success. The trudge back down the bare ominous slope was done in good spirits, and the taste of success spurred us on for the next assault.

The government blokes were amazed at how their machine went up that hill in a rush, with a shower of mud, to the first bend. It was beginning to go sideways and off over the side.

So, stopping with the hand brake on and the motor idling, I began to cut and lay bladey grass, bush trash and bark to the wheel tracks. When the others caught up, we continued this program of corduroying the way ahead.

Things were looking up. You could see by the look of the two woebegone refugees that they were taking on a new stature. They were filthy, wringing wet, mud spattered and dripping fatigue. The discarded town shoes were in the vehicle, and they had just discovered their toes, as they gripped and clawed their way about their tasks with boyish enthusiasm. Maybe for the first time in their adult lives they were doing something basic, and with dedicated purpose. Pitching in, in order to survive, I saw two men grow up before my eyes.

Everybody was a team now. There was no way this vehicle was not going to the top, and all the way out of there. Just for a moment, as I took a deep breath before easing the clutch out again, a vision flashed to mind of that magnificent double Victoria Cross winner, Charles Upham. In the middle of the night, in a pitched battle in the western desert of Egypt, he had actually convinced enemy soldiers to help push his truck out of a sand bog, then driven his men to safety.

I had a great team backing me up as well, and away we went. Heaving and shoving, busting their boilers, clawing and grappling with every resource their bodies could muster, keeping that machine going upwards; they earned every yard. We faltered a couple of times. The vehicle slewed sideways and threatened to give up the ghost, go backwards, or slide over the side and do a 'sugar-doodle' all the way to the bottom. Then the tyres would grab traction and go again, onward and upward and, finally, over the top.

There were no cheers; no time for looking about or enjoying the view. We were physically drained. Chests were heaving and burning from exhaustion. Now our bodies were becoming instantly cold and it was obvious we would have to get out of there and head for Alcatraz as quick as possible. Nothing would stop us now, not even a couple of 'humpty doo' crossings of creeks that would by now be well and truly swollen.

'You OK taking the Rover up in front by yourself?', I asked Gordon.

'Sweet as a nut, mate—sweet as a nut.'

He meant it too, as he had a great deal of affection for that old green good-as-gold machine. Its reliability gave him all the confidence in the world. It was the first time I had seen him smile all day.

Alcatraz, as it was known, had been a base camp for the electricity pylon gangs. The compound was surrounded by high steel-mesh netting and barbed wire. It had never looked a hospitable place, on the little flat clearing in the scrub, not far from the Daintree River crossing. And the area was now overgrown with bladey grass and bracken fern. However, it was a welcome sight that day, in the rain, wind and drifting fog.

Inside the neglected camp building, it was dreary, dark and damp. Miscellaneous belongings were scattered everywhere, and it looked like a boar's nest after a bad night. I could smell the vermin, and it was a haven for 'kooty skeeters' and 'wonga bugs'. At least the roof didn't leak. I was able to get a fire going in the old wood range, out of bits and pieces. Then we drew a couple of old steel camp-stretchers closer to the fire and sat around sharing what tucker we had, and waiting for the billy to boil.

'You got anything else in that tucker box, mate?' asked one of the government men. 'I'm as hungry as Hell!'

Words could not describe the look on their faces when I stood a bottle of Bundy and four pannikins on the table, then punctuated that with a packet of tobacco and some Tally-Ho papers.

'Well, look at that, he's even got the makin's!'

I have been called many names in jest over the years, but what came next was beyond all those.

'If I hadn't kept that up my sleeve, we wouldn't have got you fellows to move. You certainly did pull your weight, and now it's payback—Cheers!'

As we sat around the gathering fire, sipping our enamel pannikins of rum, the world began to come alive again. Relaxed now, I was going back over the events of the day, and what a day it had been. Then I fastened on to the vision of Gordon, stripped and testing out the depth of a crossing on our way in.

The creek was coming out of a tight gully. It was swollen, and rolling through in a consistent wave motion. Gordon went across and followed the same path back again. Blue with cold, arms outstretched for balance and striding ever so slowly and purposefully, he was a picture of dedication and focus. One stride, then another, left and then right, swinging his arms in unison. It was a gallant effort, and as he was about to leave the water I was shocked at his appearance. His body looked like a gaunt and twisted carcass and his face was distorted in a grimace against the driving rain. I had barracked him in and home again, knowing full well that it would be my turn next.

He came from the creek and stood looking at me through the open window, and he could not speak. Frozen, he looked from me back to the water and then back to me. Looking at my mate in the darkness of that musty camp, I saw the flame's flickering reflection across his now cheerful face.

'Gordon; Gordon G–R–I–M–W–A–D–E!'

'Yeh,' he said, 'that's my name—so?'

'GRIM WADE', I said. 'Sure was mate, sure was. Cheers all round.'

'I'll drink to that, mate,' said Gordon, 'I'll drink to that!'

THE WATERMELONS

Steam billowed across the platform, momentarily dampening down the dust, as the big engine pulled itself to a stop at Charters Towers, on the North Western Queensland line, in 1942. It might just as well have been 1914, as very little had changed in this goldmining and military town. A wave of khaki-clad soldiers disembarked, creating a tremendous noise with hustle and bustle, kitbags and gear.

Soon everyone was gone, save a lonely bedraggled vagrant, a ten-year-old boy whose sole possessions were under his floppy hat and locked in an old Gladstone bag he clutched to his chest with both hands. Around his neck he wore a kind of dog tag, attached to a loop of butcher's string. The Salvation Army captain walked quietly up to the lad, put one gentle hand on his shoulder, and with the other turned the piece of cardboard over. A message read, 'Please deliver me to Old Sandy Station. My name is Alan.'

The homestead where Alan's new Aunt Steff and Uncle Jebb lived was a big old wooden building, a haven of contentment. Inside, it was all smoky, stained and polished, with high ceilings. Outside, on the verandah, it was cool compared to the heat haze that danced across the dry grass of the plains. In the shade hung a canvas waterbag, plump, with the sweat dripping off it. An old enamel pint pot hung from the rolled-leather bung. Alan didn't take the pint pot down, he just stood spellbound at the view and held the cool canvas to his cheek.

The bushland seemed to extend forever. Not a tall building or a train in sight; just the mournful repetitive cry of a crow as it passed overhead in jerky flight. Like the crow, Alan was aching from loneliness. Sure, Dad had to go to the war, but Mum never had to go and die.

Under the canopy of affection, freely given by his new family, whose own two sons had gone to war, the young battler was able to shed his grief and come to terms with the tragedy in his life, and gradually grow within himself. He soon settled into the security and routine of rural life. It was great in the country school, with kids to play with, 'miggles' at little lunch and cricket at big lunch, then home again to the station in the afternoon.

As the weeks and months went by, the chores became easier and even more interesting. Alan got to know all the farmyard animals, even the chooks, by name; and he liked the smell of the woodheap, where he used to sit on a stump and eat his afternoon smoko of a fistful of Aunt Steff's brownie cake and a pannikin of homegrown milk. That was before he set to with Uncle Jebb's old Kelly axe to cut the wood, which fired the huge wood range in the kitchen.

Going to bed at night in this big old house was something of an adventure for Alan. He had a full tummy, a nice springy bed and a room all on his own; not like the orphanage. In the quietness he lay awake thinking about his father; and memories of his mother, too, flooded his mind. These would come to life in the middle of the night, as Aunt Steff shuffled slowly along the hallway in her sloppy slippers on some mysterious mission, carrying a candle before her. The light of the candle cast a giant shadow up the walls, which seemed to linger in the darkness even when she had passed his doorway.

Huddy, one of Alan's schoolmates, had invited him to stay for a week in the Christmas holidays. This was to be a most joyous occasion, with plans to go exploring in the old gold-diggings down along the Burdekin River. There was a rickety shack down behind Huddy's place, which looked out over the river. Unpainted, with a verandah round one side and a rusty witch's hat roof, there was a tin chimney on one end which always had smoke curling out of it. It was a quiet place most of the time, but sometimes in the evening the sounds of a button accordion came from the verandah and would float out over the water, hang in the wood smoke for a while, then fade away into the night.

All the kids at school said there was a retired Swedish miner living there, a huge cranky old coot who grew the best watermelons. He never sold them, but gave them to the sisters up at the convent. Alan and Huddy were about to change that, as a matter of necessity.

The kids at the railway end of town made the deal: watermelons, or Uncle Jebb's chooks were to get the chop! That would have broken Aunt Steff's heart. There was no other option. The two happy-go-luckies were forced into minor crime, which they would otherwise not have considered.

It was out of the question to sneak up past the shack in the dark, carrying the watermelons in a sack. The ambitious plan adopted was to roll the melons down the bank and into the river at night, and pick them up downstream at the weir in the morning.

In the morning, due to a fresh, the water was lapping the top of the weir. Luckily, the boys had taken two pairs of grown-ups' woollen socks, to grip the concrete of the weir as they walked out across the river to collect the bobbing watermelons. Hooking those slippery melons out of the river, carrying them across to the bank one at a time, keeping balance and trying not to fall down the six-foot drop on the downstream side of the weir, was a tedious and frightening task.

By the time there were nearly a dozen plump melons safely on the bank, in a heap under a quinine bush, the fear and the butterflies had gone and things were falling into place. The sun was well up, so the bullies from the railway gang should be down any time.

'There they are now', said Huddy, as he lifted the last melon from the river. Twenty yards away on the bank, it was not watermelons but a Waterloo about to take place.

With a quick eye and consideration for his friend, Huddy suddenly dropped the melon over the weir and, with a fistful of Alan's shirt, dived into the river. Huddled against the weir wall, frantically treading water, Alan gasped, 'What the hell was that all about?'

Huddy had his eyes fixed on the bank, the melons, the kids, and the huge frame of a man. He had his arms outstretched, with big hands open like turkey's tails, blocking any retreat for the boys—who were standing mute, with a melon under each arm, mouths open and truly in a state of shock. Over the gurgle of the water draining out of their ears and the lapping of the water against the weir, Alan and Huddy heard the big man demand, 'Vot ist your farder's names?'

There was hardly a ripple as the two lads slid under the water to swim as far and as fast as their bursting lungs would allow. As they scrambled with some difficulty up the distant bank, they realised for the first time how they had been hindered in their escape by the dragging drapery of Uncle Jebb's woollen socks.

A Class of his Own

Massey Rowan was a cattleman, but then again, he was everybody's man. He could do anything, and he would, for anybody at all. He was tall, neat and tidy, a nice old man whose good manners put him in the chivalrous age of Australian stockmen from 'way back'.

I first met him when the family still had Emu Plains, a holding on the upper reaches of the Bowen River. It was just a stone's throw from Tent Hill, where there was once quite a prolific silver-mining field. The diggings were evident everywhere across the flat that nestled under a conical hill, from which the field got its name. It looked for all the world like there had been a wombats' picnic. On any account, it would have been tough digging, going by the look of the hard rock rubble in the mullock heaps.

What was special to me about Emu Plains Station was the construction of the homestead and the out-buildings. They were all grey, and all timber—constructed with the adze, the axe and the cross-cut saw by men who obviously knew what they were about. That the buildings were still well in use was testimony to their workmanship.

~

It was one of those lovely, rare days in the bush, when there is not a lot to do. Massey and I were sitting under a tree waiting for the billy to boil on dinner camp, at the washpool on the junction of the Bowen and Broken rivers. The country around had been his lifetime stamping ground, and he belonged there.

Sheep had once been washed in this waterhole before shearing, as was the custom; and where the sunlight danced on the broken water as it skipped around the rocks and cascaded into the main pool in an endless melody, Massey had lost a horse to a crocodile. His horsetailer, unknowingly, had put the horse plant in too far up at the crossing and, before he knew it, it was all over.

The wool industry had long gone—spear grass had probably put the death knell on that—and all that was left was the old woolshed scales which, as far as he knew, were still on the verandah outside Ted Cunningham's office over at Strathmore Station. 'Strange they should be there,' said Massey, 'Ted being a cattleman and all. He suffered sheep and sheepmen lightly.'

The billy had boiled and Massey tossed in a bit of tea, let it roll over a few times, then took it off to set. As he gave the billy a couple of taps with a stick, to settle the tea leaves, a broad grin crossed his face. He had obviously remembered something that stirred his fancy. Still looking into the billy of tea, he told this story.

~

'Tell you one time,' Ted says to me, 'I'd like to go and have a look at some country that is offering. We'll take the plane; won't be away more than a day or so. Would you like to come? I'd like you to if you could get away.'

Anyway, away we went. Ted used to fly that plane on the seat of his pants, like sitting on a stockyard rail. Nothing fancy; nothing bothered him at all.

Well, eventually we came over this property in question, and Ted did a pass over the homestead. He knew where the strip was, but was a little concerned as it had quite a heavy covering of dry grass even though the owners had given notice that it had been grazed recently. He made one more swing around the strip area and, having made up his mind which way to come into it (as there was no wind-sock showing), announced: 'Hang onto your hat!'—which seemed appropriate safety instructions, even if not encouraging. Then, in we went.

Well, we went up that landing strip like a drover's dog under a swag cover on a cold night. Could not see a thing for grass. How the plane never stood on her nose is beyond me. Somehow, he managed to keep her going.

Then, what do you reckon. Through the blur of the prop I could see that there were sheep going Hell west and crooked, parting in leaps and bounds. We went straight through the lot of 'em at a gallop. They must have been having a midday camp in the middle of the strip, and dead set asleep. Didn't they liven up their footwork quick smart! Definitely a sign of an early spring, I'd say.

As we slowed down, Ted spun the plane around, short of the fence, and as the dust settled I got my wind back. I looked across the cockpit at old Ted, who was as calm and cool as a cucumber, and he said to me, 'Quickest bloody shearing they've ever had!'

~

After dinner camp we went south, over to the other catchment and on to the Bowen River proper. Between the hill where the old woolshed used to be and Exmoor Station there was, in a timbered gully, a natural stone bridge, or so Massey had said. As a matter of interest we were off to inspect it.

Sure enough, there it was; quite a span really. It was a great shelf of rock that had been left high and dry, spanning the gully while the creek, which only flowed during the wet season anyway, continued to erode the gully deeper and deeper each year.

'This used to be a feature in the garden where my wife grew up', Massey said. 'Her and her folks used to live in a slab house, just over there on the knob. It was known as Quilban. Beautiful it was in those days.'

As we walked quietly together now, across this natural bridge, I had a vision of the past and of a beautiful bush garden, and I felt that Massey held the hand of his bride and also heard the voices of yesterday.

'The old man died and the house was burned down eventually, in a bushfire', Massey continued. 'Sad part was that the old lady's ring was lost here and had never been found. Some years later I got one of them metal detectors and came back in here looking. Blow me down if I didn't up and find it. When I scratched the dirt away under the detector and picked up the ring, all these memories of my courting days, the trips out here in the sulky and the great meals the old lady cooked over the open fire came back to me. They were battlers; we all were in those days.'

'Looking down at what I had found, I could not believe my eyes. I felt like I was holding my youth in the palm of my hand. As I rolled that ring around a few times in my hand, it was just like I was fumbling a set of harness reins. It made my fingers tingle for a while there.'

'I took the ring to the hospital in town, where the dear old lady was fading fast. Would you know it, that ring snuggled up that wedding finger as her hand lay flat on the white counterpane, like it too had found a long lost friend. I could not describe the look of happiness that slowly grew on that familiar, lovely old face. As she lay there, a glorious peacefulness came over her, just like a magnificent sunset you sometimes see in the bush, at the end of a hard day.'

Massey turned to walk away, off the knoll of the old homestead site, still reverently holding his hat in his hand. It was then I saw one of the jewels of that ring, as the sunlight caught it, making its way down the cheek of his weatherworn face; and then it was gone.

BANJO'S FRIEND

I can see her yet. It was quite late, and the elderly Aboriginal lady I had come to know fondly as Nan Ruby was sitting sidelong in a well-worn chair, backed up to the warmth of her blackened wood range. Her hands were folded, almost reverently, in the lap of her tidy candlewick dressing-gown. The firebox door was open and the flickering firelight played on the black velvet skin of her cheek, highlighting the silvery hair that fetchingly escaped her crocheted bonnet.

She had nodded off, with one foot resting on the chair brace and the other snug on the warm coat of Banjo, her old dingo house-dog, curled up asleep at her feet on the bare floorboards. This big knocked-up, yellow-eyed dog was her shadow, even on cloudy days. I was envious of Banjo, as you could kind of tell that he knew all the stories, and there was no way he would betray a trust.

As hard as I tried, it was impossible for me to come to terms with her life. It was a waste of time assuming anything at all, so it was important to be there at story-telling time. That could be any time. Sometimes, some of her life would unfold when we camped on the upper reaches of the Barambah Creek, on the Petersen Dam, fishing all through the night.

There was always a main campfire glowing, with a billy swinging handy, but Nan always had a little fire of her own close by, down at the water's edge. This was ever so small, just to give her a little comfort and keep those djungerie away. The kerosene lamp, on her other side, gave all the light that was needed for the fishing.

As the night wore on and the water became still, bird-calls would carry across its great expanse, and eventually drown in the distance. The frogs and insects of the night would let everyone know how important they were, until they too finally gave up. Then there was only the occasional call from an owl, the cussing of an enraged possum and the twinkling star's reflection, bouncing off the water, for company. Through those long hours of darkness, when the short, hairy djungerie people of Nan's world kept their distance from the firelight, her stories gave her life a reality for me.

The family had come down from Wave Hill country in the Kimberley, but with the forced relocation of her people for the last three generations she now had family across Queensland, at Yarrabah, Palm Island, Woorabinda and Cherbourg. She too had been taken from her mother and deprived of her language and culture. From her early teens she was submitted to the Christian dormitory existence. But her Aboriginality never left her; she never forgot the kindness of her people, the magnificence of the corroboree, the firmness of the social discipline and the great purpose of her people, living in harmony with natural law.

Morning would come and, as the light lifted across the lake and the early shift of air came towards the land, the water would ripple and the first flight of black ducks would rise, heading for the feeding grounds. There would be a honking as pelicans exchanged acknowledgments, followed by the ritual of bill clapping. Stiff from inaction, we would make secure the chaff bag in the water containing our live catch, and head up the bank to the main campfire.

I should have been there hours ago, but never wanted to break the spell of the long night vigil, Nan's story-telling, the song and the prayer-like dirge, broken intermittently with 'Hey, lookout, Yakkai, got you, big ole fella!' Then back we'd go to a state of semi-slumber, curled up on the ground, one eye shut and the other focused on the little white paper atop the flimsy stick held vertical in the ground, across the top of which, passing through a slit end, was our line. Any action on the line and we could see the movement of the paper, even on the darkest night.

A billy of tea around the stoked-up campfire was the beginning of a new day. The night-time was dead and gone, and now the djungerie would be down at the water's edge warming their bodies by our little fishing fires that had been stoked and left burning, especially for them.

Sometimes those night-times would be happy times, sometimes terribly sad. On one occasion I found her high up on a ridge near some caves in a state of despair, crying such a mournful cry of absolute sadness. I could not bear my grief at the sight and came away unnoticed. The pain of suffering through her lifetime was mostly hidden by her sheer will to portray kindness and goodness in all things.

I found it hard to understand that there was never a conflict in her life between the love she had for the true Christian teachings, and the great scars which stockwhips had left on her back. Little wonder the corroboree 'Yarraman, Yarraman! Guddigidah, Guddigidah!' persists, for it portrays the movement and sound of a galloping horse.

Over the years I had come by various Aboriginal artefacts, two of which are authentic corroboree headdresses. 'Don't you ever let them "oogee" out of your sight, Brian', said Nan. 'They real you know, they special.' They are made from paperbark and garlanded with twisted fur and hair string from top to bottom of the conical shape, painted with brown and white ochre in vertical stripes and topped with the plumed brisket feathers of an emu.

~

One morning at home there was an absence of the customary twittering of the willy wagtail that frequented our garden. I went outside and there he was, most forlorn, sitting on a twig, no busyness about him at all. I mentioned to my wife how strange the bird looked, then it came to me: something had happened to Nan. Sure enough, we got word that the old lady had just died.

At that time there was a drought on, and we were going downhill fast. We cut our stock numbers down and couldn't plant any crops as there was no soil moisture. The wind had blown away the soil we had cultivated the previous year. There was no hope anywhere in sight. In the previous twelve months we had had only seven inches of rain. Trees we had planted were under stress, and even mature trees in the forest were shedding their leaves and dying. Some jovial people suggested I don my corroboree hat and do a rain dance.

In a state of desperation I took the suggestion seriously and confided in the memory of dear Nan Ruby. Armed with a corroboree hat and with the kindness and sincerity of that wonderful lady sitting easily in my heart, I sat down on a log and seriously contemplated the drought. A process of inner questioning and of enlightenment concerning the well-being of all living things is the best way I can explain what took place in my mind. That old Aboriginal woman led me by the hand through her spiritual land of the soil, the plants, the trees and the birds. Of course she had taken me there before, but only a little at a time.

Now, every living thing was screaming out for rain. The drought had a stranglehold, wringing the life out of the tiniest creatures. The spirit of the land was in jeopardy. On my journey of awareness I seemingly visited all those plants, and the tiniest microbes in the soil, and the roots of the trees on their fruitless search for moisture in the arid soil.

Some time later I managed to walk away in a somewhat dazed and exhausted state, and put the corroboree hat back on its pedestal in the house. To clear my head, I decided to go for a walk about the property.

Struth, it was dry. I stopped my wandering and leant on a crusty fence post, noticing that the lichen had dried, died and curled like the end of a Bedouin's boot. I stood there with an empty feeling and looked to the sky in faint hope of something, anything at all. There was nothing; just the blue overhead, the haze in the distance and the godforsaken parched earth. Not even a Molly hawk; just a swirl of dust as a willy-willy went past, grabbing a roley-poley bush and tossing it into the air in a dizzy spiral.

Pondering on the good seasons, it did seem a long time since I had seen swallows, those gallant little warriors, herding flying ants. At storm time, ants would sprout wings and go skywards in countless numbers to migrate and form new colonies. They relied on strong air currents to assist in their migration, and rain-softened earth enabled them to build quickly their new habitat. This was feast time for swallows who, in their great numbers, would muster the masses of flying ants and then feed on the wing, in the same manner as do sharks on bait fish in the sea. The closer the weather was to rain, the heavier the atmosphere became, bringing the swarming ant masses closer to the ground. Thus the magnificence of this natural phenomenon became even more apparent.

Leaning on the post, I mused over times past when I had witnessed other battles of the sky. From a wisp of white (known to the Aboriginals as 'jombok', from 'jumbuck'), seemingly organic storm clouds grew like mushrooms, then became dark, ominous, cold and frightening. Great thunderous claps belted around inside these billowing tinderboxes, then the most amazing drench bucketed down, seemingly from nowhere.

How long now had it been since my shirt stuck to my shoulders and the water ran down my face? Brand spankin' new water, straight from the heavens, you could say. The only consolation that came to mind was that as each day wore on, we were one day closer to a rainy day.

A movement on my hand drew my attention. I looked down at a most inquiring wingless ant. He was busy negotiating his way around, in the faint hope of finding something useful. I rolled my hand over to accommodate his busy search. We each had nothing to offer the other; only life itself prevailed, and I guess that to the ant at least was hope.

Then it happened. Away to the west I saw a flight of pelicans. 'Funny,' I thought, 'this is not pelican country.' As I watched, they lost height and came down towards me. There were eleven birds, and they looked so graceful, holding their wedge formation and gliding so effortlessly. They came down even lower, and to my amazement did two complete circles right above me. They were so close that I could almost see the expression in their eyes; then they flew away eastwards.

As I watched them go, something grabbed me, and I said 'Thank you old Aboriginal lady for talking to me.' I now knew that in eleven days' time we would get two inches of rain. Just for a joke I told a near neighbour that I could get him two inches of rain in eleven days and that it would cost him a thousand dollars an inch. Sure enough, in eleven days we got the rain, two inches of it, and not predicted by the meteorological people I might add!

In the early morning following that deluge, I went down to the creek, just for a look. I heard a horse tread on the sodden ground, and saw a horse and rider coming down along the track. The sun was rising through the trees behind him, presenting a classical golden silhouette. Even before he pulled up, I knew who it was; it was the 'old fellow'.

Reg Williams sat his horse like no other that I have known. Confidence, balance and patience; his tranquillity was emphasised by the collected stance of his grey Arabian. We exchanged greetings, and then he said he was heading for the stock route, where he reckoned some of his cattle would have gone, as all his fences at the creek crossings had been washed away. We discussed the wonderful rain, and I couldn't resist telling him that I had contributed in a way. My old friend sat and listened attentively to my story.

This great old bushman had known Ruby Bond, and over the years at Rockybar Station he had employed members of her family as stockmen. The glint of his stock-knife handle, held in place on a well-plaited belt, reminded me that he and Ruby—arm in arm, shoulder to shoulder—had once cut a cake at a multicultural dinner with that same stock-knife.

That was a special day, 8 August, the day I remember as the anniversary of the death of Albert Namatjira.

When I had concluded, Reg just sat his horse, fingering the reins and nodding his old brown hat in acknowledgment; I would like to think in approval.

Since that time, whenever or wherever I see pelicans, there is an opportunity for me to say, 'Hello. Hello Nana Pelican.'

THE BRUMBY MARE

No sooner had I juddered my way across the wooden-railed cattle grid, off the Garnet road and into Wallabadah Station, than I knew something extraordinary was happening out on the flat.

It was still early morning, and the ironbark trees were casting long shadows towards me on the powdery vehicle tracks. Over to the east, a great cloud of dust-filtered yellow light hovered over a big mob of Brahman cattle. Driving quite slowly so as not to disturb the mob, I went as close as I could, then stopped the motor to observe exactly what was going on.

There were about 150 head of breeders in the mob. They had formed in a circle, which was about fifty to sixty yards across, all facing inwards and watching most attentively. As the dust cleared a little, momentarily, I saw two calves in gladiatorial combat; they were all of three days old, as the umbilical cords had not completely withered. One was a magnificent white, the other an apricot and yellow with a white head. They were all ears, legs and loose skin, but hearts as big as bulls.

First head to head, then head to flank, they charged, bunted, hooked instinctively as though they had horns of massive proportions. Dust that had accumulated on this traditional cattle camp was being dug up and hurled into the air with rare abandon, quite out of proportion to the size of those doing the stirring and digging.

Reaching a state of temporary exhaustion, there was mutual consent to a pause, just for a breather, then it was on again. The spectators gave approval with the occasional nodding of heads and swishing of tails, but the attention to combat was constant. There was definitely no intervention, for this was real grown-up cattle business, being decided and sorted out. That's where I left them, with the cloud of dust and sunlit haze rising even higher.

This property was only fifty square miles, but a great place to do a couple of days' mustering, run the cattle through the yards or shoe the horses up for the work ahead. It's always a pleasure to poke about a good piece of country, well run, with good stock. Besides, this place has quite a historical background, in that many of the clearings have sizeable stone fireplaces, remnants of military encampments for soldiers heading to the New Guinea campaign.

That day I had three horses to shoe, then it would be out to the shady verandah to drink tea and tangle with some of Merle's magnificent scones, listen to the daughters playing duet piano, or watch them ride the station pet, a full-grown silver Brahman bull, about the lawn. The same bull, with bucking straps and a Condamine bell swinging under his belly, was unrideable at the Mareeba rodeo.

It was a good feeling to be made welcome and to know that I was contributing towards the running of this lovely place. I took pride in shoeing the station horses, one of which we had taken down to Ted Cunningham's Bowen River races and rodeo weekend. The mare had won the seven furlongs and the mile in good company. To ride the same mare through the timber, to the lead of a running mob, was exhilarating to say the least.

After smoko Mick said, 'Right, I want to take you up to the yards and show you some brumbies that those fellows from the Millstream ran on the weekend, from the scrub and timber country up on the goat track stock route.'

The horses were in the wire yard, and hanging in one corner. They did not like where they were and wanted to go home. They stood stock still, not wanting to be seen, these hijacked refugees from the wild. I walked around them and they trotted close-shouldered into the timber post-and-rail forcing yard. Mick opened the gate under the capped rail and they went through and up towards the pound yard.

They milled around, not knowing which way to turn, and then wheeled in the dusty yard and faced us where we had climbed the seven-foot high panel of rails to get a good look at them. They knew they were boxed in, throwing their heads and manes, snorting and swishing their tails as they suffered the agony of confinement.

In quiet tones we discussed whether or not they would make saddle-horses.

'Tell you what, Mick,' I said, 'I'll run that big roan mare up into the pound, if you could fetch a rope for us. I'll put a rope on her and see how she handles.'

'Right,' said Mick, 'she might have just a touch of clumper, but I agree she's worth a look.'

I went around and opened the yard up. Being the leader, she was first through. I blocked up and shut the gate. Walking back to open the other gate for the rest to go back to the wire yard, I was thinking about the mare and how she moved. She was in great condition, legs looked clean, no scars anywhere to speak of, no brands or saddle marks. She was a brumby for sure. She'd look all right settled down, with her tail pulled and her feet tidied up.

When I got back to the yard, Mick was still on his way from the saddle shed with some gear, so there was time to have a real good look. She had great stature, front legs well spaced out, held her head well, lively clean face, good eye—not too much white showing, and watching me most intently. It is very important, and an advantage, to handle an unbroken horse that has good focus.

'Hang on to the halter, Mick. I won't be needing that just yet. Just give us the rope.'

With that, I slid through the rails real gently, so as not to cause alarm, coiled the rope comfortably in my left hand and stood still for a considerable time. The yard being quite small, the mare stood her ground in questioning anticipation. From then on, it would be a two-way search for a communion on safe ground.

She shook her head, stamped a front foot and pawed the sand in defiance. After several repeats of this, and no reaction from me, she appeared to relax a little. I commenced to talk gently and quietly, maintaining the same tone of voice. Just when I thought I was getting through, she began to behave restlessly again, throwing the sand.

'Phew!' I thought, 'this is tight.' Never had I felt such tension. I could have thrown the rope and handled her that way, but I just had a feeling that I was going to put my hand on this horse.

In spite of being a brumby, she had a special stamp about her that deserved a different approach to the 'catch 'em and tie 'em up' method. The words of a long-passed ringer mate, one of my early tutors, rekindled in my ear: 'You've got 'bout as much chance as a celluloid cat chasing an asbestos rat in Hell.'

'No worries Jim, old mate, I've got this one in hand', I said to myself, as I inched ever so positively, yet cautiously, towards the mare.

The concentration was so intense; it all came down to indirect eye contact and smell, I guess. Closer, ever closer, I became aware of the salt sweaty smell of her body. I inched one boot slowly and softly through the sand, followed a little later by the other, hardly bending at the knees and all the while keeping the balls of my feet as firm as possible on the ground for balance—or, should the need arise, to leap in any direction to avoid being run over.

The mare's face was about four feet away now, and ever so slowly I began lifting my right arm. With the elbow akimbo and fingers half clenched, the back of my hand was slowly rising up to the level of her muzzle.

The mare's hot breath hit me in the face as she snorted and shook her head. Pausing momentarily before gaining contact again, I noticed that her ears were forward, which was quite an encouraging sign. Not so my hand, which was now beginning to shake, ever so little. I was becoming increasingly aware that my whole being was reacting to the tension building in that yard; I was entering a realm I had never been in before. So close now, I could feel the power of this horse.

My continued sweet-talking in monotone seemed to help me as well. With hand held close, not too far away from her nostril so she could smell me, I noticed the hair on her flaring nostrils was quivering and damp. The mare was either going to succumb and accept my touch, or leap straight at me. I was in no position to avoid the charge, and I remembered a horse I had faced that had reared up and belted me about the head and upper body with its front feet.

It was no man's land now. We were at each end of a very short fuse. Two against one, for it seemed that there was both my intense psychological mind game and my body reacting with quavering voice to the demands of progress and keeping control. She was watching, watching my every movement, sensing, yet seeming now to accept her predicament, while displaying a proud, defiant eye. I would have liked to cup my hand over her eye and soothe her down. Time, time, just a little more time.

When I felt the time was right, I moved the back of my fingers ever so close to the cheek under the eye, feeling the hair. Then ever so slowly, I opened my hand a little so as to gently rub her face. Unblinking for long periods of time, all of me was now aching from rigidity. Soon it would be all over. Finally I would put my hand comfortingly on her face and soothe away all her fears, then perhaps walk away for a time.

'This is it!' With such softness as I was able, I breathed out ever so gently, anticipating a wonderful conclusion, and put my hand down, lightly until firmly, onto her face, and looked into the gallant eyes of this yet untamed brumby mare. With a great spasm and a couple of throws of her head, she dropped dead at my feet.

I cannot begin to describe the horror, nor the pain of anguish I experienced then, as I stood back from what had just happened. Pathetic, soul-destroying grief. In disbelief I looped the rope over my shoulder and climbed the rails, took out the makings and tried to roll a smoke. That was a waste of time, as my hands were shaking so much that the tobacco just fell away. Never have I been so disturbed at an animal dying as I was about that beautiful brumby mare. Unbelievable.

Mick joined me on the top rail. 'Well, you never gonna handle any more fresh horses for me, young fellow!'

I turned and looked along the rail at Mick. He was sitting there, with the heels of his riding boots hooked on the second-top rail, his chin on his chest, his shoulders rounded and his battered hat pulled down over his eyes. With one hand on the rail and the other running slowly over the stubble on his face, he looked a very sad man. He was trying to find the right words, one friend to another.

Mick slowly lifted his gaze towards me, from the catastrophe that was sprawled grotesquely on the sand in front of us, and our eyes met. In that instant, I recognised something in my friend I had never seen before. There was a mutual acknowledgment, and then he said, 'Let's go and have a drinka-tea.'

BOXING DAY

I was at home among the tussock and the shingle, sitting high on the side of the mountains and looking far away into the haze. It was cold and wintry and blowing as always, but I was warm in my woollen clothes, sou'wester oilskin hat and a special jerkin Mother had made from a corn sack and edged with bright wool in blanket stitch.

I was revelling in my accomplishment of having just pulled a full-grown rabbit out of a burrow. Holding him firmly, but kindly, in my lap, I knew that even though I admired him, I would probably take him home for a rabbit stew. This was the way we lived; we ate what we could catch.

I was known as Porky, the bush kid, and I knew heaps of things! I could tickle trout, shoot a shanghai, and I understood why hens laid eggs shaped the way they were and that cocker-bullies turned into frogs.

The shearers, fencers, trappers and even the blacksmith who came to our property always had time to teach me something. But, I could never fathom why they drank their tea from their saucers when Mother gave them smoko. Yep! For a nine-year-old yunk, I reckoned I was going OK. BUT, I had never seen the sea. It was still a mystery to me. The sea was out there, further than I could see from up here on the mountains, but my time would come, Mr Rabbit. And it did, as soon as the summer season shearing was over.

The only time I'd been on a real picnic with other people was the once a year Sunday School picnic. They were pretty good as a rule; the tucker was always great, and I usually won lots of lollies in the running races, especially the three-legged race with Jennifer Joy. But today was different. All the families from the valley had gone out to the coast for a real slap-up Boxing Day picnic.

As soon as the hour was up after lunch, I planned to bolt over the sandhills to the sea. Lying in the shade and looking up through the branches of the trees, I noticed there was no movement above.

'Struth!' I thought, 'If there's no wind, maybe there won't be any waves, and the sea will be as flat as old Harold Sage's duckpond.'

But I could smell the salt in the air, so there must be some drift, for the smell to come inland. The other kids were flat out too. I wondered what they were thinking. 'If they think they're going to race me to the seashore, they'll have another think coming.'

The adults were sitting on the ground in a comfortable circle, chatting and laughing, the ladies with their nice billowing summer-print dresses on, and their faces shaded by broad-brimmed summery kind of hats.

The men mustn't have had as much lunch as me, because they still had room for a few more beers. Uncle Kelly was fixing up the crayfish pot he said he was going to drop off some rocks later on. Two of the eldest children were tying knots in the drop-pot rope, and then sitting back on the rope to make sure the knots were set fast. In no hurry and with not a worry in the world, I closed my eyes and listened to the drum of the bees in the flowering trees. The giggling girls worried me none; I'd just have a little rest until the hour was up.

I woke with a start, and looked to where I had poked a twig into the ground to gauge its shadow shift onto what I reckoned would be an hour. 'Good enough', I thought. Rolling over and over a few times to where my mother sat, I looked up into her shaded blue eyes and tugged the hem of her dress, to draw her attention but not to interrupt the conversation. Mother looked at her watch, then at the other sleeping children, and said 'OK!'

I was on my feet and running, and on passing the edge of the trees and onto the first sand dune, I faintly heard Mother call, 'Don't forget, be careful of the …' I missed the rest.

Running down the other side was hard going, but I managed to hold my pace over the shallow sand and through the tufty grass and scrubby bushes up the next slope. I reached the top, but could not see the sea. Without faltering, I raced on down into the hollow, arms flailing. A ground bird flew off its nest, almost from underfoot, momentarily putting me off stride. The sand seemed much firmer now, and hot, as there was less cover. There was no scrub to offer any shade to the dunes. My legs were tiring and my chest was burning.

On reaching the top of the last dune in a half-crouched position, a strong, fresh draught of air hit me in the face and a massive blue expanse opened in front of me. But nothing had time to register before my world dropped out from under me. I went down the sandy cliff face in such an odds and evens, heads and tails fashion that when finally stopped, I could not move. I desperately tried to sit up to find out where I had come from and, most of all, where I had arrived.

But I couldn't figure out which way was up because I was so disoriented, giddy and shaken.

I rolled over and saw that I was in the shade of a huge sand dune, and that sand dislodged in the whirlwind descent was still cascading down on top of me. Through this shower I turned to face the beach. The sound, the colour, the smell, the freshness and the size of it were frightening. The sea, the ocean; I had finally arrived.

The waves were all connected, right along the water's edge. As soon as one came thundering in, another was ready to take its place. I sat spellbound, just looking and getting my breath back with huge gasps of that lovely air. As I ran my tongue over dry lips, I could taste the salt. Everything was amazing! Everything was new!

'What made the waves? Who made the wind?', I asked myself out loud.

A huge black and white gull, gliding almost motionless overhead in the sea breeze, looked down on the new arrival and seemed to answer the question: 'Haven't a clue, clue, clue'. Then it dipped one wing, caught the breeze, glided effortlessly towards the sea, lifted over the first swell and was gone.

I scrambled to my feet, palmed my pants on either side and, with a flurry of sand, was off again. Galloping, jumping, waving my arms and yelling with joy, 'I've got a clue, clue, clue', I headed for the water.

I pulled up as a wave rolled threateningly up the beach, then, as it receded, walked out into the shallows. I enjoyed watching my toes shimmering with the movement of the water, and felt the sand move under the soles of my feet. A small shell rolled past, but as I leaned over to pluck it from the water I heard a building roar ahead. A mountain of blue water was getting ready to tackle me head on. I forgot the shell, turned, and bolted up the beach.

The way north along the beach was hindered by the out-pouring of a river, so I decided to wander southwards and in search of anything that could be found. It was my day, and already it had passed all expectations.

My fear of the waves disappeared. The air was quite still, and the crashing of the rollers was like a friendly taunt. I could run easier on the damp sand and soon discovered a game. Each wave rose a little higher, as the water rushed up the steep beach then ebbed like milk froth in the cheese factory vat. I charged through the froth at a half gallop, with knees raising high to make the biggest possible splash as I went.

So engrossed had I become that I barely noticed two women standing together on the sand. As the sound of a crashing wave died away, I heard screams that pulled me up dead in my tracks. Turning to look, the next wave bowled me clean over, rolling me up the beach like long hair wrapped around curling tongs.

With eyes smarting from the salt, and sand and water dribbling from my clothes onto bare feet, I shuffled un-comfortably to where the ladies were now running on the spot, with hands clenched to their breasts. They both pointed out to sea, yelling, 'Help! Help! Save them! Save them! Please little man can you help?'

I looked out beyond the breakers and could see two, no three, black spots floating in the water. One turned, and I realised that the spots were people and that they were in real trouble. 'Struth! They're drowning!'

I looked at the ladies again, and for the first time noticed that they were dark skinned. They looked down at me and then, together, we all looked out to sea. I looked at the waves and felt sick. No way was I going in there past the friendly froth. I remembered Mother's call, 'Don't forget, be careful of the ...'

'I'm just Porky, the bush kid! Whadam I s'posed to do!' I said to myself.

Then, from somewhere, I gained inspiration. I held up my open hand in front of the ladies as a gesture of absolute confidence, and said that I'd go quick-smart to get some help. Racing back along the beach, there was a transparent haze away ahead. It was hot, and I knew I had a long way to go. I ran till my feet hurt. I ran till my legs ached and my tummy burned. Not to give in; not to give in. Never had I been infused with such a compulsion. 'Mother would never catch me with the straw broom at this pace', I humoured myself, as I strove ever harder to keep going.

I spotted where I had come down off the sandhills, onto the beach. Wheeling around that sandhill, and going down the other side, my stride miraculously seemed to lengthen. Another couple of dunes and I'd be there. But down the last one, my vision faded with exhaustion. I bounced off a tree and fell, like a rag doll, at the edge of the clearing.

Rolling over, I managed to get to my hands and knees, and gasped, 'Take the rope off the craypot and head south along the beach; some people are drowning. And hurry, please hurry.' Those words cleared the camp.

The rescue was well under way by the time I got back. There were people everywhere. Two dark men were sitting down on the sand with rugs around their shoulders. Another was lying out flat, while Aunty Margaret pumped his chest, trying to get him to breathe. Some ladies were crying, while others were still looking out to sea. I asked Jennifer Joy, 'Who's still out there?'

'It's Father,' she said, 'it's Father!' Tears were running down her face, and she was biting her handkerchief. 'Mr Mason, the war hero, got everyone out, but Father has been washed away trying to save them.' Sunday School prayers came to mind, but not a word could I remember. I felt ill.

Then someone gave a shout, 'Look! Look out there. It's Cyril. He's walking! He's walking on the water!'

'Oh dear God!' someone else exclaimed.

'It's the rip, it's the rip!', someone yelled. 'It's built up a sandbar as the tide's gone out and Cyril has landed smack on top of it, way out there.'

There was a flutter as Jennifer Joy threw her handkerchief in the air, and Malcolm Mason made it far out into the tide and helped his old friend safely to shore. Without warning, my legs buckled and I flopped down onto the sand. The sound of the sea suddenly seemed a long way away, and I thought I was going to cry.

When the ladies whispered, 'We think the gentleman is dead, Margaret', then I knew I was going to cry, but I was going to do it alone. I headed back along the beach. When I had gone a safe distance I let my body heave, then gave my dribbling nose a long wipe with my shirt sleeve and pushed the tears from my eyes with the heel of my hands.

I jammed my eyes shut tightly; I did not want to see the world. Suddenly it had become a cruel place. Thrusting thumbs into my pockets, I bounced my pants up and down on elastic braces as I trudged along through the shallows.

Then I remembered the shells I had in my pockets, and felt a few more tears coming as I recalled what fun there had been in gathering them. Stopping, I placed them in the palm of one hand, turning each one over. They were beautiful, and I wondered how the sea creatures had made them so perfectly. But I did not want to keep them, suddenly feeling unworthy. This was their home. As I let each drop singularly to the sand, I said a little-boy prayer.

I would remember those shells. Already I knew I had learned something by giving them back to the sea. A rush of happiness tore away the shroud of uncertainty. I thrust my hands deep into my pockets and turned them out like white sow's ears, to show the waves that not one shell did I keep. Then I turned and bolted for the picnic camp, with pockets flapping.

Sunday Dinner

Splinter cast a long pathetic shadow in the late afternoon as, like a beast of burden, he carried his swag from the plane to the shade of the old mango trees beside the homestead garden. His presence was swallowed up by the hustle and bustle of goods coming off the plane, mail bags, and people going out again on the Bush Pilots service. A long sigh behind him interrupted the progress he was making in rolling a smoke.

'You the new bloke came in on the plane?'

'Yes sir.'

'I'm Charlie, the manager. The Bushies will drop you off at the out-station, where you'll be working in the breeder camp. The head stockman will meet you on the strip. I'll wire him and let him know you're on your way.'

With no time to finish rolling that elusive flake-cut tobacco, Splinter was back on the plane, with his knees up around his ears, someone's dog between his shins and his hands braced against the seat in front. There was still quite a lot of daylight as they flew out, but the shadows on the ground were lengthening and it was nearly dark when they landed on the out-station strip.

Before Splinter had his swag on the back of the battered tray-top ute, the plane, pelting dust and gravel in its slipstream, was airborne and lost from sight through the trees.

'Bushies!' said the head stockman, still holding his hat on. 'Land a plane in a flour drum if you took the lid off! My name's Mac. We better get—this old bus hasn't got any lights and it's a fair step into camp.'

They were off towards the final destination of Splinter's long day and the beginning of what already had promised to be quite an extraordinary experience.

While sitting at the slabbed dining table with all the other young stockmen, who were playing cards in the light of two standard carbide burners, Splinter was taking stock of his new surroundings. Mac had said that the out-station had been a gaol, back in the gold-rush days, which would account for the bars still in the windows and a faded '4' on the huge wooden door leading off from the kitchen.

These stockmen were serious card players. There was hardly a sound as the tins of tobacco they were using for chips changed hands. The room was warm, as the cook still had one more batch of bread to draw from the big blackened wood range. The air was sweet with the smell of tobacco smoke, and comforting sounds of nickering horses came through the porch door, which opened out onto the night-horse paddock.

The conversation turned to food. Splinter, who was still enjoying an almost intoxicating feeling after wrapping himself around the biggest meal of fresh beef-steak and onion gravy he'd ever indulged in, asked the cook, 'What have you got on the menu for tomorrow's Sunday dinner, Alf?'

The cook's reply was simple: 'Burdekin ducks.'

'Great,' said Splinter, 'I'll get up early and take that old .22 from above the mantelpiece, if I may, and go and get the ducks for you myself. I'm a good shot you know.'

The card playing stopped, and all eyes were on Splinter. The players exchanged glances, but not a word was said, and the game continued. Taking this acknowledgment as a gesture of approval, Splinter stood up, stepped back over the bench seat and said, 'OK, that's settled, good night everyone.'

Everyone lifted an empty hand in a farewell gesture, but concentration on the game was not lost on Splinter's departure. From the doorway Splinter spoke to the cook, 'Oh, excuse me Alf, could you please leave some bullets and the rifle on the table for the morning? Thanks mate.'

It was a happy hunter who strode off down through the horse paddock at daylight, well endowed with enthusiasm and an unquenchable appetite for adventure. The horses gave Splinter a questioning look as he climbed through the wires of the fence and commenced to follow the dry creek bed down off the tableland.

As the evening dinner bell rattled out over the bushland, it was a thoroughly dishevelled Splinter who dragged himself through the wires with leaden feet and, with a dangling arm, carried the unfired rifle back up through the horse paddock. He washed and quickly changed his sweaty and dusty clothes, then took his place at the table.

Alf, his day's work done, took the sweat rag from his belt and wiped the trickles from his brow as he leaned up against the door jamb, looking out beyond the dusty yard to the black silhouettes of the ring-barked trees against the gathering dusk He gave a sigh, let the flyscreen door shut, then turned and walked around the huge table, threading his sweat rag back through his belt as he went. He put a firm, kindly hand on Splinter's shoulder.

'Right now is the time in your life to look, listen and learn, for the ways of the bush are strange to those who are strange to the bush.'

'Yeah, thanks Alf, but what the hell's that?' Splinter jabbed a finger at something on his plate which resembled a huge, disfigured sausage roll.

Poor Splinter. He had walked and toiled, sweated and strained in the heat all day. He had done his best to provide a duck or two for his new-found friends' Sunday dinner. He had hoped for something a little better than what confronted him.

All the men at the table turned to face him, and answered his question in unison: 'Burdekin ducks.' It was corned beef rolled in batter and cooked in the camp oven. 'Burdekin ducks, mate, can't beat 'em!'

THE EKKA EXPERIENCE

It was that time of year again, when feathers get ruffled and people in the rural industry thrust their tails into the air with confidence. The blood runs a little faster, the town mocker comes out of the wardrobe for an airing and The Hat gets its annual stiff brush.

Country people, moulded by their surroundings, tend to be placid in nature though firm in commitment and truly inspired by competition. They revel in the challenge of the arena for supremacy. Win, lose or draw—to compete is to belong, and that's about as good as it gets. I refer to the Brisbane Show, the Brisbane Exhibition, or the Brissie Ekka as it is fondly known.

'Country cousins' is not said in jest, as most Brisbane families used to have a family connection of one kind or another, and many still do, somewhere out there in the bush. These relationships are rekindled on an annual basis where possible, when the country cousins come down to town for the Ekka. Some of these relationships go back such a long way, and even those that may have been by adoption, through one circumstance or another, are regarded by subsequent generations as 'true blue'.

My Ekka story—and everyone has one—happened in 1984. I had joined the annual migration, and had rolled my swag and headed to Brissie to stay with my 'town cousins' for the duration. My purpose was to promote two projects of significant national interest. I was deeply involved in the establishment of the Stockman's Hall of Fame (The Hall) and the development of a national horse trail, subsequently to become the Bicentennial National Trail.

It was already ten years since Hugh Sawrey had announced to Gill, his wife, that his intention was to establish a Stockman's Hall of Fame. A lot of work had already been done, and there was still a long way to go. Likewise, the National Trail, a brainchild of that great Australian, R. M. Williams, had also been under serious consideration for ten years. It would be of heritage and recreational value, and its continuous route of 5,200 kilometres along the Great Dividing Range, from Melbourne to Cooktown, was gathering support.

Dan Seymour had done a feasibility ride over the distance, and in 1978 a relay ride involving five hundred horses had covered the distance from top to bottom, to promote the idea. It was now my turn to front up and publicly proclaim my devotion to both these causes.

As far as the National Trail went, I was it. I was the trail co-ordinator, and had been involved for just on ten years. As I had been over the entire proposed route, promoting the trail was a 'spruik' I did with great passion and endless zeal. My entire family were life members of The Hall, so I was doubly committed.

Jane Paul, executive director of The Hall, had organised an amazing presentation of photographs and historical documentation, and the central focus was Hugh Sawrey's painting, *Vision Splendid*. The venue for my week-long sojourn was a corner of the wool pavilion, at the Exhibition grounds. This did not sound to me a very exciting place, but it proved to be quite the contrary.

In the bush, from personal observation, most tracks commence by animals following ant tracks from one place to another. Those millions of tiny feet eventually carve a pad through whatever groundcover lies in their way, to establish their highway of to and fro. Well, it soon became apparent to me that my corner of the wool pavilion was on such a pad, a human one; for they came and went in their thousands, several times a day. The object of their quest was to see the wool combing and carding, and spinning on traditional spinning wheels. Cottage industries used this humbly prepared yarn to make into the most useful and attractive garments.

However, the big draw was the main stage itself. On the hour, every hour, the MC would welcome the throng with great gusto—certainly a centre-ring performance. Then, a child selected at random from the audience would be welcomed onto the stage and, to everyone's delight, bottle-feed a tail-wagging lamb. To country kids, this was as much a home chore as feeding the chooks, but to their city cousins it was nursery rhyme personified.

Then a fanfare would announce the arrival of a stud Merino ram, which would stand and stare at the rabble with disdain. He would show his indifference by chewing his cud a few times, looking blankly left and right with the majesty of an ancient pharaoh, until led away by a uniformed courtier—until his next presentation.

Now the performance really began. That music! That beat! Should it pulse in the body of primitive people, it would send them either into a state of ecstasy—or off to war. There were no rafters in the pavilion to ring, for the construction was totally of steel. The vibration, the penetration, the intrusion into one's very being had to be experienced to be believed.

Then, out they would come, one after the other, defying description—these cats of the catwalk, strutting their stuff in the latest creations of creation. These mechanised frames of seduction, wearing woollen garments which, would you believe, were suitable for almost every occasion. Some were so sheer, they were hardly even there. The last segment was presented by a stable—we'll call them—of Chinese models who had come to present to Australia a collection of garments made from our finest Merino fleece. This presentation was the be-all and end-all.

Early on that first day, I took time out to watch the entire wool promotion presentation. A man who was doing interviews for The Hall with old-timers in the bush said, 'Let's get up close and have a good gander at this mob.' So we did. Towards the finale, when the most exotic oriental creature came down the catwalk, gliding like some liquid stick insect, she froze quite abruptly in a shimmering pose of feminine perfection. In that instant our eyes met. 'Look at me and you'll fry—touch me and you'll die!'

My face flushed with embarrassment. So disturbed had I become that I paid no further attention to the mannequin parade. I became bored with the whole procedure, barely tolerating the noise, and wished they would all go away and leave me in peace to get on with my job. But that was impossible, as I needed this continuous throng to provide me with new faces to talk to. That pulsing music haunted me for the rest of the week.

I settled into a corner of this world, doing my thing with anyone and everyone who showed the slightest interest in my display. Some people showed a glancing interest, and others would stay quite a while. They'd sit on a seat or a bale of hay, and appear enthralled by the stories I had to tell. Some would even wait patiently until the main attraction had run its course, the noise subsided, our hearing returned as near as could be to normal, and our conversation could continue.

Amazingly, it wasn't a one-sided affair. There were bush people who were only too pleased to tell me stories, spend the time of day and show genuine interest. There were also city cousins who had wonderful family history and were glad to share. This all helped me quite considerably, and my confidence in publicly proclaiming the causes grew every day. I felt we were making progress and, if not, lots of friends.

The dreaded hour was approaching again and the building was filling up in readiness for yet another presentation when a little stooped lady, with tired old feet on tired old legs, shuffled nearby. Dressed almost in period costume and wearing one of those old-fashioned bag-of-fruit hats, which framed her kindly face, she stopped and looked all about. Noticing my attention, and with a firm freckled hand on her walking stick, she pointed to a handy bale of hay. 'Nobody would mind so much if I sat for a spell, would they?' 'No,' I replied, 'please do.'

I sat down nearby on my bale of hay, and that seemed to make the old lady feel welcome. She took her shoes off, checked through her crocheted string bag, and produced a small lunch parcel. Having laid a linen cloth neatly across her lap, she began to enjoy her sandwiches.

There was a rare old-world dignity and charm about her. Aware that I was also enjoying her lunch break, she paused, lowered her sandwich, dabbed her mouth with a linen serviette, tilted her head knowingly to one side and gave me the most disarming little grin.

That was the nicest lunch I had had for a long time, and never a thing to eat. What's more, so enthralled had I become with my guest that the repetitive stomp of the fashion parade music had become inaudible. The audience finally having dispersed, my guest regained her walking stick. She used it quite capably to line up her shoes, which she then slipped into; she shouldered her bag, and made as though to leave. Then, having second thoughts, she drew a handy chair up alongside me.

As a gesture of silent acknowledgment, she tapped the sole of my riding boot with her stick, and sat thinking for a while. Looking me straight in the eye, she said, with a pained yet rascally little grin, 'Let me tell you a story.'

Sensing that she already had a captivated audience, there was no introduction and I was immediately taken back, with vivid description, through her life and times in the Australian bush. The closing chapter was her move down to Brisbane. Widowed now, she lived in solitude, surrounded by mementoes and the warmth of her memories. Hers was a life of a bygone era.

Her great joy was to be the hostess for a younger generation of bush people who migrated down each year for the Ekka. She had become the city granny, and this is her story.

~

We city grannies have so many mouths to feed, and Oh! the shopping, and Oh! the meals to prepare. I do really enjoy it all, and my lovely big old home becomes a festival at this time of the year. The trouble is, I am so much slower now, and really it is becoming a burden. But I must not let such trivia deter me from the great joy it all brings me.

Now, take this morning for instance. Bushies! They still have to have their corned beef, even when they come to town. Oh how I remember on the station we used to salt the beef with coarse salt and 'quick cure'. Rub the salt into the meat on those great wooden slabs in the meat house, then leave it to drain, turn it and, by and by, hang it up to dry. Such a long time ago now.

Anyway—so this morning, off I go down to the shops. It's a fair step, so I left early, as soon as the house was clear. I do walk a lot, but it's always an effort coming home, uphill, with as much as I can manage from my shopping. This morning, something quite extraordinary happened, and to be quite honest young man, I do believe I haven't got over it yet.

My last call, as usual, was at my butcher's to collect a sizeable piece of silverside. They always wrap it ever so nicely for me, so that it's still fresh when I get home. As I left the butcher's shop, I had to step around a big black and tan dog that was standing in my way. Never had a collar on, and he wasn't one of those nice and kind-eyed dogs at all. In fact he almost appeared threatening. Passing him by, I put the dog out of my mind and headed up the hill towards the bus shelter, where I usually have a pull-up for a spell, half-way home.

I chanced a look back down the street and, lo and behold, there was that dog again. Having gained my attention, he looked away in an almost uninterested fashion. Revived now, I headed for home.

As usual, I shut the gate, checked the mail-box, and went up the two flights of steps to the verandah, through the front door—I always leave that open—down the hallway to the kitchen. Oh, it's always good to be home again; it's such a peaceful, cool house. I left my shopping on the bench and went to the bathroom. On returning, I sensed something was amiss in the kitchen. There was a noise on the other side of the table. I couldn't see beyond as I had spread a lovely old lace cloth and it does tend to droop at the sides.

Well, the next thing, would you believe, there was that great terrible black and tan dog heading down my hallway with my butcher's bag in his mouth! Strike me pink! I could not for the life of me contain my wrath. I headed after him with an umbrella I'd snatched from the hall-stand on my way past.

He went down the steps in a couple of bounds. He must have feared for his life, for he lost grip of the bag when attempting to clear the gate. My voice now was at fever pitch. With that, he hurriedly snaffled the meat out of the bag and, with the tattered white parcel firmly in his great mouth, cleared the gate and headed back down the street.

He was not travelling well at all, for his front feet had trodden on the unravelling butcher's paper, slobbery oddments of which were left in his wake. The dog's carriage was almost victorious, but his tail was down, giving indication to me that he was quite aware that robbing an old lady was disgraceful behaviour!

As I leaned over my front gate and looked down the street at my vanishing corned silverside, quite unable to continue the chase, I distinctly heard my dearly loved deceased husband quietly say to me, 'Well stone the crows!'

∽

The story-teller gave the sole of my boot a kindly tap with her walking stick once more, stood up, gave me one more of her special little grins, and moved slowly but purposefully through the doorway to join the endless tramp of feet at the Brissie Ekka.

HATS

The unwritten laws of the bush are a definite code of ethics. Some day, someone may compile a glossary, which would without question enlighten the populace on, among other things, the good behaviour, manners and courteousness of a chivalrous age. It goes without saying in the bush that a man's workmanship is his trademark and that his hat is his brand. This, to me, is a noteworthy quotation from bush law, for I have always found it to be true.

Hats, having been bashed into the required shape in an instant, spend the rest of their working life being carefully caressed to acquired perfection. To insult, deface in any way or even mishandle a man's hat can be taken as a personal affront to the owner's integrity. As a result, the wrongdoer could suffer grievous bodily harm—just for starters anyway. Funny thing is, I have seen all manner of things done by a bushman with his own hat that, should they have been done by another, would have cast more than a cringe of fear.

I was riding down to the yards one evening to check on a big yarding and came across the head stockman on his way back to our wagonette camp. We greeted in the customary way, sat on our horses in a comfortable fashion and exchanged pleasantries in the cool of the evening as we looked down into the valley at the big mob of cattle we'd yarded that day.

Then something dawned on me. Bob's hat had taken a turn for the worse. The whole front had gone! A great crescent-shape had been taken out of the front. It looked for all the world like he'd gone for a drink at the creek and a 'gator had taken the front out. Bob wore an exceptionally wide-brimmed Akubra, flat brim, flat crown. Sometimes I thought it was only his big ears that kept it from falling down over his shoulders. But somehow it always sat there, dead square and flat. In or out of the scrub, racing for the lead or throwing a cleanskin mickey in a shower of shale—she was always in place and on top.

The only time I ever saw him take it off in action was in the yards one day. A particular cow had built up quite a reputation amongst the ringers. She'd come through the forcing yard on her way to the pound yard. She saw Bob, and went straight at him. He stood stock still till the last minute, then did what you'd call a half-passage. Still erect and feet together, as the cow went past he gave her such an elegant slap on the rump with his hat and bowed in her wake as she went straight through the pound yard and up the dip race. He carried on like nothing much at all had happened. You could say a competent bushman is like poetry to watch, on or off the ground.

Anyway, so I questioned Bob about the gaping gash in his lid. 'Oh,' he said as he turned to ride away, 'the pump for the dip was in need of a new flange. Good as any, I guess, she works now—well.' That was it. The only thing I could never fathom was why he cut it out of the front and not the back. Tell you what, no one asked him either; after all it was His Hat.

~

Most men in the bush wear felt hats, but there are exceptions. One I knew of was a teamster. He was a big wagon man to the north of Cloncurry. It was claimed he built the first hospital as such in Camooweal. On one trip he had a cargo of grog, among other things. His daughter (now aged well into her eighties) had put all twenty-four horses into nosebags and settled down for big dinner camp. The old man had decided to lighten their load for the evening haul into camp.

Going to sleep against a wheel, his hat (a hand-plaited grass straw, kangaroo-lace braided, and his pride and joy) sat on his knee while he slumbered. When he awoke he made a gesture for his hat, and it was gone. Can you begin to imagine the language, when all that remained was the leather braiding, sitting like a halo over his boot. A plague of grasshoppers had gone through and eaten the lot.

~

There was a young fellow, working for the R. M. Williams company in Sydney, who wanted some bush experience, so he duly turned up at our droving camp. He was a likely looking sort, and had a bit of presence about him. Big lump of a fellow and, I might add, very well dressed for the job. At that time we were walking close on six thousand head of sheep on their return journey along the Barcoo stock route, from Augathella up to Barcaldine.

The young fellow's new hat was getting on the works of Loose Wire Lloyd, the droving plant's fencer and cook. So a suggestion was made, and reluctantly accepted by the jackaroo, to place the hat in question in front of the mob when we dropped the side of the pen break on the following morning. By doing so there would be a fair chance that 'that hat' might gain some respectability, according to Loose Wire.

Well, we went ahead with the plan and out they went in leaps and bounds, all bunched up and eager to go, straight over the top of the jackaroo's hat. Merinos tend naturally to leap at anything untoward, especially through gates. When the sheep had all gone through, and the dust had cleared, the whole camp of drovers went to the middle of the break, and there was the hat—covered in dust, but not one sheep had stood on it.

The jackaroo picked up his prized hat and began dusting it down, ever so carefully. Then he said for all to hear, 'What the Hell!', banged it on his knee a couple of times and jammed it on his head amid cheers from the men, who obviously now regarded him as one of the team.

～

I did strike a couple of blokes who wore Panamas. One was a bore sinker on Wando Vale Station. Wild and wiry, he looked like a rusty bolt. He was as tanned as you could get a white man; broken-down sandshoe boots, and a red-braided Panama hat. It was his one grasp at the 'good life', so he said. He did, in later life, go on a Pacific cruise—I guess he bought a new hat for that job. Quite a change, sinking tubes instead of bore casing.

The other scrubber I ran into, in the late 1950s in Winton, who wore a Panama was a swagman, and I believe the only 'true blue' I ever came across. He was an old, old man. I can remember he was quite swarthy and walked with a most unusual gait. His clothes were nondescript. His boots were like marble cake, layer upon layer were the soles. He spoke almost incoherently to himself, it seemed.

Nevertheless, his little foxy dog always answered with admiring eyes and a jerk of his stumpy tail. When in doubt, the dog would blink. The two were a perfect blend of the animal and human intellect. The swag he carried was tidy and hung off his shoulder under his arm, and was held by the strap across in front of him.

I watched him trudge into town and head determinedly up the main street to the old Central Hotel. The fascination of this old man caused me to follow him in. He had a beer in the pub, and then went outside into the street and lay down on the green irrigated grass under a young coolibah tree with his hat over his face, and the dog with his chin on the old fellow's swag. They both were enjoying a well-earned pull-up and a camp through the heat of the day.

I ventured close enough to notice that the dog had one eye shut and the other on me. Never mind, close enough to get a good look at that hat. She was all frayed about the brim, long since worn back past the wire stiffener. The lid of the crown would, it seemed, have lifted out on numerous occasions had it not been so tediously repaired. The paraphernalia that adorned the crown was like a storehouse of important small hardware.

There were cobblers tacks stitched through, fishhooks, a length of fine cord wound around, a needle and thread wound round in a tidy figure 8, and safety pins of different sizes. One held a remnant of rag, for what I'm not sure. It seemed to me more likely than not a remnant of feminine apparel. Perhaps that remnant was the essence of the old man's story. I never asked and he never told me. But he was a grand old man, he had a grand dog, and no doubt about the hat.

~

Like most, I too have had the occasion to put a hat to good use in time of emergency. A few years ago we were bringing a big bunch of horses down the old Douglas track from Thornborough to Cairns. It was a horse and rider, packhorse mail, in celebration of the centenary of that track being blazed to the new port of Cairns, for a township to be called Smithfield, on the Barron River. The township was named after big Bill Smith, another track blazer, who had horses shod with gold and terrorised the town where the notorious Palmer Kate plied her trade.

Well, on this ride there were all of two hundred riders and about fourteen packhorses carrying the mail. Conditions were arduous, as the heat and humidity on the peninsula in October is tough going. One young lady's horse started to 'crack up' and showed signs of rapid dehydration on the first day on the track. We were miles from anywhere, the horse was distraught, the young lady in tears, and I was in a jam.

Leaving a couple of good mates behind, I sent the main contingent on the pre-arranged route and I headed across country to where the overnight camp and vet supplies should be. If ever I needed a good horse, this was the time.

We made great time, rounded up the vet, who had some saline solution, and back we roared in a four-wheel drive. The sun was going down, the horse was still propped; a slim chance we had of saving the young lady's tears. Sure, we had saline solution, but a means of administering it? The following is a brief account of aptitude.

We had two needles and three syringes. We put one needle in a bottle, one in the animal, and kept the syringes going like a chain gang. We thought we were going great for a while, but the vet said, 'The pulse is not changing and the horse is going to go. We are not getting the saline into the animal fast enough.'

'Strewth', I said, 'how fast has a man got to go?' We were all fingers and no thumbs and going like steam.

Well, we had to make a change. Of course the ideal is a funnel, a hose, and drenching the horse up the nasal passage, trying not to get it into the lungs (which is fatal). In a few minutes flat we had coupled up the two air hoses out of the four-wheel drive and the vet had inserted those up the horse's nose. We could see the end travel down and sit in the horse's neck. We tried to get the solution poured down the hose. To do this, I was standing on top of an ant bed and two fellows had the horse propped by the shoulders and an ear each. The vet held the hose. We were wasting too much fluid, time was running out and there was no doubt we were going to lose this horse!

Then it happened. One of my mates took off his hat. It was an old army slouch, pure fur felt, ear-marked and tattered like an old blue dog's ear. The crown was sound, except for a hole in the front that had worn through with years of wear. With a couple of clouts, a punch up the guts and a squeeze to bring the front in, we had the best-looking funnel you ever did see. He held it out for the world to admire; the result of a bushman's ingenuity, the trademark of our heritage. With a cooee of delight we set about our business.

We saved the horse, and made a young lady smile. Well, how else would you rather spend a day?

A New Dawning

Charlie Chambers was, above all else, a proud Aboriginal man. He was tall, strong, quietly spoken, a personal kind of bloke. He cared about his family and friends, and knew the bush like his own pulse.

Together we had sat in the darkness and watched the moon rise over the Arcadia Valley bushland, and studied the paintings and hand prints on the walls of ancient galleries in that country. I had watched in silence as he too ground the coloured sandstone with his teeth and spasmodically spat the saliva'd emulsion over his own spread-fingered palm pattern, onto the rock walls among his ancestors' epitaphs.

Although he had been a drover and long-time head ringer for R. M. Williams, I most of all appreciated his friendship and his ability as an artist. Even though untaught, he excelled in almost any medium. He had allowed me a glimpse of his culture and spirituality, which really grew on the same tree. I honoured his trust.

Over the years my association with old tribal Aboriginal men, many carrying the welted scars of initiation on their upper bodies, had influenced and guided my learning and comprehension of many things. I had been fortunate in benefiting from their wisdom, and my life was enriched. It is in times of solitude that their memory comes strongly to me.

Charlie had often spoken of his wish to help the young people, and now I had accepted his offer and was camped with a bunch of youths down at the coast near Bundaberg, at Iluka Gardens, awaiting his arrival. The anticipation was immense—how infrequent were the opportunities for young people to be influenced by such a great, yet humble, man.

It was my friend Pete's place, and at the bottom of his garden I lay in my swag looking at the patches of sky through the flower-laden sprigs of a bauhinia tree. What a peaceful yet exhilarating place to camp. One felt almost purified, breathing in the scents of all the flowering trees, not recognisable in the dark. There was such a blend of fragrances; and overhead, a panoply of brilliance was strewn across the sky.

The moon had set early and all the stars had come out to play, and I detected the chirp of an ever-vigilant willy wagtail. Sleep was impossible; too many questions and not enough answers. Over a lifetime in the bush and through nights such as this, I had tried to gather the answers that I craved.

Imagine ... a frog sits on a lily pad, and it stays afloat. A dragonfly alights on a lotus flower; it also stays afloat. A scrub turkey lays its eggs in the mounds of leaf mould it has scratched up in the rainforest, and the natural organic heat hatches the eggs. Yet, wherever man sets foot, the earth and the clay crumble beneath his feet. The plants wither and die, and the cascading crystal waterways are no more, as he builds his New World.

Slowly my mind came back to the immediate environment. Feeling refreshed and invigorated by the night air, I slipped out of my swag and into the night. As I walked slowly along I soon could taste and smell the sea, and with it my youth. The she-oaks overhead whispered in a soothing chorus. Then, away out on the now-defined horizon was the gathering light of dawn. The morning star was brilliant, like a biblical sentinel, its promise reflected towards me on the placid sea. The sand dunes ended abruptly, and there was a blackness where the frozen roly-poly flow of volcanic lava, millions of dawns ago, had cascaded down and into the sea.

Breathing deeply this fresh air of the sea, I was enveloped by a need to belong, in both a physical and a spiritual way, to all the beauty and promise of that new day. Surveying from beachhead to beachhead, from horizon to horizon, I thought how lucky were the creatures of this earth. Why had man, in his selfishness, set himself on the course of its destruction?

Down through the basalt flow, stepping lightly, I moved towards the sandy shore. The gentle lapping of the water left shiny ribbons reaching far away, like tracks of giant nocturnal snails. Lost to the abstract inquiring of my toes in the damp sand, I heard again that messenger from the night, the willy wagtail, with its nine-note concerto.

The bird was there ahead, dancing on the sand, not too sure which end of its little body its head or tail should be attached to, as it pivoted this way and that. Clearly the bird had some news to share as it moved up the beach towards the sand dunes, continuing its two-foot shuffle and chirping as it went. Entranced, I followed.

Sometimes it is possible to live a lifetime in an instant. This is how it was when, on looking up, I saw in my mind's eye the form of an elderly Aboriginal lady. She was kneeling by a blackened tree stump, which was the site of an ancient Aboriginal midden.

The pinkness of her opened mouth and the lines on her face could be clearly seen. Her eyes were tightly closed as she seemed to pray, arms outstretched in front of her, with palms down on the sand. Her back was arched and her head at first hung forward; then it lifted to the now brightening sky, which threw a dash of pink through the long mane of silver hair that draped to her waist.

I felt drawn towards her, but stopped at a respectful distance. I could hear her voice, a mournful yet melodious chorus like the soft whispering of the she-oaks I had walked beneath before daybreak. The willy wagtail, satisfied with his mission, now took a perch on the stump and waited. Not a sound did he utter, nor a movement make.

The lady, now prostrate, was acquiring a golden presence. Glancing over my shoulder I could see the sun just peeping over the horizon, and felt a chill go over my body. Hunkering down into the sand dune, I closed my eyes and considered what I thought I had seen. I could feel the power about me in this place.

The willy wagtail startled me with a shrill chorus, and I was instantly aware that the old lady had gone. Getting to my feet, I walked to where she had been. There were body marks in the sand: shallow impressions where she had knelt, and palm prints where her hands had been. No footprints left the scene. But there were other marks. A broad mark with deep cut and drag marks on either side headed down towards the sea—the obvious tracks of a female turtle returning to the sea, having laid her eggs.

The shock of understanding hit me. Had I not, indeed, witnessed the old Aboriginal lady's passing to the Dreamtime? Wide-eyed in amazement, I lifted my gaze to the shoreline. There, sure enough, was the old lady turtle, ploughing in such an agonising way towards the sea. Cut and drag, cut and drag.

In an instant I was running after her, calling her to stop. All to no avail, for I had only the language of man, not the language of the spirit. As she reached the ripple of the tide, her head lowered into the water, ever so slowly. She hesitated, lifted her head; the water breached once over her rounded back, and she was gone.

Spell-bound, I stood and looked out to sea for some time, waiting for something to happen, a sign of some kind. Nothing. Accepting my helplessness and trying to keep everything alive in my mind, I turned and followed the turtle's drag marks back up to the midden. I was greeted by my friend the willy wagtail, who gave a couple of almost spent chirps and sat his ground on the old stump, as much to say, 'I told you so.'

Then I was surprised by a voice a little further away. It was Peter, my mate from the tree garden. 'Gidday! So you did find the old Aboriginal midden after all, just above you there, by the old stump. We don't tell anybody where it is as a rule. It's kind of special to us.'

'Oh no—no! Never knew anything about that. I just came down early to see if there were any turtles.'

Peter looked straight at me, in such a strange and knowing way.

As we walked silently together, back over the dunes, I could feel the penetrating warmth of the sun on my back. But then, passing through the belt of she-oaks, the whispering from the needled boughs in the breeze sent an uncontrollable shiver up through my body and out through the top of my head. There was no need to look up, for I knew that the willy wagtail was about somewhere, or had he already gone on another errand?

How was I going to tell Charlie about my vision? Was there really a oneness of the spirit like the old people had told me? Maybe it was possible for a white man to comprehend.

THE EXPERT

I can recall old Bob Nimmo making reference years ago to a neighbouring new head stockman.

'You know what Brian, that new head stockman they got on the Dozey muster, he's a good man.'

I said, 'And how would you know, mate?'

In a kind-hearted manner, old Bob grinned and replied, 'Well, he said he was.'

You meet them everywhere, which is not to say that we don't all have lots to learn.

I had gone into the Great Dividing Range country just north of the Head of the Condamine and above the Steamers. The Steamers are a run of massive rocky outcrops, so called, I imagine, due to their likeness to a line of funnels on an old coal steamer. I had a saddle-horse and a packhorse, a bit of tucker and some tools. The job on hand was to cut a track for saddle-horses up a ridge to a set of sliprails in a saddle on the main ridge.

There was a well-intended bloke who had heard of this excursion. Looking forward to a good walk in the bush, he had encouraged three middle-aged and similarly inclined ladies to accompany him. Having followed my directions, they all arrived at my camp, looking forward to their adventure. I was ready to go, so away we went. It was a lovely morning, and as I rode along, leading my packhorse, I mused over the idea of people walking along to accompany me as I headed out for a day's work.

The ladies were most intrigued by the horses and pack gear, and could not wait to see what was stowed away in the pack bags. Likewise, I was quite taken by the gear they wore: trendy hats, little backpacks, and oddments of gear that appeared from time to time—all part of the bushwalker's mocker, I suppose you could say.

When I got to the bottom of the ridge I had to work up, I unsaddled, stripped the packs and went about my work. The understorey of the scrub was wet and shady and cool on this southern side of the main range. The bushwalkers went walking, and that suited me fine.

By around dinner time, progress had been good and I could see where I had been, so I knocked off to go down to the creek to boil up. No sooner had I gathered a handful of dry bracken fern to commence to build a fire than the bushwalkers and the 'expert' arrived back at the dinner camp.

I was going about my business in a practical manner when, in a little while, I realised there was a running commentary on what I was doing. The expert was ensuring that his entourage was made aware that he himself was well endowed with all the basic bush skills. He was doing well, for when I went to the pack bags to get some tea to throw into the billy, I noticed he had a captivated audience.

My water hit the boil and, just as I was moving closer to the fire, I heard the voice saying, 'Sometimes it is advisable to have a green stick across the top of the billy to keep the smoke out of the tea.' I threw the tea into the billy, and the expert lifted his voice to inquire whether or not I was going to throw in a gum leaf, and was I going to swing the billy at arm's length over my shoulder to settle the tea leaves.

'Neither', I said. Presently the water came to the boil again and I lifted the billy off the fire, put it down near where I was going to have my dinner, gave the sides a few taps with a stick to settle the tea leaves, and thought that was that.

Not so. The expert was still holding forth, with his jungle green, light cotton, long trousers and his two-tone walking boots, fashion-label shirt and dipstick floppy hat. His arms were outstretched to emphasise some notion that had the ladies spell-bound, by their expression.

What happened next was so bad that my tea was cold before I got around to pouring some into my pannikin. Unbeknown to the expert, he had taken his stance on an ant pad and, at that most triumphant instant, was made painfully aware of the fact. They hit him where ants hit the hardest, all at once it seemed!

How do you remember which are the stalactites and which are the stalagmites? Well, the answer is, 'When the 'mites go up, the 'tites go down'! That's exactly what happened. The present company didn't even rate as the expert frantically dropped his daks, kicked them off, made severely damaging swipes at his body front and back, stamped his feet and began running on the spot. Gathering his daks by the lower leg, he commenced to flail them onto the ground.

On realising his undignified position, he made a soundless gesture of anxiety and apologetically bolted for the scrub, unaware of the equally inadequate gestures of sympathy from his once captivated audience.

THORNBOROUGH

My great grandfather came to Australia in 1859 on the *Great Britain*, a steam and sail ship, to work on the goldfields of Ballarat and Bendigo in Victoria. Mustering cattle from the hills of Piccadilly, one of the earliest goldmining sites out from Charters Towers, was as close as I had ever come to the goldfields.

The long-since vacated goldfield on the Hodgkinson River, a hundred miles west of Cairns, seemed a nothing at first glance. Bob Norman, a Bush Pilot pioneer, changed all that. He introduced me to the cemetery on the flat amidst the ironwood trees, at the Thornborough town site in 1975. I became intensely interested in this harsh and rugged country.

The captivating stories were on the headstones: young lives snatched away, young mothers dying in this country while trying to give life. I could feel the pain and the weight of hopeless despair in this place of horrid isolation, a hundred years ago.

Looking all about, there must be many untold stories in these dry gullies and rocky ridges where once thousands of people lived, worked, strived and died. It is now a lonely, voiceless country.

The collapsed mineshafts, the overhead gearing at the Tyrconnell mine and the once steam-driven Kingsborough stamper battery seemed only to need a nudge to begin their rhythmic pounding of the ore, accompanied by the resounding 'woof! woof!' of the bellows that forced air down the shafts for the underground miners. The stone-pitched crossing on Caledonia Creek was a sentinel of witness, as was the leaning, lonely, grey, weatherworn post, once the corner of a lady's garden, which stood monumental among the ever-encroaching rubber vines.

These Madagascar rubber vines, dense and tangled, covered the barren slopes where streets had been. Rusted iron, broken concrete slabs and heavy mining hardware were littered all about, almost shamefully abandoned. Over there, stark and grey on a barren flat, stood the seemingly ancient, weatherworn Canton Hotel.

Who were these people who carted the great ten-ton steam boiler now rusting on a mountaintop at the deserted General Grant mine at Kingsborough? What manner of men cut and carted the wood that fed all the steam engines on the field? Where did they get and store the water that was vital on such an extensive field? How did they get all the necessities for life and work over the ranges and into this godforsaken place? How did they survive? These were the questions I asked myself, just for starters.

Making it my business to find the answers, and having already decided to be a custodian of their memory, I did a lot of research and rode a lot of miles, and made some good friends along the way.

~

By 3 October 1976 I was ready. Over two hundred people from all walks of life had come together at Thornborough cemetery for a commemorative service. The insistent striking of an anvil by my infant son Glenn provided the summons. This Longhorn anvil had been Ned Crossland's, a smithy on both the Palmer and the Hodgkinson goldfields. Colin Cusson, Archdeacon of Cairns, who was born on the Ravenswood goldfield, officiated. Nearby stood a simple wooden cross and a wreath of golden flowers in the shape of a horseshoe. As the sun was going down we said prayers, and hymns were sung as they may never have been sung here before. This congregation had prepared itself well, and was in a determined frame of mind to commemorate with enthusiasm and dignity.

Early that morning, horse riders from five to eighty years old, having camped on the flat, saddled up and were taken on a conducted tour of the goldfields and the adjacent townsite of Kingsborough by Fernley Marshall and Tom Volkman. This was the beginning of a wonderful day, to honour the memory of the pioneers and to substantiate the purpose behind this tremendous bush gathering.

During the ride they saw in the dry hills many graves with headstones of rock, marble and iron. Their horses' hooves stirred the dust of the once busy streets and wagon roadways. They saw the site of the 700 foot General Grant shaft, and the mighty Tyrconnell that yielded 52,753 ounces of gold. Signs of previous habitation were everywhere, and under their scrutiny the goldfields seemingly came alive and the Australian colloquialism 'hard yakka' was passed along. The spirit of humanity rose from the rock, dust and desolation of the lives that had gone before.

A bonding taking place among the riders became manifest on the visit to Carl Axel Egerstrom's grave. The one-time gardener and baker had carved his own grave from solid rock and constructed his own headstone, on which a friend had placed a bronze plaque. The gravesite was surrounded by succulent plants, which Carl had planted seventy-six years ago. It was as though they had survived the harshness of all those years so as to be recognised now.

And so we prayed and so we sang those hymns, for the women and the children, for the miners, the teamsters and all men from everywhere, including Carl from Sweden. 'We nearly blew the leaves off all the trees with our singing', someone was heard to say. Late that night, in my swag, I went back over the past eighteen months. What a journey of discovery it had been. Hard work, solid planning, absolute focus—and now it was all happening.

~

Lying in my swag, I remembered standing at Kamerunga with Bob and Ron Norman, looking up at Glacier Rock, high above the Barron River and the Kuranda railway line. 'Well,' I said, 'if that's where the miners went up from Palmer Kate's at Smithfield … that's where we shall come down.'

Finding the hundred miles of pack track through the goldfields from Thornborough, Kingsborough and Beaconsfield, down towards Northcote on the Leadingham Creek, was no problem. The wagons had left it well defined. Away towards Mareeba, around the southern end of Granite Range, the old way became apparent when wheel ruts across great expanses of granite were discovered. Further eastward to Emerald End, and the considerable distance of open forest and hilly country to Speewah, took quite some time to define.

There had been a telegraph line in the early days, and the odd cypress pole with a tin cap, immune to white ants, had survived the bushfires. These were definite signs that gave us direction, as the line had been constructed adjacent to the pack track.

Once on the right route, interesting oddments kept turning up, such as barred heel-plates off old-style working boots, and heavy horseshoes that had been cogged for steep hill work. Even a pressure gauge for a traction engine was found, and a discarded pack-saddle frame in the fork of a tree, and now and again a beer bottle. A prospector may well have carried water in it over the latter stages of his journey to the goldfields. Did he make it to the next water? This was always the question I asked myself.

The real test was rediscovering the track from Speewah through the rainforest to the top of Glacier Rock, and down that massive slope to Kamerunga. Of all those to whom I was grateful for their support, it was Alex Sandilands and young Laura Collier who were game to take this one on, when others thought it an impossible task. I had been in there before and knew what was in front of us, and it wasn't good. I knew what to look for, and together we found it, but nothing prepared us for the daunting sight from the top of Glacier Rock. Did we really have to go down there? It drops about 1,400 feet in a mile, I'd guess.

To add authenticity to this task, we each had a saddle-horse. Our escapade of discovery through the rainforest was equal, in trauma and satisfaction, to the trips of Bill Smith and Inspector Douglas all those years ago, when they marked this track from the goldfields to Trinity Inlet. It had long since become overgrown.

Once getting on the line, by identifying the track ex-cavation around the steep sidings, progress was good. We came on what we thought was a huge scrub turkey's nest. Can you imagine the surprise and elation when, on scraping away the deep leaf litter and layers of debris, we discovered a huge heap of green concave-bottomed beer bottles, all broken. We three cheered loudly, our exhausted bodies, torn by lawyer cane, shed all the pain, and we gained stature as we looked into each other's sweaty, dirty faces in absolute delight. We had done it; we were sure that we had the track. Two more telltale heaps were discovered on the descent to the railway-line level.

Some weeks later, we had pre-arranged for the Kuranda train to stop above the line, at the bamboos on Packer's Flat, and I hijacked a special passenger, Evelyn Maunsell, subject of the book, 'Spose I Die. I piggy-backed her up to this spot, boiled the billy and made her a damper for smoko, then put her back on the return train to Cairns. Some picnic—some lady.

Mrs Maunsell had come from England as a young lady in the early years of the twentieth century. She had gone up this range to live with her husband on Wrotham Park cattle station on the Mitchell River, northwest of Chillagoe. She stayed on the property, with her Aboriginal friends to support her, while her cattleman husband went to the First World War. She reared a son, who became the celebrated Senator Ron Maunsell. As a tribute to her, we chose to use the pack saddles and bags from the Wrotham Park droving plant to carry the packhorse mail on the Cairns Centennial Trail Ride.

Having marked the rainforest track, six of us went to Speewah with a packhorse, Brandy, to cart our tools and gear. In one day we cut that track wide enough for horse travel down to Kamerunga. A well-meaning Cairns reporter followed our track and caught us up when we paused for a breather in the stifling heat. He supplied a pannikin of OP rum, which was passed around. My great mate, Bill McFarlane, of the Gilbert River, passed it straight on to me. I said, 'Ain't you going to have a tug, mate?' With a quizzical look he replied, 'There's not enough in it.' That kind of explained how we all felt, but we carried on and got the job done by each taking a turn in the lead, the last man having a spell and leading the packhorse.

Then there was the question of access to Thornborough from Dimbulah. There was no road from Gordon Morrow's gate on the old Mulligan road, so we made one. Together with some great mates, we cleared the sleepers off the old Mt Mulligan railway line, then had the railway embankment graded down to road width. With the old railway bridges all long gone, we made the rocky creek beds trafficable with a huge bulldozer, compliments of the Dimbulah Shire Council.

At Thornborough we now had access, but what to do about water? With the ingenuity of Glenn Steel, Lancaster pilot and now civil engineer, we plotted the deep sandy bed of the Hodgkinson with a long steel spike. We then sunk a hole and were able to pump 1,100 gallons an hour from a reservoir of water we had discovered, which was banked up by a reef of rock in the depth of the riverbed.

~

Tomorrow we would be an army on the move. Leadingham Creek the first night, then the second day spent on the more recent wagon road around Granite Range to Mareeba and on to Emerald End. This is the site of pioneer John Atherton's home, where we would stop to lay a wreath on the family graves, and then on to the caravan park, where the biggest bush dance ever held on the grass in North Queensland was going to take place. I had had the Mareeba fire brigade burn off all the surrounding bushland, and since the rain there was now a carpet of emerald green grass.

Yes, it was a long night in the swag, as I absent-mindedly watched the stars shift across the sky, but the time passed as I went over those eighteen months of preparation. I was grateful for all the support I had had from my family and loyal friends, who had also come to believe in this big undertaking. To think, on the dawning it was all going to happen in earnest. And this is the ride song that would go day and night:

There are hoof beats ringing out on the Douglas Trail again,
Bringing down the pack saddle mail again.
There will be campfire stories told
About Hodgkinson gold
And about the men who came to work the land, etc.

~

I have the fondest memory of dear old Mrs Volkman standing on a ridge, watching the packhorse mail and the endless string of riders on fresh horses pass her by in a cavalcade, heading for Cairns. She was the last of the Thornborough residents, still living in the Canton Hotel.

As the riders passed by, it must have been a time, in sadness or was it joy, for her to ponder on her life. It is a crying shame that such as she had to survive in such isolation, where deprivation dawned with every new day. Let us always remember these women of the bush. They left a nugget in the dish of our Australian heritage.

Being the last rider, I had time to dismount and give the old lady a small posy of wild flowers, a gesture of farewell from us all. Mrs Volkman stood there, lonely and frail, and received the posy with great dignity and humble charm. The look on her face told me that ride was a fitting tribute to her and those of her kind buried down there on the flat at Thornborough, and also for those who lie in unmarked graves about this sometimes harsh land. It was also a tribute to the beginning of Cairns, and I am thankful that I was able to contribute.

THE MAN IN THE BROWN HAT

The custom-made chair, hand-fashioned from a stump, was rounded and polished to a satin finish. It was not so much the shape as the magnificent grain that gave that special appeal, highlighted by the early morning sun which was filtering in through the treed garden and beaming into this sanctuary of creativity.

The old bushman sat there under his brown hat in a pose of concentration, peering through his low-slung glasses at the tail ends of some kangaroo-leather lace he held in his corncob hands. Those hands had done more than their share of hard rows and were knuckled, battle-scarred and strong but, even so, they had a softness about them.

In the later years, when I came to visit, he was able to give the hard work away and concentrate on his leather. Hand-cutting lace from selected tanned kangaroo hides was an art. With the use of the leg of a wooden clothes peg and a specially notched thumbnail, he ran the knife over it to bring the leather down to the right gauge for the job at hand. To watch him take the shoulder off that narrow lace, yards and yards of it, running it past the blade of his razor-honed pocket-knife as he walked away, was something else. He took great pride in leaving such lengths of unbroken selvedge on the floor.

Having finished the Scobie hitch plait he gave a sigh, cut the loose ends and passed the whip handle to me, where I had pulled up a chair at his hand-adzed work bench. This in itself was a work of art, crafted by the master of his trade, Cyril Dahl. It was kind of special to sit there and run my hand over its uneven earthy finish. Somehow the timber had a warm feel about it. Now the handle I held was not only good, it was magnificent. Only master craftsmen can create poetry with leather.

'There's whips and then there's whips', he said. 'Tell you what, I was in on camp early one evening and this drover came through, watered his mob and then steadied them up for the night. It wasn't so much the way he handled his cattle that I admired; it was earlier, when the horse plant came through the timber and across the flat to the tanks; it was the bells. A couple of saddle-horses had those bells that had a special something about them—way different than anything I'd ever heard. They just stood out from the other Condamine bells. They kind of made music in the evening air. You spend a lot of time listening to bells when you're on the road with a droving plant, as you know. Camped by my fire in the swag, I decided that I just had to have one of those bells.

'I rode over to his camp real early next morning and put it to the drover. All I had to bargain with was my best whip, and that was a Henderson, nearest thing to a black snake you have ever seen. Beautiful. He agreed to give me one of his bells, but it was going to cost me two whips. We did the deal. I still have it; kind of alloy it is and inscribed "Success to the Horse Teams".'

'Well fancy that,' I said, 'I picked one of those up when I was shifting a mob down the Barcoo. I got off my horse and there it was, lying amongst some shedded bark at the foot of a tree. It wasn't in perfect condition—the tongue was gone and a little piece had been chipped out of the side of the bowl—but the inscription was quite recognisable.'

We sat there for a while in silence, I admiring his workmanship, and the old bushman, no doubt, drifting back to that cattle camp and those bells making music for his memory down through the years.

It was then that I became aware of an aura of beeswax and sandalwood sap. He turned to me, his moustache as shiny as a whistle, and I can still hear him saying quietly, 'That was a long time ago; but it was a good time ago.'

A GOOD DROP

It was one of those odd occasions when, for no reason at all, I felt a compulsion to look up and check my surroundings. Some second sense told me something was going on that I should know about. Couldn't see a thing and so, busy as usual, with a horse to be shod, I continued to shape a shoe on the anvil. Then I paused, to have another look.

It was a peaceful valley, still damp and dewy at this hour of the morning, and the mist was hanging heavy on the rainforest-clad, precipitous slopes of old Father Clancy, barely a mile away to the south. What a great old mountain weather watch it had proved to be over the years.

Then I saw a movement. Sure enough, a lone figure was walking in off the road and heading up the long gravelled driveway towards the house. I couldn't imagine it being a social visit as there wasn't much to offer. Our house was a fairly humble dwelling made of unpainted grey ripple iron, with an equally grey corrugated-iron roof, and on a morning such as this it almost disappeared into the damp greyness of the landscape. It wasn't a very hospitable-looking place then, and there weren't too many people about.

I put down my tools and watched the person walk on in. He was a fairly tall man, not stooped, but walked with his chin on his chest as though deep in thought. He didn't have a hat on, which was strange for this part of the world. Then I noticed he was grasping something in one hand. As he strode along it hung downwards and swung, as though he was carrying a dead cat by the scruff of the neck.

That was it. I knocked off and just had to go and meet this person. Our paths met at the back porch. He never said a word, merely lifted his open hand in a gentlemanly gesture of acknowledgment, and bid me with his silent motion to enter the house. This I did, and he followed. I noticed that he had the decency to remove his boots.

During that brief but silent encounter I recognised that the object in his hand reminded me of my dear old grandmother, who had spent her youth in Deniliquin. He held a 'Deniliquin dilly bag' by the scruff of the neck—in truth, a sugar bag, the contents of which were yet to be divulged.

While the kettle on the stove began making progress, the stranger introduced himself: Ken Lewis. He was the new owner of a property further along the road towards the Beatrice River, and he had walked along this road with a dedicated purpose, to meet us.

The object of his mission was now taken from his dilly bag and presented onto the table with firmness and sincerity. This bottle was obviously of some rare commodity. It sat there, perhaps a little dusty, on our humble kitchen table; stark, dark and threatening, like a charge on a short fuse.

'This', says our new acquaintance, with yet another masterly gesture of introduction, and spoken with goodwill, 'is to square up for any trouble my stallion has been causing your mares. Perhaps we can talk this thing over, as I understand any further unwelcome visits by our dear George and you were intending to take the matter rather seriously.'

Well, what a relief that was. Such an unusual beginning to what has turned out to be a rather special friendship, which has lasted for twenty-five years.

I wondered who this bloke was. It was obvious that he hadn't fallen out of a tree in this neck of the woods. It has taken years for his story to unfold, and to me it has been like the weaving of a most fascinating tapestry of events.

His grandfather had been a teamster, and I had crossed the tail-end of his tracks many times, where the old wagons used to lumber eastwards from Clermont to St Lawrence. I had become familiar with the old track that continued through Funnel Creek, Boot Hill Creek and on to the Eighteen Mile. This led to a massive incline for the bullocks to drag and snig their loads of mineral ore, up the Vinegar Hill and onto the tops of the Connors Range. Then that terrible descent, of unbelievable terrain, down the wagon road adjacent to the original telegraph line, on to Connie's Creek and so eastward across the plains and Saline Flats to the smelters and loading jetty of St Lawrence.

Ken's father, too, had set an example of accomplishment and personal discipline to his family; never a display of dash or debonair. Not until Ken himself, in the officer's uniform of a Lancaster pilot, visited the great halls of his English ancestors while on furlough, and stood facing the most formidable of portraits, did he recognise those qualities in his father. In a prominent place in the ancestral home hung a portrait of a young colonial man in the Digger's uniform of the First World War. Crisp, smart and invincible; there was nothing dowdy about soldiers of his time. They were men of the past with a promise for the future.

That most coincidental yet extraordinary visual encounter, so far away from home, set the tiller of the journey ahead for this young man. This young pilot strove to survive, and in gallant fashion carried the infusion of his family's spirit through life. Countless numbers of people, in all walks of life, have benefited by his association.

To my knowledge, the Agricultural College at Clare, in North Queensland, was a special place of interest for him, as was the rice industry on the Burdekin delta, and Burdekin Shire Council administration. His experience as a cattle man, sugar farmer, rice farmer, and soils and irrigation mastermind, gave him a wealth of knowledge which he shared with humble aplomb. He was also a great fisherman, a wonderful organiser, a special kind of father for his family, and a great mate.

Above all—he remained a flier. He did prepare a manuscript of his experiences as a wartime pilot, especially for his family, though it was never published, to my knowledge. It was a presentation of kindness; he never dotted the 'i's or crossed the 't's. Absent were the horrors of death, the dying, the instant obliteration of his friends alongside him in the aircraft formations of battle. Sometimes they were literally gone in less than a blink.

The smell of fear oozed out of every pore of the skin as the razor's edge of battle came closer with every throb of those magnificent engines; onward, onward. He had used it as a tool to hone his skill beyond excellence and to protect his crew. His thirty-five operational missions as a Lancaster skipper are an unquestionable testimonial to his ability.

I carry around with me a pocketful of Ken's anecdotes and snippets of his fellow fliers' experiences, and I shall try to do two of them justice.

~

In a briefing room in Britain during the bleakness of the Second World War, Ken is about to fly on yet another bombing mission to Europe and is collecting his parachute issue. With his mind on countless serious matters, he hardly pays attention to the casually spoken 'Bring 'em back, lads, if they don't work!' from the cheerful elderly orderly.

The mission was completed before dawn, and having safely landed his shrapnel-shredded aircraft, Ken was once again thankful to be alive and to shed the tremendous responsibility. Chill darkness and an inhospitable icy wind ripped across the airfield as he, last of all, left the aircraft to join the transport taking the aircrew back to the briefing room. Mentally, he was shedding the horror of it all. Time enough yet to be jubilant about getting back in one piece.

With his parachute harness slung over his shoulder, he stepped up to the back of the rear-loading vehicle, which suddenly took off. With a firm stance on the footplate and his hands locked onto the handrails on each side, he hung on for grim death. The monotonous drone of the vehicle lulled him into semi-consciousness.

Then it happened, as quick as a flash and with devastating effect. Ken said it must have been the rush of freezing air on his face as the bus took a turn. His subconscious, spurred by that icy blast, must have sensed that they had taken a hit and he had been blown out of his aircraft. He was in mid air, and going to die.

Instinctively he reached for his parachute harness. In doing so, he let go his grip on the handrails and plummeted backwards onto the airfield, where he landed with such force that the parachute release was activated. The chute billowed to its fullness, and the icy blast propelled him along the airfield from whence he had come, with quite devastating effect.

Almost immediately, Ken became conscious of his predicament, but it was some time before he was physically able to haul in the bottom shroud lines, to collapse the chute and halt his unceremonious journey. It was too late to avoid being thoroughly mauled by the experience.

The occupants of the bus, quite unaware of the catastrophe, continued on to their destination in the dark.

When, eventually, Ken did make the briefing room, on foot and against the head wind in the darkness, he was in a bedraggled and painful state. He paused inside the doorway to inspect the damage under the electric light, and then proceeded towards the dispatch area. With the ruffled and unfurled parachute gathered under one arm, the other hand produced a gesture of total surrender to his most disagreeable circumstances.

He dumped the parachute onto the table and looked straight into the eyes of the now horrified elderly attendant. The poor man first observed his beloved parachute, then lowered his gaze to the torn and bloodied knees and elbows of the flying suit, then back to the face of this determined, haggard, war-torn Australian warrior.

He stood motionless, spellbound and speechless—then sprang to attention and reeled back a couple of paces when Ken announced the worst: 'The bloody thing did not work!'

~

Another of Ken Lewis' classic stories, as near as I can recall, goes something like this.

A friend, who aspired to be a modern-day Cobber Cain and was always eager to get a better plane, had gone away from the family property, quite some distance, to take delivery of his new acquisition.

He flew the plane homewards with great zeal, and on approaching the property came in low and at a more than reasonable speed. He pulled the nose up and did a victory roll right above the homestead. His wife, a most excited spectator, waved her acknowledgment and then watched the plane gain height, turn and bank around in the normal approach to the property airstrip.

The plane, having made a good landing, was taxiing in a most unusual fashion, not towards the hangar but straight towards the homestead. His wife sensed that this was cause for alarm, as did all the poultry in the yard, which scurried for cover.

Eventually the motor stopped, the propeller finally came to rest with a chuff, all the dust in the yard settled, and a muffled call came from the cockpit. It was an almost inaudible plea, but his wife comprehended: 'Bring the scissors, love!' Whatever the situation, it must have been desperate, so she bolted up the steps into the house quick and lively, and came down armed with a pair of dressmaking scissors.

The pilot, having slid the cockpit canopy back just a little way, ever so gently, pronounced through gritted teeth and with an expression of absolute agony on his face, 'Please cut my hair off!' On looking from her husband's reddened face to the top of his head, she immediately recognised the problem and complied, ever so carefully.

This is what had happened. Quite characteristically, the pilot had been flying with his harness comfortably loosened. When he had spontaneously sped over the homestead and done his victory roll, showing off his new plane to his wife, he had quite simply dropped out of his seat. His head had smacked into the perspex canopy of the cockpit, which had instantly split, and fastened onto a good handful of hair.

The implications of the predicament had not been appreciated until this manoeuvre was completed and the plane became upright once more. The approach to landing had then to be made, and the landing executed, all in a most delicate fashion. The pilot was suspended, so to speak, with his scalp held firm; his backside could not reach the seat, and his toes could barely reach the foot pedal controls.

'Best bloody landing he ever made'—or so he said!

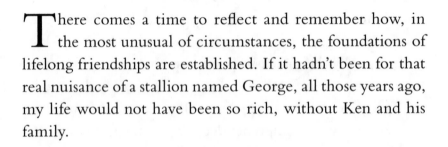

There comes a time to reflect and remember how, in the most unusual of circumstances, the foundations of lifelong friendships are established. If it hadn't been for that real nuisance of a stallion named George, all those years ago, my life would not have been so rich, without Ken and his family.

THE OLD JALOPY

The family Ford jalopy sat slumped, covered in dust, alongside the spring cart in the long-forgotten dray shed. It was many years since it had had a smile on its face, a honk on the horn, air in its tyres and the wind whistling over its canvas canopy.

Once affectionately known as Henry, it was like an old mirror, in a way; in the fading blue-bottle paintwork, reflections were stored away and locked in metallic memory. Thrills, laughter and the joys of children, not to mention rolling along the endless miles of country roads; the sad times and the good times. It had been an integral part of the family's life in those days.

Although up-to-date by the engineering standards of the times, it was now such a sad sight to see, this old symbol of a family's togetherness. Should there be a pause, people of that era could spend forever telling of their lives, when they too had such a vehicle; and they would say, 'What about the time ...'

As I ran my fingers over the arch of one of those graceful mudguards, and ploughed a flat furrow through the dust, I thought to myself, 'What about the time in Ernie Carter's hay paddock ...'

It was haymaking time, 1941. I was four years old and keen as mustard, out in the paddock with the men and thriving on the atmosphere of continual and exciting activity. The paddock had been mown by friction-drive mowers drawn by pairs of horses in harness, and left in the swathe for several days to sun dry and ripen.

That day, the quietness of the countryside had been disturbed by a hive of activity. Farmers from the area had been alerted, and each one of them had a speciality to contribute, as was the custom, towards the neighbour's haymaking. Hard yakka, but nevertheless almost a festive occasion.

There were men on single horse-drawn spring-tine trip rakes, which raked the swathes into rows of heaped loose hay. There were others who drove horses in pairs with steel-tipped wooden-shafted hay sweeps, which bulked the hay up at the main camp.

Some of the bulked-up hay was put into huge loose hay stacks by men driving a single horse in harness, pulling a rope and grab which ran through a pulley on a gin pole. The simple steel grab lifted bundles of hay up to the stackers. These fellows, with pitchforks, working diligently and with great delight, built the haystacks higher and higher, almost right up to the sky; or so I thought.

The real steady workers forked the balance of the hay from the swept heaps into the stationary hay press, or baler as it was sometimes called. This grotesque red monster sat there, roaring and bellowing all day long. The great nodding neck of the feeder rose and fell, perpetually feeding on some unknown. The grinding, throbbing, thumping of its insides was beyond my comprehension. It was a mystery, and quite a frightening one at that. The only time it stopped its perpetual motion was when the motor was cut out for smoko.

The massive internal plungers of those early machines were horrendous, as was the steam-driven machinery of that time. Power was visible, and often accompanied by special sound effects; they punctuated a way of life that was strenuous yet pleasantly rewarding, and most activity had a certain rhythm. The product at the end of a day's work in such a rural community was rewarding, as everyone had contributed, not least of all the women folk.

Right on the dot, one or sometimes two lovely old jalopies would waddle in through the gateway of the paddock and ramble their way across to the main camp. They found their way in as direct a line as possible through the maze of windrowed, raked and drying hay. What a sight for tired and dusty eyes they were. The driver had a firm hand on the horn, and the sound of 'honk, honk' or 'ooger, ooger, ooger' would encourage the men further out to cut short a run and head in. When the apron parade turned up, they needed no further encouragement to knock off.

In no time flat, horse collars and hames were taken off and those marvellous gentle giants were tethered, to water and spell. The picnic hampers were unloaded out of the jalopies. Everything that the women had prepared had been cooked on wood-fired stoves, and in the ovens where miracles were made. Such tremendous respect and cordial goodwill was always accorded these women, who toiled to feed and pamper the harvesters.

I remember the happiness on those faces as they poured out pannikins of black tea and unfolded the linen covers to reveal great mounds of fresh buttered scones, and pikelets as big as buggy wheels. There were slabs of hot corned beef, homemade pickles, 'giz-gog' sauce and mustard; food that the men could fill their fist with, then sit anywhere at all and get 'stuck in'.

Some sat on the running boards or on the bumper bars of the jalopies, some on loose hay and others on the bales out the back of the press that had not been stacked as yet, ready for carting to the shed for storage. This was tucker time, plenty of everything for everybody. The only limiting factor was time. 'You gotta make hay while the sun shines' was a fact of life then.

Now that the great roar of the press motor had been silenced, the dinner camp was a peaceful place, punctuated by friendly and complimentary conversation, the rattle of teaspoons stirring sweet black tea, and the most appealing fragrance of new mown hay in the stack close by. The massive Clydesdales never moved a muscle, hardly twitched an ear; theirs too was a most welcome and well-earned pull-up.

Still time enough for a bit of a blow after having such a terrific tuck in. The men lolled about, or stretched out on the stubble with their hats over their faces. Others took time to roll a smoke or fill the pipe.

During the lull after dinner in the hay paddock, something that gave me great pleasure as a young fellow was to lie on my back, all by myself, in a bunch of hay. I would sink into its softness, breath in its sweetness, and watch the tiny grey skylarks twittering and chattering in sheer delight. Bolstered by their own joyous melody, on fluttering wings in vertical flight they went higher and higher into the blue of the sky until they would practically disappear. There they would hover for some time, in continuous chorus. For no apparent reason, they would plummet in silence down, down again, as a falling stone, to alight and disappear in the stubble of the golden hay. Then others would take up the challenge.

The haymakers were a fairly ordinary bunch, in that most dressed the same. Striped denim trousers held up with fireman's braces, and a belt on which to thread a leather pocket-watch pouch. Open-front cotton shirts with sleeves rolled up over the working men's arms, which were like huge legs of mutton. All wore heavy leather hobnail boots, and the older ones even wore waistcoats. It was mostly the hats that made any variety at all amongst these jacks of all trades.

What this bunch couldn't do! They were all familiar with the local cheese factory, and could cut curd, cheddar, set the cloth and press the cheese, and roll the great round fifty-six pound maturing cheeses on the shelves in the curing rooms with the flick of a wrist. They could plough straight furrows while walking behind their teams of heavy horses, or pull a pair of footy boots on and go as good as the rest on Saturdays. They could rear, raise and dress a pig, or sink a well; turn around and milk fifty cows by hand, and go out and dance all night. It was wartime, and so it was necessary that all the able-bodied men not called up were also actively involved in the home guard. I can't imagine anything that was beyond them.

Among all the crew, it was the men who worked the stationary hay press whom I was most interested in. They seemed to have time to talk to such little fellows as me. As much as I admired the men on the pitch forks who fed the loose hay into the Nodding Neddy (as the press was commonly called) it was the two men who made the hay bales who were my favourites.

Before the automatic bill-hook system was developed for tying knots in the string around hay bales, bale length and tying was all done manually by these two experts, who sat at each side of the bale chamber. At regular intervals of bale length, they would insert a division board into the baling chamber, then thread the two bale wires through and twist the knots. The bale section progressed along, as the piston-type plunger forced through more hay. If the men on the pitchforks were doing their job and keeping up, there were about ten to twelve plunger strokes to the bale. The bales sprung out as they escaped the pressure of the machine and thudded onto the ground, and the wires were immediately drum-tight. Although the press wasn't terribly speedy, it was constant, and quite demanding of attention.

The baled hay was easier to transport, store and feed out to the cattle than was loose hay. In agricultural terms, it was quite revolutionary practice for that time.

~

Many years later, I was sitting in a hay paddock with my Dad, discussing a hay crop which was about to be baled by a mobile hay baler, the operation done by one man. 'Do you remember,' I asked, 'the two pressers who worked on that stationary baler of Duncan McPhee's during the war years?'

'Sure,' said my Dad, 'a couple of old returned fellows from the First World War.'

'Well,' I said, 'one of them, who always wore one of them long-sleeved pink woollen singlets and smoked a pipe, he was the toughest I have ever seen, before or since!'

'What makes you say that?' asked my Dad, as he twisted a handful of hay in his hands to check the moisture.

'Well, I remember one day at Ernie Carter's place, he told me how tough he was. He said to me, "You wanna see how tough I really am, well, watch this!" With that, he took one of them ballpeen hammers out of the press's tool box, got a nail, and with about four clouts drove it straight through his trousers and into his leg; dead set!'

After all the years I had never questioned what I saw that day, and that old bloke had been a kind of hero to me ever since.

My old Dad got a grin across his face, and on taking the stalk of cocksfoot grass from his mouth, which he had idly begun to chew, said, 'Well, strike a light. You were pretty young at the time, but I do remember that cunning old codger had a wooden leg. So what do you think of that?'

~

On looking back, it was a hard yet humble, furious yet in some ways fortunate way of life. I saw my exhausted Dad's head nod over his dinner at night-time, and quite often saw him grimace with pain. There were times when all he had left, it seemed, were a few crumbs of tobacco in his old polished tobacco tin. But I never heard him say that he was mentally stressed, or needed pumping up on multi-vitamins, or had to take a couple of weeks off to go to some refuge and imbibe some mental and spiritual program, for the purpose of restitution. Perhaps somewhere between then and now we got it wrong. But I do know that here and there, there are those trying to get it right.

BOB NIMMO

During the Second World War, useful men were at a premium in the bush. As well as station duties, Bob Nimmo had the mail contract from Hughenden north into the basalt country. The roads weren't flash—dry, dusty, corrugated and basalt; bog, black soil and floods in the wet season.

Bob's job entailed a lot more than dropping the odd letter into the odd hollow tree along the track. For from packhorse days, the mailman in the backcountry had always been the lifeline. Mode of transport changed, but the bush mailman was always a character in some way or another, and had to be self-reliant.

Most people in the west of Queensland, especially in the basalt country, have heard of Bob Nimmo. And the name 'Nimmo' has been associated with all manner of wonderful deeds—horsemanship and revelry—since the first whip was cracked in that country. Bob was well educated and the family were established graziers. Nevertheless, he had his own brand of 'outbackery' to add to the flavour of the bush scene.

In the general run of the mill, he was asked to do a job with his mail truck. A crawler tractor had rolled and killed a man, and Bob had to go out and fetch the machine back to town. As it was wartime, Bob's truck was probably the only one not commissioned for service of some kind.

Having fortified himself for the journey ahead, he set sail in a cloud of dust. Some distance from town, and travelling in the dark, he came upon a section of the road that was well defined. In good spirits he went faster, and on passing the judge's box for the third time, he realised where he was! In quite a dazed state, he corrected his mis-manoeuvre and continued on his way.

The tractor was on its side. With tow ropes and tackle wedges and blocks he righted it, built himself a humble ramp, dug the wheels of the truck in to lower the deck, and commenced to load the tractor. People of the west still speak of the strength of this man, who could carry a cornbag of salt under each arm from a railway wagon to his truck. Not to mention what he couldn't do with a paling from a fence in a donnybrook.

He took the compression off the motor, put her into gear, and with the crank handle he cranked that great hunk of machinery onto the truck. In need of several spells on the way up, he had cut a forky stick and, when the need arose, he would jam it under the handle and hold it firm until he got emotionally prepared for a further onslaught.

Bob loaded it all right, and on his way back into town he bypassed the track through the bush where recently the bush race-meeting had been held. Improvisation is a talent inherent in the bushman, and the only way of measuring its success is whether or not it is practical; it works or it doesn't, and there's not much time for a second chance.

On another occasion, Bob had a six-ton wagon loaded and a good horse team out in front when they 'did a wheel'. As a matter of course, the wagon was unloaded and jacked up with lever rails. Then Bob felled a good strong tree, and hit it with the axe where it was needed to fit nice and snug under the deck and over the front axle assembly. He Cobb and Co. twitched her into place, loaded the wagon up, and away Bob went. Nothing special—just a breakdown situation in the bush that had to be overcome, and that's the way it was done. It was rough travelling, but at least he was travelling—on three wheels and a drag pole.

Incidentally, I should make the point that Bob was born a cripple, and until the day he died he had trouble with club feet. He had been subject to many operations in order, at least, to stay mobile. A normal person would have spent a lifetime in a wheelchair; not this bloke. He represented his college at Southport in gymnastics and was also in the rowing team. He could not run at all. In the bush he never was able to jump off his horse to a beast. His technique was to slow them down, then grab the tail and let the beast drag him from the saddle. As long as the tail was held, the beast was as good as down.

Once on a cattle rush I was first to the lead and stayed there. Presently we were among the timber and holding a decent turn of speed. There was a bellow over my shoulder. I chanced a glance, and there was the most fearful sight I can remember. About to run me down was Bob; his battered old sombrero hat, forced flat against his brow, seemingly was restricting his vision. With his teeth bared, his jaw struck firm and his face coloured like a shattered hunk of amethyst, he went past me as though I was standing still, taking everything in his stride like a great mountain of molten metal. One thing I do recall about that ride was his reins; he rode on a loose rein.

There is only one thing that I reckon could beat Bob from the jump, and that would be a quail. Old man cock quail hangs onto a thicket branch until his wings are doing about eighty kilometres an hour, and then he lets go.

There was a time when Bob was reminiscing about the real close shaves he'd had along the way. Accidents just happen in the bush, even to the best. On this occasion the Aboriginal ringers, who had done a great day's work on the cattle in the yards, were told to knock off and head back to the station. Bob was going to count the mob out, extinguish the branding fires and check the yards.

When it had been dark for some time, the head ringer became concerned that Bob had not ridden in. He caught a horse and rode the considerable distance back to the yards. There he discovered the main gates still open, the cattle gone, and in the dust lay the horse with Bob pinned beneath. The ringer cut the girth and the saddle made free. In what was a delicate operation, to say the least, Bob's severe hold on the reins was relinquished, the ringer took charge, and the horse, now able to lift its head, got to its feet.

'I think that was my worst day', said Bob. 'I knew when the horse spun around and we went down that my leg was busted. My old boot had gone through the iron. And I also knew that if I let the horse get up, he would have dragged me all the way home, because the yard gates were open. Tell you what, mate, getting on towards dark I felt like making a bad decision, so in case I was to do anything stupid, I got my stock-knife out of its pouch on my belt and threw it away. Never found it again.'

There was a humorous side to Bob as well, as demonstrated when he attended a muster on the Black Braes – Wando Vale boundary. When two camps come together for such an occasion, it is customary to take turns at killing one's own beast to share. Wando Vale killed first. When it was Bob's turn, some cattle were cut out of the day's yarding, with at least one of the Black Braes cattle to be considered for slaughter. There were, of course, a couple of Wando Vale 8FL cattle there as well. All hungry for some fresh meat and anticipating a good roasting of rib bones that night, ringers plus neighbouring head stockman lined the rails.

With all the action, and mutterings of dedication to do a good job, Bob at last took his stance. He laid the rifle firmly on a post, took deliberate aim, and fired. Down went a Wando Vale 8FL beast. With a most pained look on his face, Bob glanced over his shoulder at the neighbouring head stockman, hesitated, then in a most apologetic tone of voice said, 'Struth, I'm a bugger of a shot!'

~

Years later, Bob was hospitalised in Cairns, where a young lady friend of our family was nursing. Right from when she was a child I had told her stories about the bush and the men I'd met along the way. One day at the hospital, when she had just come on duty, this poorly clad mountain of a man came lurching out of an ablution cubicle—swinging his hairy arms about and demanding somebody's scalp for the insufficient plumbing. With a wonderful command of the English language, his spurts of oratory blended with the colourful colloquialisms of the bush.

Young nurse Elizabeth stood her ground and, to her own amazement, eyeballed the rampaging patient. 'You've gotta be Bob Nimmo', she said.

'And how would you know, girlie?'

'Coz I just do!'

That was the ever so subtle beginning of a special friend-ship that lasted until old Bob passed away. When he did go, all those who knew him were saddened, none more than the Aboriginal people whom he had employed over the years at Oak Park or Black Braes. I took time to write to Senator Neville Bonner, a one-time employee and special friend, and gave him the sad news. The letter I received in reply was from a gentleman, acknowledging his respect and admiration for another.

A Vision Splendid

We had been mustering cattle at the station, and everybody who was going to Longreach had already left, except me. I was left to hitch a ride in a private plane later in the day, for the two-hour flight. The next day, Longreach was going to be packed for the opening of the Stockman's Hall of Fame.

Dick Whittington and his cat walked all the way to London to see the Queen, and that was a long time ago. Right now, I was climbing into the cockpit of a pretty smart twin-engine aeroplane—dogs and swags over in the back seats, Snow and I in the front. He swung the plane around on the end of the red dirt strip, and momentarily the deep blue sky was lost as we were enveloped in a cloud of dust.

As both engines accelerated individually up to maximum revolutions in a test boost, the machine rocked on its brakes and the dust was blown away by the now invisible blades of the propellers. A roar of power bounced back off the ironbark trees lining the strip and we rocketed skyward over the basalt wall of the Rainbow Station tableland, heading west in a steep climb, bearing ninety degrees, on our way to Longreach to see the Queen.

Having never flown a plane before, and rather nervous, I managed to keep this highly technical and sophisticated lady airborne at ten thousand feet and on course for the last two hours. My meagre instructions had been: 'That's the trim, compass on ninety degrees, keep her at ten. The throttle is set; wake me when you see the lights of Longreach. Oh yes, that town down there under our wing, by the mountains, is Springsure.' It took me some time to realise that by looking to the right and to the left I could actually check if I was flying level, by the distance of the wing tips above the horizon.

It has always seemed that just when one gets the hang of a new job, the job's finished, and sure enough it happened again. I was enjoying the sunset dead ahead, which was sending shadows sprawling across the landscape, when the radio jumped into life with a loud gaggle of incoherent jargon. As I was about to give Snow a nudge he stirred, grabbed the earphones and, almost in the same movement, swung the controls in front of him. We went over the side into a swinging cutaway dive that brought the very trees into focus before we levelled out. On the way down he said, 'Just in time, there's an airforce jet about to kick our pants. There he goes just above us now!'

As we were landing, I thought that perhaps Dick Whittington had had a less interesting trip to London. Nevertheless, when Jack Makim of the Light Horse and I welcome the official party into the Stockman's Hall of Fame at the opening tomorrow, we will be just as humble as he.

Next morning we walked slowly across the dry earth towards The Hall, and already there were countless thousands of people in a paddock. Although dressed the same, in stockman-cut working clothes, I shouldered a tidy canvas swag roll while Jack carried a furled whip in his hand. With great pride he had made it in kangaroo hide, with the name 'Philip' plaited into the handle. My swag seemed appropriate, for twenty-nine years previously I had carried one through this country as far west as Winton, looking for work. Now, wending our way through the throng, I thought 'Who needs a job!'

I saw Cyril Dahl and his wife Dallas in the foyer, standing near his own hand-dressed pioneer cottage construction. To my astonishment this great bushman was wearing a suit. It was immediately suggested that he come back 'suitably attired', and he later appeared dressed like the bush-timber master craftsman that he most certainly is, and obviously much more at ease.

A handful of us welcomed the official party, and we were a great team. When Queen Elizabeth II and her escort, Sir James Walker, started up the ramp towards us, my hat came off immediately, almost as a compulsion. Her Majesty offered me her hand and, bowing, I kissed that tiny gloved hand. Still holding it, I looked into those beautiful eyes and said, 'A gesture of affection from every bushman in this country!'

Everything after that was easy. It was a most wonderful occasion of genuine conversation. With her interest, her knowledge and humour, not to mention her regal presence, she won me.

In turn I met the Duke of Edinburgh, Prince Philip, escorted by Jane Paul, the executive director of The Hall, and later the Governor, the Prime Minister and their wives. Oh, what a lovely time we were having. It was so friendly, so personal. Everyone was rejoicing in this special occasion, and the surging pulse of the crowd could now be felt even inside the building. It was party time at Longreach.

As Sir James Walker led the way across the mezzanine floor towards Dame Mary Durack, Hugh Sawrey, R. M. Williams and his two long-standing Aboriginal friends, Wally Mailman and Charlie Chambers, I paused to reflect on Hugh's dream. This dream was portrayed in his painting, *Vision Splendid*, which depicts the sunlit plains extended to a western horizon, and a mob of cattle on dinner camp. There's a small fire where the drover is boiling his quart pot and, as the smoke lifts lazily into the blue sky, it crowds in to form a great mansion, one could say a shrine of remembrance for those that went before—a stockman's hall of fame.

On exiting the building to hear the Queen's speech, the first people I met were Geoff and Delphi Atkinson from Gunnawarra Station. 'Oh', said Delphi, 'I'm so glad that you boys wore your leggings, you do look so smart.'

~

Now, that's my story of Longreach, but to be quite truthful, there is a sequel.

After returning to Toowoomba, my wife Carene and I went to visit Jane Paul, who was in hospital. There was a question in Carene's mind to which, to be quite candid, I did not know the answer.

'What did Brian say when you introduced him to the Duke?'

'Well, I'll tell you indeed what he said' was Jane's reply, as she sat bolt upright in her bed, intent it seemed to deliver a 'coup de grâce'. 'Having made myself ever so presentable, with gloved hands, a beautiful hat, spent hours on my personal appearance not to mention my curtsy, in preparation for escorting the Duke, I present Brian to him, and what does he say? Well, I'll tell you. Right off the cuff he says, "Gidday, pleased to meet you mister", and that floored everybody!'

MULLIGAN'S COUNTRY

A quick run down along the Great Dividing Range in Queensland, and it is amazing the number of pioneering arterial routes there are, not including many stock routes. I got to know many of them during years of planning the great National Trail for horse riders. The Bump road up from Port Douglas to the Hodgkinson field, and later branching to Mareeba and the Georgetown coach road; John Moffatt's Stannery Hills to Irvinebank railway line; the Valley of Lagoons to Ravenswood, joining the Charters Towers wagon road across the Burdekin River to the port of Bowen; the Conners Range to St Lawrence wagon road and the initial telegraph line.

Then there is the Mt Morgan and the Dee Copper mine roads to Gladstone; and the Golden Fleece wagon and coach road from the coast westward through Musket Flat, into the Biggenden / Mt Perry mineral fields. Further south there's the wagon and coach road down the Blackbutt Range from Nanango to the Brisbane Valley; the Gorman's Gap roadway up to the Darling Downs; and then, right down near the border, the convict-built Spicer's Gap road up onto the Darling Downs.

~

I shall endeavour now to take you with me on one day of a trip along the old Bump road to Thornborough, which was done with a mate, Fernley, and a representative from the Queensland Government Mapping and Survey. We had saddle-horses and a packhorse, just a good size plant for poking about.

We had ridden up onto the knob adjacent to and on the northern side of Dora Creek, to get a real good look at the Mitchell River catchment basin and beyond. Away across to the east, on the horizon, is where the Bump road comes over 'the top' from Port Douglas onto Mowbray Creek. This is where the rock in the creek bed still shows ruts ground out by the iron wheels of the coaches and wagons which passed that way on their journey to and from the Hodgkinson goldfield and others further out, a hundred years ago.

It took a team of thirty-six horses to get a wagonload of four tons up the Douglas incline. In October 1877 thirteen wagons left Port Douglas carrying over a hundred tons of stores and, pulled by tired bullocks, wheels turning ever so slowly, made it to Thornborough eighteen days later.

This route up from Port Douglas was charted by a remarkable bushman called Christie Palmerston. He was, reportedly, a fierce-eyed man, always well decked out in red flannel shirt and moleskin trousers, top boots and well armed. He somehow survived the rigours of his nomadic lifestyle and managed to establish the major arterial routes that became the lifeline between the west and the Queensland coast. The Bump road superseded the original pack track to Trinity Inlet, which became Cairns.

This side of Mt Molloy, itself an old mining town, on the Font Hill Station road, just a little way east of Dairy Creek, is the local cemetery. It is the burial place of James Venture Mulligan, the north's greatest prospector. He discovered the Palmer River and Hodgkinson goldfields. His gold discoveries alone yielded just under four million ounces. Humbly, he became the first postmaster at Thornborough on fifty pounds a year.

Away to the north is the great pedestal rock that gives Font Hill Station its name. The headwaters of the Mitchell pass below to the east and are contributed to by Dora Creek, which comes in from the west. It is up this Dora Creek that we will proceed onto the original stone-pitched wagon road. This section was perhaps the greatest test of endurance for the teamsters, and the main part of our journey for the day.

The narrow insignificant creek bed is quite a placid place in the daytime, adjoined by useful flats for grazing animals. How the pioneers managed to get this far inland in the Wet is beyond me. Some stayed here, for there are a few mango trees and old galvanised water tanks. There are even a few graves away back out on the flat, near a dry sandy creek bed. As we moved further upwards it became very hot in the valley, which does not seem to catch any breeze at all, due to being cradled under the massive blunt end of Granite Range, to the south.

We pulled up for dinner camp, unsaddled the horses and took the pack off the packhorse. It was great just to have a spell under the river oaks in the heat of the day. The rocks in the dry creek bed were radiating heat, the ground was hot even in the shade, and the air was uncomfortably hot to breathe. Fernley took a sacking roll from a pack bag and, with a flourish, unfurled it onto the carpet of she-oak needles where we sat, displaying the beef for dinner. Then, taking his stock-knife from his belt, he gave the blade a couple of strokes across the leg of his trousers before laying it alongside the meat.

'Nice bit of corned brisket, Brian. I thought you'd enjoy that. Bring back old memories? Help yourselves.'

I could tell at a glance, by the colour, that he had cured it himself with coarse salt and 'quick-cure-it'.

'Great, mate, some of your own?'

'What do you reckon?' replied Fernley, with a rascally grin.

'What about tea?' said the government man.

'No tea,' says Fernley, 'we never pack water through here. We should come onto water tonight, on the East Hodgkinson if we're lucky. There's some oranges in that nearside pack bag.'

I suggested he help himself, and that he might put a couple in his saddlebag because he may be in real need of them this arvo.

The horses were enjoying the break, standing hipshod and heads drooping. They had all been here before and knew what was ahead. The old roadway is rough and rocky as it climbs ever upwards. It is amazing how the stone-pitched bed of the road has stayed together, having been neglected of maintenance all this time.

We pulled up for a breather half-way up the last leg, and our horses were grateful. The saddlecloths dried on the dinner camp were now running with sweat. Standing on a bit of level ground and looking all about, I recollected how I had pulled up here some years before. A mate's horse had cast a shoe and it had to be re-shod.

~

Good was the memory of my first trip through here: sweat running off my nose like water down a drainpipe; hardly able to see to strike the nails. It was storm time of the year.

Bending over, looking at the sole of that hoof held between my knees, hammer in one hand and shoe in the other, with half a dozen nails in my mouth, and in that instant being jolted by my subconscious …

Bullocks pull into their yokes in silent agony as the huge wagons pass. There are shouts of encouragement, and the whip crack; blowing horses strike the flint-like rocks with every stride of their pounding iron-shod hooves. Those massive animals burst their chests and drive their bodies almost beyond the supreme effort. Shortened trace chains sing under the strain, and swingle trees are ready to snap. There is the creak of dry harness leather and the tortured screech of steel. Somewhere, a baby cries …

'You OK mate?' asked Steve, as he held the reins in anxious anticipation of getting his horse shod. I blinked a couple of times. With the back of my arms I wiped the sweat out of my eyes, and with a puff blew the drops off my nose. 'Oh, sure mate, just went a bit dizzy for a minute there … must be the heat. I'm OK now, but.'

How could I tell him in an instant that I'd been on a life's journey.

~

I had been over this track on three occasions, and never ceased to be inspired. Cobb and Co. coaches ran this route for years. It is amazing that that company alone harnessed six thousand horses every day, Australia-wide.

It's always good to reach the summit, where we enjoyed a bit of a blow. There is a good flat stretch of country where even a sizeable team can rest. There is always a breath of air, and the views are far away. I think it is the relief of getting to that stage of the journey that makes the surroundings even more appealing. Even the gnarled old box trees have a certain artistic appeal.

I could feel the company of those giants of yesterday as we hit the top at Dora Gap, on the crossing of Granite Range. There would have been shouts of triumph from parched throats, and teams backed up off the strain. Teamsters had just been to Hell. Heaven was standing on aching, fatigued and trembling legs, and grasping a slab-sided canvas waterbag, and draining the lot.

I was aware that my companions had also been deep in thought, as hardly a word had been spoken. It was time to move on now, for it was still a way to our overnight camp on the East Hodgkinson, at the junction with Roman Creek. Our horses, over the worst of the journey, began to step out a bit. I guess they knew, with the massive Granite Range rising up and quite forbidding on the left, that Bulls Pinnacles, their home paddock, was dead ahead.

Fernley is a busy kind of bloke. Even when he is just riding along, covering the country, he has to be doing something. So he was just riding along out in front, swinging his split reins and rolling a smoke.

'Going pretty well', he said, as he pulled up to lick his cigarette paper. 'Should be in camp 'bout dark, or bit after.'

The government man, having pulled up alongside, was taking the opportunity to write a few hurried notes on a pocket pad he held in the palm of his hand. He stopped what he was doing and said in quite a shocked tone, 'You're not dinkum are you Fernley? Tell me you're not dinkum.'

'Pretty right, mate,' says Fernley, ''bout dark-time the rate we are going. We're travelling pretty well.'

'You bastards are trying to kill me', says the government man.

'Not really,' says Fernley, 'that's just the way it is.'

'Right,' says the government man, 'let's get going, but sure as hell I could go a cup-a-tea!'

'Going to be an early moon tonight', says Fernley, as he turns to ride off into the south-southwest. 'Should make for good travelling if we get held up.'

As soon as the sun went down, the heat of the day lingered long enough to remind us that it had been a hot day; then the chill soon set in. And what a great day it had been!

'There she is now,' says Fernley, 'I just saw a glint in the moonlight, so there's water holding down there near the junction.' That was good news all round. 'Should be some still holding up by the wire yard', Fernley continued.

Once in on the gravelled creek bed, the orderliness of the camp just rolled along. Saddles off and lined up, saddlecloths spread out over the top to dry, pack bags off and laid out in a row, pack saddle on end and spreadeagled, three swag rolls out in front. The government man was already getting a billy from the packs as Fernley marshalled the horses. Meanwhile, I was scratching around and getting a fire together.

'Go straight up the gravel there,' says Fernley, 'you'll come to a tight rocky gully—should find water there. I'm just going to check the wire yard, then I'll water the horses.'

My little fire of dry grass and driftwood rubbish that had been left high after the last Wet had just taken. The flickering firelight drew the horses' attention and they seemed to nod in approval. They too were going to enjoy having a camp. As Fernley struck a match and lit a smoke, his classic bushman's features were as a sculpture, shrouded in the white moonlight. He turned and strode off into the timber.

'Well, that's the best cup of tea I've had for bloody years', says the government man. 'Can't beat a billy of tea, can you.

It's just different! I can handle this hunk of bread and corned beef. Wouldn't call the king my uncle, as the saying goes.' He looked as content as any man could be, sitting on his swag, the firelight dancing across his happy face while he ate the humble meal and nurtured his second pannikin of tea.

'But tell you what, I won't be long out of the swag. My legs are sore, my bum's as stiff as a board, but I'll sleep the sleep of the dead in this creek bed tonight, for sure.'

I lay in my swag wide awake for a while, just thinking, as the moon shifted around. Perhaps, in fantasy, I might hear again the travellers of yesterday. But hardly a sound did I hear; just the odd crackle from the fire close by and the snicker of horses as they grazed through the night.

Just after daylight, Fernley was bringing the horses down, I had stoked the fire and the camp was alive. I heard a heavy crunching of gravel, and on looking up I could see the government man walking towards me down the old creek bed. He was carrying the tea billy. 'Odd', I thought, as it was swinging in his hand as he walked. He stopped as he came into the camp. Fernley pulled the horses up. We both sensed something was about to happen. It was the way he stood there, with the obviously empty billy.

'That water,' said the government man, 'ain't fit to drink!'

Fernley just shook his head, never said a word, and rode up the creek bed to water the horses.

THE SEARCH

It had been a long day and, as was anticipated, going to get a lot longer. The sun had long gone down, the moon was fairly well up over the bushland and the earth was just coming alive.

A shift in the cool night air onto my face as I walked along was as refreshing as a splash of spring water after the intense heat that had driven me to rest in the shade of a gnarled boxwood tree for most of the day. This was God's own country if you belonged here; if you didn't, it could be Hell.

The clapping wings of a hooded owl broke the silence, as it left the fork of a dead tree and went off on its now silent mission for prey. There was a thump, thump off to the side, as a rock wallaby sounded the danger with his foot on the hollow ground before he too leapt off into the night.

I cast a long, irregular and dancing shadow in the white moonlight as I picked my way down out of the rugged basalt-flow country and onto the dry, sandy dunes that were the riverbed. The horses coming down Anthill Creek from the waterfall camp should have crossed here. However, as the water had gone underground some distance back, at the junction with the Burdekin River, there was sand, miles of sand.

Circling around, trying to define any tracks, I thought, 'Surely the children in the group would have put their horses into the sand for a frolic here somewhere.' They were, after all, on the last couple of days of a bush ride that had taken them from Cooktown, south, on an epic six hundred kilometre journey through some of the toughest, yet picturesque, country about.

This was the first group to cover the top end of the mighty National Trail. It was a familiarisation journey for those who were keen to ride in the National Mail Relay Ride the following year (1978). Until now, it had been a wonderful overland adventure for everyone. However, now they were well overdue.

I had been their leader for the entire journey, then had made a bad decision and had entrusted this section to a fellow I had faith in. Our nine-year-old daughter was one of the riders. What a great trip she had had. This was her answer to her elder brother, who had done a droving trip across the gulf when he was eleven years old.

Trying not to disturb the ground as I searched for tracks, I thought perhaps this was like walking through the calmed mind of a sleeping giant. For signs of the forces of destruction and devastation were everywhere, from when this river serpent last rose up from its sleeping bed of burning sand, fuelled by the torrential wet season rains. It had raced its way from the upper reaches, passed here, then dragged in all the tributaries west of the Divide to cascade over the falls from Ravenswood, then down through the delta to the sea.

The younger trees of the riverbed community had boughs that were bowed and bent. The force of the water's rush had left a tangled mass of dried vegetation fastened onto and adorning the branches a good twenty feet up. At the downstream side of the buttresses of the giant gums were huge excavations where the river's force had sucked at the sand and torn away all support from the massive roots, and which now cradled stagnant pools of water. Nope, there was not a sign here.

The Southern Cross was nearly vertical, so it would still be around nine o'clock. The moon was full, no chance of any cloud, so I reckoned on having good light until the moon set. That should allow enough time to cross all the country between here and the top lagoon by two in the morning. The map of the country was in my mind, and the smell and sounds of the night were like a soft touch on the tiller, which would guide me onward in the search for the lost horse riders. 'Where are you Tania?' I whispered into the night.

The dead trees on the dry swamp plain shone ghost-like in the moonlight, clawing in grotesque fashion at the dark sky like frozen bolts of forked lightning. These tombstones of the bush were victims of a big Wet some years ago. Some day those rains would come again and flood the lagoons, float the lily pads, and again swans would build their reedy nests in this land, which pulses with the timeless spirit. The confectionery of nature would appear as if from cracks in the ground.

The cygnets and ducklings would follow the breasted waves of proud parents as they promenaded the lagoon waterways, attended by an entourage of dragonflies and applauded by the clapping of pelicans' bills and the honking of the vigilant brolgas.

It was on these waterways that Ludwig Leichhardt witnessed the corroboree of the lotus eaters in the middle of the nineteenth century. Sadly, the tribesmen have all gone, but the land pulses with the throb of foreverness in the swamps that remain, and soars in the velvet flight of the brolgas in the evenings. The sounds that go into the night are those of the creatures that belong.

Thousands of whistler ducks, all whispering 'Wheat Bix, Wheat Bix', herded themselves like soldier crabs before me across the firmed mud, which had cracked as it dried into a grey mosaic paving. Going into the dry season, the tops of the dried mud, once the bottom of a flourishing lagoon, would flake and crumble, then blow away, reminding one of the pattern of all life.

Coming to an accessible point to water, I searched for tracks. Nothing. The whistlers, totally confused and in a screech of disarray, took off and then wheeled as one across the sky, like the sweep of a broad brush-stroke across the heavens, blanketing out the stars as they went, and were gone.

Then I could smell them. The warm, sweet smell coming down-wind was that of a cattle camp. Tracking that smell like a dung beetle, I left the clay-pan and followed my nose across the bare plain, right onto the camp. Anywhere there was a chance of water and feed for travel-weary horses was the object of my quest.

Without a sound, a big stag bullock rose to his feet, stood his ground, and slowly swished his tail. He sensed a foot traveller's nearness. Seldom had he smelt man alone, unaccompanied by the sweat of his horse. Lifting his magnificently horned head, his wet muzzle glistened in the moonlight as it nodded this way and that, quietly testing the wind. Standing stock-still I presented no danger, and the massive animal resumed his composure.

A flight of pygmy geese slid across the moon in a 'V' formation, the white wing feathers reflecting iridescent flashes through the darkness as they wheeled and came back, bunched up, with legs down and necks well forward. They went close by overhead with a rush of wind from their extended wings, as they see-sawed into a landing on the water just beyond the cattle camp. There were sounds of welcoming abuse from the inhabitants of yet another lagoon. There was a honking of brolgas, and red-billed water hens screeched. Their familiar paddling could be heard as they ran away through the shallows, loudly applauded by the black ducks, which didn't care anyway. Then, all was peaceful again.

By giving the cattle a wide berth and coming in towards the water, with the low hills to the east behind me so as not to present a silhouette, nothing on the lagoon was disturbed. There were fresh horse tracks here, unshod ones, which had come in to water. They were not brumbies, nor were they the tracks of tired horses dragging their feet. They were the tracks of good stepping horses, probably station horses, which had been bushed after a muster.

Now seemed the time to have a good look at the total situation. Moving back up towards the hills, away from the marauding mosquitoes, I sat on a log by a burnt-out stump. With a stick I proceeded to draw a map in the dust and ashes, on a 'clean page' I had levelled with a scrape of the side of a boot and a sweep of the palm of my hand.

Looking out to the northwest from this vantage point, the lagoon waters on the plains reflected mirror-like in the foreground, while the black hills towards the Undara basalt country stood stark against the skyline, and there was a twinkling of the stars all about. What a pity such a beautiful night had to be shrouded in anxiety, as alone I tried to piece together the puzzle. Which way had they gone, those with gullible innocence on horseback?

I began my mud map, drawing in the dust and ashes the Anthill Creek, down, down from the waterfall camp, in behind the basalt walls and onto the Burdekin arm; then the other tributaries coming in from the east over towards the Herbert River side. Then I filled in all the plains south of Lamond's Lagoon, the Lake Lucy lagoons out before me, and the long line down the middle, which was the Wairuna Valley motor road.

I could see old King, the Minnamoolka Aboriginal drover, with his two equally dark, blue-shirted offsiders, drawing a similar mud map in the dust by a dying campfire in the early hours, two days ago, on the shoreline of the Gunnawarra swamp.

Feeling along his mapping stick, this wonderful old man had said, 'Stay on the creek, take him this way and that, stay on the Anthill Creek. Plenty time to catch black bream on dinner camp. When you get to the Burdekin, go upstream, little bit long-way, past Lamond's Lagoon to where Clarry wants to camp by the old log bridge, on the Wairuna motor road.'

That seemed a long time ago now. The riders had either not identified this, the upper reaches of the Burdekin, in its dry state and had continued down, looking for a bigger waterway—or they had run late and cut straight across the plains to the Lake Lucy road, crossed it in the dark and gone further east. The latter was quite feasible, as the 'road' was little more than an accentuated cattle pad.

The first option would have put them within striking distance of the Valley of Lagoons Station, and safe. So, choosing the second option, I decided to follow up the Lake Lucy Creek and then the low-lying swamp country back towards the head of the Burdekin.

On rising to get going, my whole body had stiffened, the perspiration in my shirt having gone cold across the shoulders, and as I stamped the circulation back into my legs I looked out at the moon. It did not have long to go, only an hour or so. The Southern Cross had rolled over and was doing a nosedive into the darkness of the distant landscape. In all, there was not a lot of time with adequate light to travel by, so I would have to step up the pace and be even more vigilant.

It was a waste of time looking for tracks near the dribble of a creek, as the banks were too eroded. So I chose to stay on the outer banks, where the country could be covered at a swinging stride. I kept my eyes peeled for cattle pads, as animals usually walked directly to the water. Travelling parallel to the water, it was easy for me to step over a possible clue, but I had to keep going.

The ground was taking on a greyness, now that the moon was not so effective. The further it went down, every bit of vegetation seemed to be laying down ever-lengthening shadows, in order to chide, taunt and tax my inner strength.

With a start, I realised my mind had begun to drift. I had become cold and my stride was shortening. 'No way', I told myself, 'was I going to falter.' Then I remembered a line I'd heard somewhere: 'Give me a ship and a star to steer her by'. All I needed was a clue, a decent set of prints in the dust, and those riders would be found.

Becoming even more vigilant now, I took a new tack, left Lucy Creek at the four-mile junction and headed northeast in the hope of cutting some tracks on the way across to the vast Wairuna plains. Well-worn cattle pads became more infrequent, as they wended their way from one low-lying area to another. As one lagoon dried up in the dry season, animals moved to the next waterhole in succession. The cattle droppings were hard on the parched ground and there were no noises in the night, no sweetness in the air. Stagnation seemed to have taken hold.

Time was running out. There was only one hope of finding the lost ones now, and that was if the horses themselves had dictated direction, which they could well have done, and put them in on the waterholes of the Wairuna Lakes.

I was a tired, hungry and leg-weary traveller when I leant my back up against the smooth trunk of a dead tree on the southern end of the lakes, crossed my legs and folded my arms across my chest. I had done my best, reckoning to have covered at least forty-five kilometres since sundown. With a big sigh of exasperation I watched the moon set and dip out of sight, down through the trees.

Blackness. 'Oh, where are you Tania?'

Where had I gone wrong? I began to feel failure where I had never failed before. The children's safety may be at stake. They would at least be as hungry as anything by now, and none of them were carrying swags. I must have missed something, somewhere. Where?

There was a huddle of pelicans out by the water's edge and I could hear the mud on their feet as they moved one leg and then the other, just for something to do. They weren't going anywhere; they too seemed unimpressed by the surroundings and looked quite perturbed at the questions being levelled at them from the darkness.

While there had been light, the sounds of the night were quite audible over the steady plod of my boots, and were a comfort. In this time of complete darkness, all the birds and living creatures of the night were no more. There was not a sound, and I was overcome by a strange feeling as a shift of cold air brushed my face. I could smell the swamp, and all the hair on my arms stood up. It seemed, suddenly, as though all eyes in the still darkness were watching me.

A long way away a bull roared. The sound seemed to hang in the heavy air for some time, reverberating amongst the timber and then slowly fading like a dying gasp down a mineshaft. Then all was still again.

Time to move. I headed west to get onto a ridge as soon as possible, for I needed to go higher to get the benefit of the morning star when it rose in an hour or so. Not only did I need its light, but I also needed reassurance of exactly where I was.

With no moon, and the stars on the blink, the landscape was as black as the inside of a cow. Staggering and stumbling, clawing and falling, I made my way to the ridge. Not being able to move at all well, my body began to cool and my feet became leaden in the heavy boots. Fatigue was now taking its toll, for I had really pushed myself hard to cover all that country.

Like a hungry, cold, destitute, mongrel dog I lay down alongside a log in an effort to cheat the breeze which threatened to freeze me. Lying there huddled, chin drawn down on the chest so that my teeth wouldn't chatter, and with palms together between the thighs, I breathed down inside my shirt in an effort to warm my body. Remembering my shirt-sleeves, with deft motions I rolled the sleeves down and buttoned the cuffs, then resumed my position. I was exhausted, beginning to freeze, and shivering uncontrollably.

When it seemed the night would last forever, the eastern sky began to lighten. Sure enough, here comes the greatest comfort of all, the morning star, my guiding light and promise of a new day. How many men, over the millennia, had gone through torment while waiting for its rising, when seemingly it put all the other stars to flight.

I wasn't about looking for any more horses; I was heading for camp. About a hundred yards along the ridge, I walked onto the Wairuna road gate and, thoroughly pleased with my navigation, headed northwards.

The sun was coming up through the trees when I came onto the low-lying country adjacent to Lamond's Lagoon. Nearly home now, I tried to lengthen my stride, but the toes of my boots were dragging. I stopped to look at my tracks in the dust of the motor road, along with those of the nocturnal animals and ground birds of the night. What a pathetic sight. Track an ant; no worries! Find twenty horses; no chance!

On the final acceptance of failure, my heart seemed to break. My shoulders went down, my arms seemed to hang to my knees, and there was little strength in my legs to keep me upright. Staggering into camp, I met Clarry's horrified look with defeat. All I could do was to lift my arms up to show empty hands. With a mouth parched and dry, I never uttered a sound as I collapsed on the ground.

Clarry Stonehouse was a good mate. He made a billy of tea and was off back to the station to put a plane in the air. He had hardly gone out of sight through the timber in his old Landrover when a vehicle pulled in from the south. A familiar face looked down at me where I lay spread-eagled on the ground, discarded boots airing beside tormented feet, and my head on a rolled swag against a tree.

As I lifted a pannikin of tea to my mouth, a familiar voice said, 'Gidday! What happened to you, mate? You look absolutely beggared, and it's not even breakfast time yet!

'We're all OK. The horses will be down at the Valley yards by now. You know,' he continued, 'we came down from the

Anthill Creek proper, like King said, and hit the Burdekin. She was dry as a wooden god. At least we thought it was the Burdekin. Then, which way to go? We were supposed to go upstream, but how the Hell can you tell which way is upstream in this country when the bloody thing is dry? So we headed south, camped at an out-station mustering hut, and Allen picked us up this morning.'

'You all right, mate?', he inquired, as he thrust his head a little further out of the window and took a good look at the tattered boots and drawn face, now shaded by a tilted hat. 'You don't look too good!'

As I sipped my tea and rolled the sweet flavour around inside my mouth, I lowered my head so as not to portray the disgust at what I had just heard. That hurt more than my aching body. Then I repeated those words to myself in disbelief: 'How the Hell can you tell which way is upstream, when the bloody thing is dry?'

Oh well, I guess we all have something to learn.

Viv

When she was just a filly foal, Viv was like a parcel of dynamite on pogo sticks. Bay, with a black mane and tail and black points, she had a look in her eye that would talk you into anything: a regular rascal.

My wife, Carene, had been doing most of the breaking-in and, when the time came, she took Viv on. Our breaking-in methods were a bit ahead of their time, with remarkable results as a rule, and were admired by most people when taking delivery of Carene's stock.

Viv was no exception, up to a point. She went right through and never put a foot wrong. She drove in long reins as sweet as a nut, and had taken the saddle and mouthing gear no problems at all. The first ride out of the yard was as good as gold. Carene rode up past a large concrete tank we were building on a ridge, giving me a proud nod as they went past. She gave me not such a happy look on the way back, carrying the bridle and saddle.

'Where's your horse, mate?', I asked.

'God knows!', said Carene. 'She just bucked like you wouldn't believe, and I landed on the ground with both feet in the irons and the reins in my hand … no horse! I had the girth fairly tight, I thought, and it was still done up when I landed. She broke the chin strap on the bridle, though.'

Well, never had I heard such a story. She couldn't be that bad! So, later in the day I caught her in the paddock, put a bridle on her, and she was quiet as can be. Feeling fairly confident, and having seen Carene riding her about the yards bareback, I jumped on her back to ride her to the yards.

Well, that was the biggest mistake I had made for some time. That mare gave me such a hiding. With a handful of mane I rode her; she was mostly going high and forward in her bucking frenzy, because I had her on a pretty short rein. When she stopped, I took her to the yards and saddled her up.

On mounting, I gave her her head and every chance. Lucky for me I stayed on, because she gave me everything in her repertoire during that third big attempt for the day. I might add that the bruising I carried from ankle to ankle was quite severe and stayed with me as a constant reminder for some time.

I guess, in a way, those bruises helped to establish the respect I had for her spirit, and we have been the best of mates for twenty-three years now. There have been a few who have come along, claiming they 'ride anything'. And Viv has had a few wins to keep a smile on her wise old face.

~

As a stockhorse, I guess she's done her job in the droving plant, camp drafting and a lot of long-distance work. There was a time when I had just got home from riding four hundred miles and had to take her to an Australian Stock

Horse qualification assessment. I arrived late, and they were winding the operation up for the day. 'Tell us about the mare, Brian', said one of the assessors.

'Well, she's three-part Arabian, sound as a bell, never ever has she come down with me in the bush, and I'll put her at anything with confidence.'

'Right', he says. 'It's late, so don't bother saddling her up, just jump on bareback and ride straight up the length of the yard there. When you get to the other end, stop, then put her along the face of the yard to that far corner. Chop her back to the centre of the yard, pull her up, then walk straight back towards us here and pull up, then back up a couple of paces so we can have a look at her.'

Quietly to myself I say, 'No trouble, easy as anything.'

I gathered my red-hide split reins and jumped on. She stood like a rock. Then I eased her away at a walk, up the cattle yards for sixty yards, and pulled up just short of the timber rails. Viv was as casual as anything. We turned and cantered across to the left-hand corner of the yards. Here, as instructed, I was to turn quickly and chop her back to the centre of the yards, and pull up.

As Viv moved across the yard, her pounding hooves on the dry ground disturbed the most unlikely of neighbours, for through the rails in the corner was a pig sty. The big old sow must have been sound asleep, but just as we were about to reach the corner, this massive animal leapt to her feet in a shower of dust, and gave the most resounding snort!

Being the most alert horse you'd find anywhere, Viv took all that in and, never having seen a pig in her young life before, took exception. I never had to touch the reins, and she cut back almost underneath herself. It was a miracle I didn't go spearing through the rails to join the sow. Viv just kind of took me with her, and we landed almost immediately in the middle of the yard.

With a touch on the rein and a sudden downward pressure on the wither with the cup of my other hand, she stopped dead. She was standing on her tippy toes, head up, tail out, all four legs propped and well spaced out, and she snorted twice in absolute defiance. I could tell she was asking me, 'What the hell was that, mate?' Once composed, she walked straight up to the assessors, pulled up and stood like the perfect lady that she can be. I backed her a few paces and she nodded her head a couple of times, as much to say, 'What do you reckon?'

'Well now,' said one of the men, 'I don't know where you got her from, but I have never seen a horse that can turn like that. She's magnificent! I like the way she walks and holds herself; what great presence she has. Just done four hundred miles, you say? Amazing! Can't wait to put the big "A" brand on her.'

I didn't bother to enlighten them.

~

Some time later we purchased a Silver Moonlight colt from Ken Atkinson of Wairuna, down at the Valley of Lagoons, and were intent on breeding from some of our good mares. The first breeding season went well, and we had the mares in a handy paddock to keep a good eye on them. Having determined they were all in foal, after hand serving them, we decided, wisely or not, to run the stallion out with the mares.

Unbeknown to us, this beautiful grey stallion of ours had a set on Viv. This became urgently obvious, right from the start. As soon as we let him go through the gate, he put his ears back, bared his teeth and headed straight for her. What happened next almost had to be seen to be believed.

The mares moved as one. They immediately bunched up in a tight circle, heads in and backsides out. Viv, the object of the stallion's wrath, cantered in a tight circle around the circumference. The mares, with their front feet well dug in, let fly with both barrels each as the stallion tried in vain to run Viv down. Every time he passed a mare's hindquarters, he got belted. The sound of flying hooves hitting those taut muscles and leg parts was quite sickening.

This circus of impromptu animal behaviour went on for as long as it took us to realise what was going on, and then to cut Viv out and shield her quickly to the gate. She made it unhurt, but in a state of near collapse and in a lather of sweat. The stallion, apparently none the worse for wear, settled down almost immediately to recover from his exhausting challenge, and to blow the froth from his mouth.

The following day it was painfully obvious that he had indeed been in a battle royal, but he showed no animosity towards the other mares. I have no reasonable explanation for the stallion's behaviour, but I do have an admiration for the spontaneous reaction of the other brood mares.

~

On another occasion, we had taken delivery of a white gelding, stocky bloke, about fifteen hands high, who on release into the horse paddock immediately endeavoured to establish his authority. His technique was to corner anything in his sights, back up and try to kick the daylights out of it.

When he had given a few of the horses a going over, Viv and her cobber, Banner, put a well-planned strategy into play. I could sense something was on, so I stood at the gate and watched. Viv got behind this rogue gelding and teased and taunted him. She was too quick for him. He would back and kick, back and kick with both hind legs, but every time the mare was too quick. He was strenuously straining his body, hitting thin air.

Meanwhile, Banner had planted his hooves firmly in the ground, just waiting his chance. Viv's taunting manoeuvre led the unsuspecting rogue, in his backward movements, straight towards the trap. The tide of this one-sided battle reversed in one magnificent broadside from Banner. His flying hooves hit the gelding and completely rolled him, and immediately everyone joined in to finish him off, one way or another. He was no further trouble, and settled down to be quite a useful addition.

Viv, this quite outstanding mare, gave me years of pleasure, until she gracefully passed away in 2003, at the grand old age of thirty-two.

ONE OF A FEW

Tom Goody is an institution in himself. He's the sort of bloke who is always a pleasure to be with. No matter the situation, he comes up trumps; a real handy bloke. He and his brother Roy are sons of Hector Goody, who was written about by Lex McLennon, the acclaimed bush poet from Thangool.

The Kroombit Tops on the Calliope Range; what a battle-ground that country has been for a select band of mountain horsemen. The Goodies and their kindred family, the Rideouts, one and all over a couple of generations, proved their mettle catching brumbies and running scrubbers. In this rugged of all rugged country, where waterfalls never seem to hit the bottom, the trees are tall and the sticks are thick, and lesser horses and lesser men would tumble at every stride.

There's a saying that the fear of a fall and of death on the rocks helps keep a firm seat in the saddle. But these were a different breed of men. 'Keep both feet in the irons, a clear mind in the middle, shake the reins up a good horse's neck and your weight up over the shoulder, and you'll ride like a mountain horseman.' These few words, spoken to me by Tom in his quiet, kindly way as we stood warming our hands over the embers of our campfire, were almost poetical; a requiem to the past.

Tom and Roy grew up quick, and they grew up keen. Appreciation of nature was well and truly nurtured in the boys by their mother Dorrie. So well prepared were they to make their mark on the landscape that at an early age they built a hut up in the hills towards Pine Mountain, a long way from home at Malakoff Station.

Their hut had all the 'mod cons' of the day, hand made from timber and no. 8 wire. Nearby, they had a picturesque ferny garden and a magnificent gorge waterhole for a bathroom. So steep were the rock walls that the sun seldom got a look in. The water, crystal clear, was always welcoming and a good place for a bogie after a hard day's work.

This was their sanctuary, a place of solitude where at a young age the boys established their code of ethics, a place for planning their future. You could cook a feed, have a camp, mend some harness, or just sit on a bench in the sun by the wash-basin stand to mend a broken sock, and see forever.

That's all a while ago now, for by the time I knew them Tom and Roy had long since pensioned the horses off. Harness from the mustering and droving days was gathering dust in the shed, and the pack bags had been slab-sided for years. The shouts of cavalier horsemen echoing their way down the ridges and up out of the gorges had gone. It was now the hum of finely tuned saws, then the pregnant pause before the trunks leapt off the stumps and the crashing as the great giants measured their length on the forest floor.

These men, who had tracked brumbies and run scrubbers, knew every nook and cranny in these rugged ranges and, initially, only they knew how to get the timber out. Once again, they were pioneers.

~

The Rideouts of that earlier generation had grown so keen that Alan had planted his new wife on a saddle alongside, and with the pack bags full and a couple of light swags had headed up Dry Creek onto Bailey's Gully, and disappeared into the Kroombit Tops for their honeymoon!

I remember Alan saddling up a horse in the darkness before the dawn at Mt Morgan. He had bred the horse himself for a stockhorse; and had bred him to run. Good enough, he reckoned, to be called Harlequin, after the horse that Harry 'the Breaker' Morant had immortalised in his poem 'Who's Riding Old Harlequin Now?'

I noticed that day, 29 October 1978, that he had two special horses to cover his selected stage of the National Mail Relay Ride on its way from Cooktown to Melbourne. One was Harlequin and the other a big dark stallion called Brown Flight, which he rode on the last stage to the Callide Dam at Biloela.

Alan got in at 7.30 that night, a great ride of about a hundred miles, having crossed the Calliope Range twice and made time on those seemingly endless plains in between. No fuss, no bother; well within his capabilities. Well I remember the flashing white fetlocks of Harlequin; his hoofbeat rhythm just rolled along, mile after mile. Alan sat his horse like a flea on a dog, or a frog on a log, and they hardly knew he was there.

~

Nine years later, Tom and I had just come down from the Kroombit Tops in a four-wheel drive. The undergrowth in the timber there was tinder dry. It had been a long dry season and could stay dry for a while yet. Still, an early storm could be on the cards. Optimism can be a dangerous road to go down, but then again, a half-full tank at the mill is better than a half-empty one, any day!

Dry country is just dry country, but when the desolation of drought is dragging the station stock down, and everything with it, drought becomes a curse. The land all about, and down along Apple Tree Creek, was littered with dry cattle droppings, like gibbers scattered across a desert. Birds, resting on the ground in the shade of a she-oak tree by a dried-up rock hole in the creek bed, stood motionless, beaks open, panting, trying to stay alive. The sandy pads where cattle had camped in the creek bed were dried and crusty, and showed no sign of a soak.

Then we passed by a big hollow-barrelled river oak, and well I remembered how, the year before, I had cut a huge wedge out of its trunk. On that occasion, going on towards dusk, I had noticed a fair lump of a bullock standing motionless up against the tree. Funny, I thought; he should be out grazing at this time of day.

On cautious, yet close, inspection, I found to my surprise that he had put his head low down and actually inside the hollow of the tree trunk, either for curiosity's sake or to get away from the flies. Then, either in a fright or simply when it came time to move away, he must just naturally have lifted his head. Lo and behold, his head had jammed in the tighter wedge of the hole above, and was held fast behind his ample set of horns. He was standing motionless, probably resigned to his imminent fate, and had not the slightest inclination to lower his head in order to escape. Going by the dung droppings on the ground, he had been there for a couple of days or more.

I cannot amply describe the noise that sallied forth from within that huge hollow tree when I deftly began to cut a huge wedge out above his head, with my chainsaw. He roared and bellowed, sitting back on his hindquarters, swinging one way and then the other, and flailing his tail like a scythe. Never have I seen an animal so angry, and he didn't mind who knew it!

The chainsaw, having done its job well, was turned off and placed behind another tree, out of harm's way. Then, with the aid of a crowbar, I sprung the timber wedge from the tree trunk. With a tremendous lurch, the beast went full tilt backwards, and with an agonising, almost sickly, bellow went down on his haunches in the dry gravelly creek bed.

He shook his head a couple of times and, on gaining focus, having adjusted his eyes to the light, he spotted me. I was merely standing there, leaning on the crowbar, but in the next instant I feared for my life.

That bullock sure as Hell had me in his sights as the culprit who had held him captive for all that time, not to mention the torment of the chainsaw whizzing around his ears. And he was about to set matters right. He had that look about him.

His initial charge scared the daylights out of me, but very soon we came to an amicable agreement. I believe he sensed that I meant him no harm, and he was glad to slope off on wobbly legs, glad to be free and alive.

The day was drawing to a close, the late afternoon shadows of the hills were coming down, and as we moved along I was going over the legendary history in my mind, as told me by Tom over the years, of the Kroombit Tops. So vivid had his stories been to me, and I kept revolving the pictures in my mind.

The old packhorse mailman's route had been from Kroombit Station up Dry Creek, then Postman's Gap and onto the Tableland. The spare coach horses were taken over the Calliope Range by Specimen Hill and then down the slope onto the Gladstone road.

Specimen Hill, where there is now, supposedly, a uranium strike, is a place that always interested me, not just for the colony of Pretty-faced wallabies, but for the sloping-drive mineshaft. It must have been tough going in to find the lode ore, because it was such a small opening. The miners had put a line of tracks in and had used billy goats to pull the ore wagons out.

To the inexperienced, this land north of the Cania Gorge and up off Three Moon Creek would appear impregnable and mysterious. So too had been some of the contents of the mailman's load, as I learned in the following passage from an old diary. One canvas bundle was dumped at the Calliope police station doorway: 'Chinaman Boss, picked him up, picked him up on the Tableland. Been dead not long. Dropped his guts out and buried them, he much more lighter to carry now!'

Some shearers who were walking through triggered the most amazing story of the gold rush on the Tableland, at the head of Callide Creek. So the story goes, they shifted the door-stop in order to close the door of a humble dwelling in which they had been offered hospitality. One of the men, having gained mineral experience somewhere along the way, sensed that the rock was a little more than heavy. On closer inspection, he recognised the presence of gold; and so it was on again. Such a thrashing did the miners give that country that today it is still as bare as a board.

Leaving Apple Tree Creek, we moved over onto the Monal road and heading homeward to Malakoff Station, which was now run by Tom's sister, Girlie, and where their mother still lived. Tom's property was further down the valley.

'Just pull up here for a bit', says Tom. 'Check the troughing; probably gotta get the engine goin' and drop a bit of water into the tanks.'

While he went about his business, I took the chance to stretch my legs and wander about a bit. The old motor looked quite a piece, mounted up on its wooden blocks, well maintained and clean as a whistle. Everything Tom did, it seemed, was always well in hand.

As he took a tin of petrol from the four-wheel drive and was intent on topping up the fuel, I recalled a similar motor we had for driving a two-stand shearing plant and sometimes a circular saw, and how temperamental it was. My old Dad used to have some quite animated conversations with that reluctant piece of machinery!

A bloke along the road never had the patience for such motors, as I recall. He used his old Morris Commercial truck to drive his circular-saw bench. He merely backed the truck up to the bench, jacked one back wheel up off the ground, put the drive belt around the bench pulley and then around the truck wheel, and that was that. Start the truck up with the crank handle, put her in gear, and that saw used to fairly hum. A great deal of attention had to be given to lining up the truck so that the belt would not get thrown.

Ready to go now, Tom took a firm hold on the crank handle, making sure to keep his thumb out of the way in case of a kick back, checked the magneto, placing the palm of his left hand over the intake, and gave it a go. Winding, winding, faster, faster; winding, winding, faster, faster. Hand off … hand on (the air intake); splutter, bang; and away she went!

Pulling water up out of the ground had never been so easy. Not like some of the troughing I had seen on droving routes, where a bronco horse was used on a rope-and-pulley system called a 'whip'. A flap-bottomed bucket would be lowered down the well, then hauled to the top and tipped into the trough to water the travelling mobs of cattle.

This old hit-and-miss motor was doing a good job, even with a most irregular, yet traditional, beat. She would fire for three revolutions, miss two, fire a few more and then miss a few more, but she somehow kept going. 'There's enough petrol to fill the tanks and top up all the troughing', said Tom, as he headed for the vehicle.

I made myself ready to travel, but no Tom. I looked back at the yards, and saw him put an old bush hat on a corner post. Then he picked up a stone, put it in the crown of the hat, and walked on. I could not fathom that one, so as soon as Tom arrived I put it to him. 'What's with the hat, old fella?'

'Well, yah dunno—yah never know. That temperamental old cussed thing may just turn around and stop, as soon as we've gone, for no reason at all. I have always noticed that when I'm lookin'—she keeps goin'. So, I just outsmart the old devil, and I puts a hat on the post, like, and that cranky old coot thinks I've still got my eye on it! Never failed yet; petrol tank's always dry when I get back here.'

~

The years seem to have slipped away since then, and I fondly look back on my introduction to Tom's family. I remember riding past a little 12 foot by 12 foot cottage up the Cania Gorge. It was just bush timber, with a well-weathered witch's hat roof of corrugated iron, a lean-to on one end and a sloping-roofed galley on the other. 'That's where an old lady used to live, and she was still tailing out weaners on horseback when she was ninety.' Her little horse yard was still standing, but the sliprails were down.

By and by, we came on the township where Tom's mother had spent her youth. All these family historical sites have been swallowed up by the waters of the Cania Dam; however, the memories remain.

Tom and I share a recognition for things of the past, and on one of our adventures we called in at the long-deserted Bluebag copper mine, on the stock route over towards Kalpawar.

Out in the middle of a clearing in the bush, where once there had been a township, sat a stumpy, scrubby little bush. On closer inspection we discovered that it was a rose. It had survived countless droughts and bushfires, and the foraging of drought-ridden cattle, horses and 'roos.

We took some cuttings home, and I now have two of them growing up the ironbark posts of the shade verandah at my home. It is an old-fashioned English pink and white rambling rose. They look pretty scraggly most of the year, but then they always flower well. Just like Tom; he's always turning up trumps.

Did that miner make a go of it, or did he die, like so many died, down the shaft? No matter, together we have kept his wife's dream alive. The flowering every year since is assurance of that.

TATTERED AND TORN

It had been raining. As I trudged along the confines of the sparsely gravelled road, the red volcanic soil came squelching up between the cloven hooves of my two newly calved heifers. They too meandered up the slope towards the rainforest, where the track then disappeared around a curve and into the drifting fog.

Something prompted me to look back to the left, and there on a clear sloping piece of ground about fifty yards away were two of the most unlikely looking individuals. They stood quite motionless, and coolly watched rather than observing my pitiful progress. They seemed not at all concerned about the dreary damp day, clad only in miscellaneous football jerseys, baggy shorts, no socks and sandshoes. The shorter, by far, of the two puffed a droopy cigarette under a drooping hat. The larger, by far, lifted one brawny arm, deftly removed an old cloth hat, and in the same motion gave his close-cropped head a questioning scratch; he rolled the straw across his mouth and called out, 'Gonna milk a few are we?'

Not too sure whether that was a greeting, a genuine inquiry or some contemptuous remark that deserved to be ignored, I just raised a hand in friendly acknowledgment and kept trudging along. I was proud of my two newly acquired heifers, and I said to myself, 'I'll show you fellows how to milk cows, just give me time, give me time.'

It was a humbling experience, taking what was the beginning of our dairy herd up to Doug Taylor's to be milked. We had purchased a 160-acre dairy farm on Middlebrook road, hoping to make a fresh start. On occupancy, the dairy inspector had advised us that the cowshed was condemned and that the Millaa Millaa Factory would not receive any of the milk until a new dairy had been built.

Doug's place was situated on a ridge that ran eastwards, and that day the misted valleys to the left and right were like swirling lakes rising and falling at the whim of the gusty wind. Even so, I could see through the now pattering rain, away down the Beatrice River country towards the South Johnstone. It was beautiful, scenic, cold and damp.

Doug and his father, Bill, came from the house to greet me. They looked dry and tidy, like they had been sitting by a wood range, eating breakfast and drinking tea. Doug had a good-looking bush hat on. He looked as fit as a kangaroo rat, with a ready smile and master of any situation. His dad was holding his head to one side against the freshening wind, and balancing over it a stoved-in corn sack that looked like a pixie hat and covered his shoulders in a most practical and ingenious fashion. He was wearing a short-sleeved grey woollen bush shirt, open at the neck and, like so many of the old bushmen I'd seen, a copper bracelet around his wrist—which was commonly believed to ward off rheumatism.

My whole day was changed by the warm welcome of those two happy faces, with the dampness already beginning to drip off them. In a natural and generous fashion they complimented me on the quality of my heifers, which they said they would gladly take care of until I had the new shed up and running. With a shaking of hands, they took charge. A wire gate was opened into a paddock handy to their old but tidy wooden walk-through cowshed. A hand wave in the mist, and the heifers and my two new friends were gone.

Relieved, yet saddened by my predicament, I set off back on the two-mile stretch for home. The bracken fern on the roadside was brown, dead and damp. The tobacco bush weeds were dreary and drooping under the load of moisture held by their furry leaves. Up in the tall rainforest, currawongs called in spasmodic chorus, which echoed far away in such a joyous song that I began to feel less saddened. I was beginning to lengthen my stride and shrug off the coldness and damp as I approached the stamping ground of the two watchers of the earlier cattle drive.

A grey featureless dwelling sat there by the roadside in an even more featureless landscape. As I was passing the gateway—for there was no gate swinging on the gateposts—a high-pitched 'Gidday!' came floating my way from out of the fog, from someone at the back of the house.

'Come and have a drink of tea.'

I faltered in my stride, and felt instantly cold, damp and hungry. Across the cleared yard, towards the back of the house, I could now see a woman of trim but firm stature. She was wearing an apron, and the sternness of her folded arms was defied by the most beautiful open-faced smile of welcome one could wish to see. She was standing beside a rainwater tankstand. This crumbling structure looked almost certain to threaten the porch, across which she disappeared as I began to make my way towards the house.

'Get in here and get that wet shirt off, and stand by the stove and warm yourself up.'

She was busying herself preparing smoko. At the far end of a bare wooden table sat the enormous bloke whom I had seen earlier. He sat motionless, with his elbows on the table, looking at me over the top of an enamel pannikin of tea, nestled in both hands. He kind of nodded his head to one side and said, 'Take a seat, sit yourself down, too bloody cold to be walkin' about chasin' a couple a coogees up and down the road in this weather.' With a pannikin of steaming black tea and a fistful of slab bread and cocky's joy, I was introduced to Ted and Trudy.

I had not been in a farm kitchen like this one for many years. The old wood range was warming my back and the smells of yesterday came back in a flood to me. I had landed in possibly the best larder in Queensland, and had been made truly welcome in the most unlikely of places.

The rain that had kept up a drumming on the unlined corrugated-iron roof eased off, and I made ready to get on my way. Trudy came through a curtained doorway with a jacket for me to wear on my way home. Holding it out by the shoulders she said, 'It's Ted's old suit coat, so it should fit you. It'll never fit him again, so keep it and wear it out.'

Over the wet seasons that came and went, and the cold winter mornings, I donned that double-breasted pinstriped suit coat and I was grateful. It became my friend.

With a wonderful wife as a staunch offsider, we got the dairy farm producing. We ploughed, fenced and cropped, building our stock numbers up. The new herring-bone cowshed made the milking a lot easier, and time and money were spent on water reticulation and gravelled raceways to all the paddocks. It was becoming a truly lovely property. Even when it rained almost continuously in the wet season there was little water lying about, as we had drains, culverts and waterways to accommodate the heaviest falls.

One day, I put on the old suit coat as usual and away I went to work. For some reason, I ran my hand around the cuff of my right sleeve, and felt something there. Most of the cuff buttons had long since come off, the shoulder seams were giving way. and there were runs down the sides where I had been snagged getting through the barbed-wire fences. It was at the tattered and torn stage, and ready to be pensioned off. But when I took the coat off for a closer inspection, away down inside the heavy lining, I made a most amazing discovery.

Without hesitation, I took the coat back to Ted and Trudy. We laid it out, cut the lining away, and there, lo and behold, was a solid gold bracelet. It was beautiful. It consisted of several gold horseshoes held together by tiny links. As Trudy laid it out flat on the table, it gleamed up at us like a child's smile. She picked it up, laid it on the palm of her work-worn hand, and gently stroked it. I could see that Trudy was holding back the tears.

'You know, I have not seen this bracelet since the day we buried Grandma. This was Grandma's bracelet, and they took it off and gave it to me that day.' Turning to Ted, she said, 'And I gave it to you Father, to take care of, and guess where it's been all these years?' Then the tears began to flow.

I did get to see the bracelet one more time, at Ted and Trudy's daughter's wedding. It had been taken apart; two of the horseshoes had been made into earrings and the others put on a gold chain to form a necklace. Whether or not the gold horseshoes brought the bride good luck, I do know that Ted's tattered suit coat was the foundation of a lifelong friendship.

STARLIGHT

There have been tremendous changes in the bush in regards to stock handling, right across the board, in the last thirty years. Even the once colourful language of the stock camps has practically gone.

Down on the Thompson, out from Stonehenge, in fairly recent times I saw a young station hand throw a beast by the tail on a clay-pan as he stepped off his motorbike. The motorbike was well broken in and didn't go anywhere; it just sat spinning on its boot peg! Having witnessed this display of competence from a modern-day cattleman, I thought, 'Well, maybe these new chums are handy; they just go about things a little differently.'

Over the years I have come across quite a few men you would call handy. They definitely are a breed of their own, and quite distinguishable. One was an Aborigine; I shall call him Starlight.

Cattle were being drafted and Starlight had to operate one of the gates going out of the pound yard. He was recognised as being a handy man, and he was good on a pound-yard gate. Unbeknown to anyone, yardmen had been over this set of cattle yards and had done some running repairs, one of which was to replace a board in the gate allotted to him.

During the course of the day's work a stroppy beast hit this gate real hard and, not being latched of course, it drove old Starlight backwards in no uncertain manner, as he was quite lightly built and short of stature for a northern Aborigine. He never got up off the ground.

Ringers rushed to his aid, and to their dismay they quickly realised that a protruding bolt from the replaced board had knocked his eye clean out of its socket. The damage had been done, and damn the yardman who had left that bolt exposed.

I spoke to old Starlight some time later when he eventually got back on the job, from the hospital. 'How come you have now got one blue eye, old fellow?' I asked him. He had especially requested it while in the hospital.

'Well now, I can see 'im allasame you, white fella', he replied, quite emphatically.

'No way, Starlight,' I replied, 'that bloody thing is made of glass anyway.'

'By Chri, you pluddy stupid, Brine. How do you think I gonna see through 'im, if he's nodglass?'

It has taken me a lot of years to come to terms with what the old tribal man said, and it has been a most enlightening conclusion.

BIG RED

Counter-lining a stockman's saddle is a specialist job. It deserves all the consideration and ability you might have. The saddle has to sit right on a horse. It has to be comfortable yet firm to ride in, and must be kind to the horse's back. Then it has to look right. The channel has to be straight, and there is a special stitch for the serge, every one of which has to be right. That is the mark of a tradesman. After all is said and done, a saddle is a stockman's throne.

I learnt this in one lesson. Having completed my first saddle counter-lining, I thought I'd done a great job. I remember my old friend and task master, Reg Williams, taking his stock-knife from his belt and, with one arm comfortingly around my shoulder, cutting every stitch I'd laid on that saddle. As my ego began to drip onto the floor, my old friend said, 'It's not that bad mate, it's just not that good either!'

Since that terrible day, I do believe that I've done eighty or so different types of panelled saddles and enjoyed them all. I was fortunate to have had such a good tutor. Probably it's not what we learn but how we learn it that determines the real value of knowledge.

Once I was leaning over my workbench and concentrating on the job at hand. Then a friendly old-looking sort of fella sidled up, took a spare wooden saddler's stool, climbed up, hooked his heels on the brace and, like a crow on a post, patiently watched as I went about my work.

He just sat there, with his old hands comfortably folded in his lap—quite motionless for some time, save for the casual movement of his head as he attentively followed my movements with the curved counter-lining needle, waxed thread and seat awl. Then he introduced himself and asked, if I didn't mind, could he sit and talk and watch me while I worked. I guess a pair of hands working diligently at almost anything is a fascination.

'You know,' he said, 'what I really came in for was to ask you if you could make me a pair of concertina leggin's. Some of my cobbers wore the Birdsville Track spring-sided leggin's. RM used to make a good set of them out of oily kip leather. All we did was send our leg measurement to Adelaide, and back they'd come in the mail—fit neat as you like; last you for years they did.'

'I won't be able to right away,' I said, 'but I will get the concertinas done for you.'

The old fellow seemed quite happy about that, and he made himself a little more comfortable on the stool. 'I always wanted a pair; don't see them too often these days, concertinas. They are the bee's knees.'

'Tell you what, one time in the cattle camps, every man wore leggin's. We were well dressed, in gabardine, stockman-cut pants or moleskins, a good pair of boots, and always tidy about the waist. I don't think men swore as much then as they do now. I think we had more of a colourful language. It was Australia's own. Everyone'd say "G'day", and you always knew where you stood.'

'Everything's changed. Funny though, there's still plenty of cattle coming down to the sales, and the wool trucks keep coming down, so somebody's gotta be doing some work, out there in the west.'

And so he began his story.

~

S'pose I was a bit of a gangly kid meself, when I rolled my swag, jumped the rattler, and went bush for the first time. Lucky for me, I landed in a good camp, out Carnarvon way. Great horse country, and a good bunch of men. It was a well-run place, and the head stockman was a top man. He took me under his wing a bit, and taught me the ropes pretty early in the piece.

Whenever we got the chance, there was a small mob of brumbies we tried to yard. Never had much luck for quite a while; they were always too fast for us. Good sorts they were too. Someone said that they might have come from pretty good stock, as they used to breed horses on a station handy to there, for the mounted police.

The ringleader was not a mare; it was a big chestnut buck. I got close to him one time, and he had a great mane and tail, four white socks, and a real proud head about him. Time and time again he beat us. Then one day I had a brilliant idea, of a change in tactics on how we could run him. I had learnt from the old head stockman, and I had built on that. On making suggestion of my new plan, I was surprised that as soon as we were able, all the men rode out to give the young fella's plan a go.

When I saw that chestnut come flashing through the timber, down along the creek, with all the brumbies right on his hammer and tack, my heart was nearly jumping out of my brisket.

Just where he used to break and go up the side, we'd built a blind. Then the ringers on fresh horses came in on the flank with a rush and swung the lead. Big Red, as we had come to call him, flew straight ahead, never faltering in his stride, down along the wing of the wire yard and into the big timber yards. They were trapped. Well, what a performance! It was unanimously agreed that Big Red belonged to me. The other ringers divided up the useful horses amongst themselves, and we bushed the mares and foals.

Now my work began in earnest. That horse taught me more about horses, and indeed myself, than any other. He was a fighter from go to whoa. But under the head stockman's guidance, I finished up breaking him in to the saddle, and never knocked the stuffing out of him.

He kept that magnificent brumby stallion spirit. We soon came to have mutual respect for each other, and indeed that led to a great friendship. He was all heart, and he was all horse. I could take him to the lead, any time at all, running either brumbies or cattle through the timber. When he was flat, he could float! There was nothing that he couldn't block, and he didn't know how to chuck in the towel.

Well, it was about that time when war broke out. Lots of us young fellows joined up, 'cause we thought it was the thing to do. Hardest thing I ever had to do was say goodbye to Big Red. He had his life in front of him; God knows what I had.

Before you could say 'knife', I was a Japanese prisoner of war, and didn't we cop it mate. Tell you what, if it weren't for those quiet times by myself, and thinking about the bush and Big Red back on the property, I wouldn't have gone the distance. That's all that kept me going, that's for sure. Lot of fellows never made it; I guess Big Red pulled me through.

Anyway, when that show was over, I came home to Australia. On a free pass, I caught the train out west again. Then, from town back to the station I went, on the mail truck. It had all changed and looked a bit run down. The main place had a caretaker on it, and he invited me over to the big house to have a drink-a-tea. He was a nice old bloke, and we talked about horses, cattle and men and what he'd done in his life.

'Yeah,' he says, 'there is a big red horse down in the spell paddock, along with some mares and pensioners, a few unbroken ones as well. Could be the one you're talking about. Don't know what you would make of him. Flat out yardin' him, let alone catch him, so he's probably never been ridden since you left.'

'Would you mind,' I said, 'if I poked on down and had a look at the horses?'

'Help yourself. You know where the harness room is if you need any gear. Make yourself at home, old digger.'

That was a lonely old walk, across the flat and down through the timber to the creek. Memories of the anxious years and torment in the prisoner-of-war camp came back heavily and seemed to weigh me down.

As I neared the creek I could smell the sweetness of the water. I heard the splash of a water dragon as it jumped off a log somewhere, and high-tailed it across the creek. Overhead in the trees I heard the sad warning honk of a wood duck, and there was a flurry of white speckled wings as a pair flew directly up along the waterhole and were gone. Then all was quiet again.

Was this all a dream; hadn't I been hurt enough …?

First I heard them, then I saw a big bunch of horses just come up out of the creek bed. What a sight to see. There were young ones, old ones, chestnuts, baldies, blacks and bays. I could smell them, and my heart began to pound. I had a feeling I hadn't had for years; this was no dream.

They got such a fright to see someone on foot that they cleared up the side, and with a bit of a chivvy I sent them on their way in a cloud of dust, heading for the station yards. When I finally arrived, the old fella had shut the gate and was sitting up on a yard rail.

In rather a pensive manner he inquired, 'Well, can you see him in the yard?' We sat there on the yard rails for quite some time, rolled a smoke and looked the mob over. He was there all right; I clapped eyes on him straight away. That proud head was quite unmistakable.

Not having been yarded for some time, the mob kept milling about, raising a whirl of dust. It was a noisy yard, as mares and foals were separated. They were all 'talking about'. Big Red had pulled up in the middle of the mob, standing stock-still, looking straight at me. He just stood there, nodding and throwing his head, just like he was trying to jog his memory.

'Yeah,' I said to the old fella, 'he's there alright. I'll just cut him out.'

'I'd give you a hand, but I know he's too quick for me', said the old fella.

When they had steadied up a bit, I opened the gate into the big yard. As they trotted away, I gave a whistle and called out, 'Whoa Red! Pull up old man.'

Would you know it, that horse just stopped in his tracks. He stood there, nodding his head and throwing his mane about. Then he struck the ground a couple of times with his front feet. I guess, in his own way, he was showing me that he wasn't hobbled. We just stood there, looking at one another. That was a sight for sore eyes. I never thought that I'd see the day. Then I thought of all my cobbers who wouldn't be coming back from the war; and that was the hell of it all.

I walked up and gave him a pat for them, and slipped a halter rope around his neck. I just stood in the yard with my hand on that horse's shoulder, and like a couple of old bushmen who hadn't seen each other in a long time, we had a long conversation; and never a word was said.

'Well I'll be damned', said the old fella, as he shuffled across the dusty yard. 'Will you look at that. I wouldn't 'ave believed it if I hadn't of seen it with me own eyes. Never seen a horse called out of a mob like that, never! What you gonna do with him, now you caught him?'

'Well,' I said, looking the horse over, 'I would like to tidy up his mane, pull his tail, and give his feet a run around with a rasp; and then bush him. Then, if it's okay by you, as soon as I get myself settled I'll come back and pick him up. I am going to make a place of my own, and I reckon getting a good horse is as good a way as any of startin' off.'

'Suit yourself digger, suit yourself', the old fella said. Then he added, 'By the way, you probably noticed he was never branded with the station brand. I guess everyone knew that you'd turn up one day.'

Well, one way or another I did get myself a few mile of country. Not a big place, but it had good water and plenty of useful timber. House wasn't up to much, but it tidied up okay.

Soon as I got a horse paddock fenced up, I went out and collected Big Red and rode him all the way home. The old overseer even gave me a station saddle and said, 'Going concern mate, going concern. You poor buggers that went away, earned your keep.'

Well, just like clockwork, next thing I ups and met a real nice lady on a trip down to Brissy. How she fell for me God only knows, but she was the prettiest thing I ever did see. We got married practically straight away. That's the way it was after the war, and being young and full of beans and dreams we went out to my place and got stuck in. Together we were a pretty good team.

We never had any children; our home, our garden and the animals were our life. We just poked along from day to day. She was a great mate, never complained and she always backed me up with any tough decisions I had to make. When I look at it, back over the years, I reckon me and my little wife made a real good go of it. Our property was a bit tucked away and we never saw many people passing through, never had too many friends, come to think of it. We just seemed to need each other really.

Then, as the years went by, I started noticing a change come over my little mate. The stillness and quiet of the bush deepened and became a stone wall for her. It became such a threat that where once she would bring me smoko down to the yards, and watch me handle the breakers, well later she wouldn't even go outside the garden gate.

She sort of grew into herself and became lonely and despondent, and the isolation must have begun to eat her away. Even the garden we made together was of no further interest. Like the roses, she too lost her bloom.

Talk about go downhill. It was a shame to see it mate. I thought maybe she was crook, but she wouldn't go and see a doctor. In the finish, one evening we were sitting out in the cool on the old wooden verandah; in the peace and quiet we were watching the big old moon rise up over the hill and beam out across the bushland and throw those long shadows through the timber. I remember there was just a bit of a breeze and the old mill down across the flat was creakin' and the air was crystal clear and you could hear the water droppin' into the tank. One of those evenings when you wouldn't call the king your uncle.

Then she just ups and says, straight out of the blue, 'Roy, this is your world, and it means everything to you, but it's killing me. Please take me home!'

Well strike me dead, that did it, the bottom fell out of the bucket. For a moment there I wished the Japs had killed me. Then for the first time in years, I saw her cry. That nearly pulled my heart out. Seeing her cry, fair dinkum; would have pulled Christ off the cross. I knew straight off, I had no option. The horses, the cattle, everything I had worked for, for us, seemed all worthless now.

I never picked it mate; she never let on. Struth, all those years, so unselfish; she did everything for me. Who was I now to pile pity on myself? I realised then, this lovely little woman of mine was almost broken. I can see her now, as she sat in that old chair in the moonlight, hands over her face, trying to stem the flood of tears. Her sobbing possessed her, and shook her whole body.

She was strong, and never turned away, and was unashamed of what she had said. I was somehow proud of her in a way, for her honesty. She lifted up the hem of her skirt and wiped her tears away. Then she looked at me, and in a voice I hardly recognised she said, 'I love you Roy, but I will die here if you don't take me home. She leant over and put her tiny hand on my arm and said, 'I am so sorry Roy, please forgive me?'

'OK mate,' I says, 'if you really want to go, that's what we'll do. I'll ring the agent in the morning.'

I could not believe I had just said that. But there's no way I would back off, having given her my word. I picked her up and carried her inside the house and put her to bed, and pulled the covers up over her, and she slept like a log.

You can imagine it was late by the time I turned in. Thinking back, I remember I sat out there on the verandah going over things in my mind. It was the first time since I was taken prisoner of war that I felt real empty. But deep down I knew I had made the right decision and a commitment to my wife.

Somehow I would find myself again. God knows where else; I was far from being a city bloke. You know, a man has a set of tools, and he takes them wherever he goes, and he makes of himself what he can. These tools are his morals, his ethics and his principles. They sit pretty tidy, under his hat.

You wouldn't guess who was first up in the morning, singin' she was, like I hadn't heard in years.

We got done like a dinner on the sale of the property. That didn't really matter; thing was we had turned the corner, and it's amazing how things look from another angle. We done all right in the city. My wife was forever grateful, but I don't reckon I ever got over it.

Hardest thing was saying goodbye to old Red. He knew. I could tell by the way he looked at me when I went down to the paddock to say goodbye. We just had a bit of a yarn, and then he nodded his head as always, a couple of times, then he just turned and walked away. I could tell he was kinda down, 'cause we had said goodbye before, me and Big Red.

~

'Now don't you forget about those concertina leggin's, young fella. Better knock me up a set of tapered red-hide split reins while you're at it. Tell you what, if you'd put a gulf knot in the end of 'em, I'd be grateful. Never know when I'll be need'n them.'

With that, he got down from the stool and shuffled off along the workbench. As he went, he ran his hand over a side of leather that was hanging on a rack. He stopped, and worked the edge of the leather with his hands. That was a lovely moment. He then turned and gave me a nod of approval. 'Nice piece of kip', he said, then continued on his way.

I looked down at my saddle, and to my surprise the job was practically complete. I could not for the life of me remember laying a stitch since the old bushman began his tale. It seemed like I had heard it all before; it was a familiar journey. But then life is not a destination, it is a journey, from go to whoa.

The old fella never did come back to collect his leggin's or to handle his red-hide reins with the gulf knot hitch. But then, he may not have needed them where he was going. Truth is, Big Red would have been there to meet him.

THE GULF RINGER

A bunch of ringers had ridden across from Bullock Dray Camp to help us bronco brand all the cleanskins, big and small, from the drafting of a ten-day muster in basalt country in North Queensland. The cattle were held handy in a fenced paddock in the bush. The Aboriginal stockmen had been tailing them out during the day to feed and water in the creek. They had settled well this evening, and were as full as ticks and contented. The ringers' camp was open, save for a fly canvas slung on poles to protect the packs. There were a few new faces, but most knew everybody by now.

Before suppertime it had been a boisterous bogie down at the rock hole in the creek. Saddlecloths had been washed and flogged clean on a flat rock, and then hung on low branches to dry. The horses too had enjoyed a washing down and had been turned out in the horse paddock. Those ridden today would have a couple of days off, then come in fresh for the journey homewards.

The camp itself was about as far away as you can get from anywhere in this country and, as always, was a reflection of the men in it. It was orderly. A large log had been snug up by a bronco horse to the fire, and all the cook's gear had been stowed away.

The men gathered around the fire after supper. Some squatted on their haunches and riding-boot heels or along a log, while others sat cross-legged on the ground. No one wore spurs into the camp.

There were no 'odd bods' here. They were all work-hardened, sun-dried Australian stockmen—'ringers'. They wore stockman-cut clothes, greased and battered leggings atop R.M. Williams elastic-sided boots. There was a grey sameness about them, save for the odd coloured neckerchief that caught the firelight.

These were Australians of bush tradition and the chivalrous age of yesterday. They never had much, but they had pride in who and what they were. They were all different and yet they complemented the oneness in this cattle camp. So important to this way of life was relying on and having confidence in each other's ability at all times. Interestingly enough, it was the hats that kind of said it all, about each of them.

Some men held a hand akimbo with a rolly smoke on the thumb and, for those on the drifting side of the fire, a hand held to shield the face from the wisping smoke, and hats at the nod to break the glare of the glowing nest of coals at the butt end of the log. Their facial features were emphasised by the fire's glow, and the contrasting shadows were haunting.

As was customary, the Aboriginal stockmen had their own little fire, away awhile. Their contentment was always obvious, as they laughed and 'yackied' till late, reliving moments of hilarity in the day's work, retelling bygone stories and always making light of the harder times, as was their custom.

The fire died down and there was only one Dee billy on the side, just ticking over for a brew later on. The cook had lifted a brownie out of a camp oven and it was on its edge, on a clean saddlecloth against his pack bags, cooling for by and by. Nearby was bread, also baked in the camp oven and already cooled for the cutting of tomorrow's cribs.

Doug Campbell was at the fireside in the circle of men. He was little, and he was different. He grew in stature as the need arose, but he could also melt into the landscape at ease. He was of mixed blood, with perhaps a dash of Chinese for good measure. From Normanton, in the Gulf of Carpentaria, anything was possible.

He had been in the bush all his life. He was a bit of a 'larrikin lamp', but he had all the bush skills. Amongst cattle, Aboriginals, the best of men and the best horses that they could breed, his ability was exemplary. He was said to have been a head ringer when he was just sixteen years old. No one considered questioning Dougy; his knowledge was legendary.

Dougy was a Gulf ringer. He had the language and the mannerisms of that hard country, strongly influenced by Aboriginal pronunciation, culture and vocabulary. God never put breath into a bigger little scoundrel. Then again, he would not make fun at another ringer's expense—he earned every mile.

You could pick him in the bunch, as he was the only one who wore the rolled-brim Stetson hat, with a Gulf bash high up the crown. He had a grin on his face even when he wasn't laughing. He was first to pick up a stick and tap it a few times on the ground and stir the dust and ashes at the edge of the fire. Everyone knew that Dougy would be first among us to talk, and all eyes turned to him, knowing full well that they were about to be entertained.

'Did I ever tell you about that Chinaman gardener bloke in Normanton, Jim, old mate? You know them old Chows, long skinny fellas, bare feet and great big hats about two axe handles across—well, they used to carry a couple of baskets on a long stick across their shoulders ya know, hawkin' round the town. They might 'ave about a hundred and fifty pound in 'em. Well, when I was a yunk, I used to get them glass marbles out of them softdrink soda bottles to use in me ging. I used to wait in the long grass, and when they trots along the street, I took good aim and whack 'em in the ankle. Struth, that used to buckle 'em up, and they'd come down—baskets, hats, poles and pawpaws and cantaloupe melons all over the street. The air went blue with Chinese curses. Us mob used to dive in, round up some tucker and bolt.

One of the gang, little sawn-off, sandy-haired, freckle-face bastard, split to the coppers. So we rounded 'im up, had 'im all trussed up to castrate the wimp—we didn't want any more of 'is breed about, now did we Jim? Well, we got lumbered in the act. Our hides were nearly tanned from the floggin' we got!'

'Well, so ya bloody ought'a been" said Jim, with a serious expression, and he stamped his boot in the dust. The statement demanded a pause of dignity and respect; then everyone burst out laughing. They obviously had no respect for the quitter.

'Anyway,' said Dougy, 'I had no right bein' in town in the first place—it's only that they took me there to get edumacated that I got into all this strife. All in all I never had much schoolin'. What happened was, I cut the teacher's stinker for floggin' me so much in the schoolyard. No more will she be breedin' 'er darlin' little goats by that long 'orned, piss-bearded billy. "That'll teach 'er," I said, "for paddlin' my arse with that bloody great waddy."'

The cook stamped his feet into his old blucher boots by way of exclamation, gave the laces a tug, stood up stiffly from his stump and turned to warm his rump by the fire. There was another round of laughter as a breeze lifted quite on cue, and blew sparks into the night from the glowing end of the log.

'Hang on,' says Dougy, 'that's not all. They gave me an even harder time. So I says, "Yez can all go to buggery". First up I drained all the water out of the rain tanks at night at the school, set fire to the dunnies and burnt 'em clean down. All that was left next day was a couple of heaps of black, twisted, wrinkly iron. But, oh yeah, I forget to mention, that was the day after I put crickle grease on the seat of the sheilas' dunny!'

At the conclusion of Dougy's story there was not a sound. He had been so engrossed in the telling, and looking down along his prompting stick as he tapped it on the ground and stirred the ashes, he hadn't noticed that we were all rolling around, holding our bellies in agony. There was dust, and boots, pannikins and hats, going everywhere.

When there was a measure of composure—some ringers still play-acting Doug's renditions—the cook pulled his sweat rag from his belt, gave his face a wipe, then put the billy nearer the coals to make a drink of tea. 'Bugger you Campbell!' says the cook, 'Let's 'ave a drink a tea, and pull a wedge out of this brownie.'

A scud of rain had gone past almost unnoticed and the stars were coming out again. A new moon was creeping up through the trees, throwing a ghostly light all about. It had become quite late, and having given the cook's brownie cake the thumbs up, we sat huddled in silence, looking at the fire, each with our own thoughts and cradling our pannikins of tea. The dew was settling now. I could feel the cold dampness across my shoulders, and it was about time to slope off to our swags.

Dougy was still anchored to the fire, and he and Jim were having one of those bushman conversations whereby they'd offer each other a glance and a nod now and again—with never a word spoken. Just as a couple of ringers got up and dusted the seat of their pants, a dingo howled in the distant darkness. ''E's nowhere near the cattle or thereabouts,' said Carmody.

Then Dougy made a statement. You could see it coming. He had been brooding on it for a while. 'I gotta confessin' to make.' The ringers sat down to the squat again; they were not going to miss the finale. 'You heard about that quiet pet stag bullock and the stumpy tailed dog that disappeared from the station? ... Well, that was me!' There was a concerned silence and then someone said, 'Well go on Dougy. Strike a light, fill us in.'

'Well now—all them stiff-necked bastards from the big house gone over to the neighbours for a couple of days playin' tennis or somethin' and I was left takin' care of the place. That great bludgin', loose-pizzled, slack-arsed, wrong-eyed bloody thing is walkin' all about the place, behavin' like a blubbin' poddy sook, 'cause he misses the missus and is all alone, and he fair gets on my works. On and on he goes, bawlin' 'is eyes out. That's not all. That stumpy tail, ankle-bitin' terrier is followin' 'im everywhere 'e goes and yappin', non-stop, I tell you, and 'e won't shut up. Well, the pair of 'em, with all that noise goin' on, I was goin' around the twist. I decides to do somethin' about it, and put us all out of our misery.'

The enormity of his story has long been left in the bush, but the hilarity of his rendition would stay forever. At the conclusion there was silence, shock. The night seemed to stand still and the fire crackled. Then each of the listeners rocked back as one off their heels, lay flat on the ground, and laughed and laughed in the dusty fireside. Someone repeated Dougy's closing statement: 'That'll teach you pair of bastards to annoy me on a Sunday!' Then the camp erupted again, and the rollicking laughter continued until we were exhausted.

Dougy lifted his head to look at the fire, seemingly unamused, then a full grin came over his face, and probably for the first time he allowed himself to see the funny side of what he had done all those years ago.

Next morning I woke early—the moon was still fairly high an hour before first light. I joined Jim and Dougy at the fire and had a quick drink of tea before mustering the fifty or so horses into the temporary pole yards we'd built near the camp. The ringers had nearly finished breakfast as the daylight brightened; the smoke from the fire drifted in the chill air, and hugged the dew-heavy grass across the flat.

The ringers had cut their cribs; a good slab of corned beef and a hunk of damper, with a little sugar and tea for their quart pots, would do for dinner camp. 'May as well get going. It's too cold to roll a smoke.' This was the business end of being a stockman, and everyone took his responsibility seriously.

Dougy was first to spot cattle in the rugged country. He just had a second sense about where to find them. We all dismounted, relieved ourselves, tightened the girths, and were ready for anything. He detailed the men out in groups to scout, and nominated the direction all the mustered cattle would be going in. When the first mob hit the clearing, Doug was in the lead with Jim backing him up. He pulled the lead around and blocked them up with one hand in the air, sitting his horse like a statue. 'Whoa bullocks, whoa bullocks, whoa'—he talked those cattle into submission. Then he put another man in the lead and they all walked away, following him, as though they were going to church.

THE CALF AND THE DINGOES

The country had come away well after the burns, and early seasonal rain had given the grass the jump. There was good feed everywhere. It was great breeder country, the cattle were in good nick, and they had mustered well. Even though it was a fair step for them coming out of the hilly tablelands and onto the flats along the river country, they had come onto camp with full bellies, were well watered and had settled real early.

Those of us ringers who had had an early supper were sitting around the fire. It was always a good feeling having put in a good day; there had been no busters fortunately, and all the horses had pulled up well. The cattle were in a wire holding paddock. Even so, they still had to be watched as there were a few touchy ones in the mob.

We had swapped the odd whip crack through the timber along the way, to keep in touch, but there had not been much chance to talk since dinner camp, where we'd boiled our quarts and had a bit of a blow. The evening was relaxed. It was time for drinking coffee and enjoying a smoke.

The camp coffee was brewed in a pack Dee billy, and made with coffee and chicory grounds as lumpy as a half handful of wheat. It sat on the edge of the fire, just ticking over all evening. Whoever needed a brew just dipped a pannikin in. Or, when a rider came in cold off 'watch', he'd drop his reins, spin his spurs around to face the front of his boots, get a brew and squat for a while, roll a smoke and tell everyone how the cattle were, in about two sentences.

Sometimes this coffee was about as tough as it gets. Some ringers liked to drop a red-hot coal in from the fire. Then when it stopped fizzing, there was a dash of salt and sometimes even a touch of mustard—to bring out the flavour. We never had milk, but it always needed some sugar or a spoonful of crickle grease.

One pannikin of this brew, when I went on watch, did me for a couple of hours. I couldn't go to sleep even if I tried, and I rode around at a leisurely pace, singing quietly. My eyes seemed wedged open wide; I saw everything and never missed a beat. Even when I hit the swag, I seldom went to sleep after being on watch.

This camp was on a clear river terrace above the cattle, but they'd know we were there. I had moved away from the friendly glow of the campfire, and perched myself comfortably on a log to enjoy the night and have a quiet smoke, before it was my turn to go on watch. My horse was saddled, close hobbled and tethered nearby, ready to go.

The moon reflected like a round yellow cheese in the still blackness of the waterhole, at the bend in the gully below. The air had cooled and become heavy after the heat of the day. The smoke was drifting downwards from the campfire, and forming a misty haze above the cattle camped down along the river. The night was quiet, and every now and then as the air shifted I could hear the rattle of the ripples as the water left the shallows downstream and ran away in rivulets over the gravel bed, to who knows where. As I rubbed the coarse flake-cut tobacco in the palms of my hands, the wonderful words of Banjo Paterson just seemed to fit:

> And the drover's life has pleasures
> That the townsfolk never know.

A cow in the mob had been calling out. Her bellow had become quite recognisable. She must have planted her calf, or it got dropped off by the ringers late in the afternoon when it had become too tired to keep up. I was about to stand up when, away up the creek, I heard a calf answer her anxious call. It sounded lonely, lost, hungry, but hopeful. Soon it called to her again, a little nearer now, and it was jogging along, judging by the sound of its call. Then all of a sudden there was an agonising bawl of terror.

A ringer leapt from the fireside, exclaiming, 'The poor little bastard has been hit by a dingo!' Together we stood, staring out into the night.

A hush had come over the camp and all the men were standing up, trying to ascertain what the situation was out there in the dark. Were there any other cattle to ring and protect the calf, and how many dogs might there be?

A scream from the calf echoed through the timber. 'There he goes again! Hell 'e's motorin'. There must be a pack of 'em, but 'e's givin' 'em a run for their money. If 'e keeps goin', 'e might just make the mob. Go little fella, go!'

The almost continuous bellow of agony and fear was coming nearer now. 'Sounds like they may be driving him towards the river to drown him.'

Then from the cattle holding paddock came an answering bellow. 'Holy sufferin' Jesus, that calf must've missed the muster, and that's its mother in the paddock. And now that poor little poddy bastard is out there gettin' chewed alive by them moth-eaten, scavenging, doe-eyed dingo bastards of things.'

Another bawl from the calf reverberated across the rocks and through the bush, amplified by the stillness of the night air. He was nearer now. The cattle were becoming agitated. The ringers were making haste, gathering their horses to go and help those on watch to steady the mob up, should they try and rush.

'There he is now! I can see his baldy head. He's heading for the waterhole. I won't put my horse into a swim in the dark, so Kevin, take my mare to the cattle. I'll go to the river on foot. There's the dogs now. I just caught a glimpse of them.'

'Jesus they are givin' him curry. Bastards!' replied Kevin, as he slipped the hobbles off my mare.

Down the bank I went, out of the moonlight and into the shadows. Tripping over yet another obstacle in my haste, I catapulted myself in topsy-turvy fashion over an embankment and down to the rocks of the main riverbed. I was intent on attacking the dogs, but aware of their capabilities when hostile.

The calf was fairly hollering, and there was a great deal of chaos on the opposite riverbank, then splashing noises. 'They've driven the calf into the river!' I thought. I was furious by this stage. Grabbing handfuls of stones, I pelted them hard and fast at the centre of the commotion. I sent a barrage of withering fire with such force that my shoulders became pained with the effort.

There was enough reflection from the moonlight onto the water to enable me to see the calf standing almost midstream, flank deep, head lowered, swaying in the disturbed water. A scattering of stones on the bank indicated that my broadsides had shifted the dogs and they were now retreating along the bank, so I added further encouragement. I had beaten them so far.

Positioning myself where I could see the calf, I waded in after it. I was soon out of my depth and was swimming fully clothed, with leather leggings and riding boots. The calf had stopped bellowing now, and I could hear it gasping. As I stood up to walk the shallows, the brave little bloke sensed my presence and wheeled about to stand its ground in anticipation of another attack. It was blowing and heaving for breath, and I feared the attackers may have punctured its lungs. Its whole body was quivering as I approached, hand outstretched and talking quietly. It seemed about to charge me, and did make a couple of fumbles that were meant in earnest but lacked energy. The calf was completely spent.

After a little more talking and waiting, the calf staggered forward and smelt my hand. He never moved away. I ran my hand along its back and up along the neck, then went to fondle its ears. They had been nearly pulped by the gnashing and tearing of the dingoes' attack. He was quite well grown and came up to my thighs in height. 'C'mon you poor little bugger,' I said, 'Let's go home.'

I had my hand on his wither, and he leant against me as together we went out into the waterhole, a bit of a swim, then into the shallows of the other side. We both stood panting. I heaved a huge sigh of relief. I don't recall ever being as close to an undomesticated animal as I was in that waterhole.

Gradually his breathing slowed and I realised how cold I had become. The mother was still calling. The ringers had done a good job holding the cattle, especially as there were some touchy ones, and a few big stag bullocks that would have run instinctively to protect a calf in trouble.

'Right-oh old mate,' I said, 'Mama's calling.' He refused to budge, so I got behind him, put my hands high on his battle-scarred rump, and pushed him encouragingly towards the water's edge, up onto the gravel and dry ground. 'Home at last, and away we go.' With that, he let fly with both hind legs, dropped me cold onto the riverbed, and careered off.

WHAD NAME YOU?

I had pulled up for a bit of a blow on Barambah Creek—
nothing special in mind, might catch a fish later on. I
was having a bite to eat under a shady tree when I noticed
a small bunch of Aboriginal children poking about further
along the bank.

As they got closer I watched them. There was an
older boy in the lead, around ten or eleven years old, and
it was he who established what they did and how they
moved along. Appearing through the tall dry grass from
time to time, at their heels, were a couple of half-grown
dingo/cattle-dog pups.

All seemed oblivious of my presence until they were
right on me. But I reckoned they had had me in their
sights all the while. They quietly gathered about ten feet
away from me, looking at everything except me—younger
ones eyeing my food and the billy of tea. They seemed a
little edgy and kept looking all about and handling their
hunting sticks, kicking the dust or toying with the coals
of my dying fire.

One of the dogs stretched himself to sniff my jacket, which was lying in a crumpled heap alongside me. I moved my hand and he darted back, only to try again as soon as he had plucked up the courage.

The eldest boy, whose hunting stick was as long as himself—straight and sharpened—stood now with commanding stance, closest of all, and jabbed the stick into the ground. He kept this up until he had dug a hole at his feet with his purposeful thrusting. When his actions had drawn everyone's attention, including mine, he demanded, 'Whad name you?' They all took up the same stick posture as a show of unity.

I lifted my hand as a gesture towards the encroaching dog, and got a lip-curling snarl for my trouble. Yet again the spear came down thump. 'I said, Whad name you?'

I looked out across the waterhole as I rolled a shirt sleeve, then looked King Billy in the eye and replied, 'I'm a cannibal.'

With that, they bolted. The dogs also got the message, for they had their tails jammed down as hard as they could. If the boys had been wearing shoes, I reckon I would not have been able to see their backsides for heel plates. As they bolted through the trees I heard one scream out fearfully, ''e's a cannibal!'

Then all was quiet again at my little dinner camp on Barambah Creek.

CHARLIE

The big mob of cattle we had mustered out of the ironbark ridges of the red volcanic tablelands were now moving like a liquid red and white mosaic across the green and grassy plains. The blue sky sat down on the horizon, for it was flat as far as the eye could see, and there were some timbered hills over to the left which put a border onto this magnificent scene. Molly hawks hovered over the mob as it rolled along, ready to dive onto anything resembling food.

Bob, the head stockman, was dropping back to speak to me on the tail of the mob. He seemed to disappear off the side of his horse and then come up again, swinging what I thought for a moment was a whip, over and around and above his head. Then he let it go, and it circled like a boomerang across the top of the tailenders towards Algae, a New Australian from Lithuania, who was making a fair fist of becoming a stockman. Algae was nodding off in the heat and from exhaustion, as it had not been an easy muster. The projectile was a six foot carpet snake that Bob had snavelled from the ground while in the saddle. Just before it got to Algae he yelled out 'Daylight!'

Algae nodded, a jerk and a blink, and then nearly died of fright as he saw what was coming after him. He took immediate evasive action and yelled some Lithuanian obscenity to Bob, then gave us both a wave and a grin and rode on around to the wing of the mob.

Bob pulled up, and gestured towards the timbered hills: 'We'll be working the mob over to the old sheep yards site for dinner camp. Nothin' much there any more; they went when the spear grass came in. This is cattle country anyway. But ya gotta take ya hat off to those old fellas bringin' sheep this far up in those days. There's a rider comin' across the plains and he's got a packhorse. If it's who I think it is, he may have mail from the station. You stay here and pick it up. I'm goin' out to the lead and give old Jacky a hand.'

The rider pulled up and said, 'This the Bancroft plant? Well, I've got some mail for you.' He handed me a small parcel of mail from one of his pack bags, and I sat my horse as I thumbed it through. There was one for me and I put the rest in my saddlebag. The mailman said 'G'day' then turned, and with his packhorse on a lead, continued on his way. I held the letter up and Bob gave me the pelican nod, turned his horse and rode back around to the wing of the mob.

My horse was glad of a spell and grazed at the reins' length, handy, while I became totally engrossed in a twenty-one page letter from my elder brother, Norman.

He was managing a big property and I was always interested in what he was doing. I folded it and stowed it in my saddlebag, gathered my horse up, mounted. As we swung about to follow the cattle, I got the surprise of my life—they had completely disappeared.

Looking at the country, I figured where they might be. Those old fellas would have needed timber to build their yards and a shack, and I could see where the timber was reaching out to the flat, following an old creek bed. The tracks of the travelling mob were easy to follow, and I picked up the creek and was riding towards the sound of the cattle.

Along the wide, deep, white sandy creek bed I spotted old Charlie Gibson, an Aboriginal stockman, riding towards me. He seemed to be studying the creek bed, for he would stop, lean from the saddle, look all about, then ride on towards me. After a while he stopped, dismounted and took his quart pot from the saddle. I thought, 'You silly old man, there's no waterhole there.'

He dropped his reins and was down on his knees when I rode up. 'You OK old mate?' I asked.

'Hey Brian, he's good all right, just gettin' drinkin' water, boil up directly at the sheep yards.'

'Fine, old mate, but where's the water?'

''ere 'e is, down 'ere—look all about you. Watch them ants, now see that bee, see that moth. They all know. Brumby been packin' the sand down with 'er front foot. That wader, 'e's been comin' up through the sand. See that insect, 'e knows all about it.'

So Charlie went about his business with his hands and dug quite a hole in that hot riverbed sand. Quite soon the sand became darker and then obviously damp. Then down went Charlie's quart pot, and he dug out a big area in the bottom of the hole. Not until then did he pause in the laborious ritualistic rhythm of his excavation.

He waited a little while, and then looked at me with laughing, black eyes, as I too had dismounted and was on my hands and knees alongside. His happy face, with an unspoken question, invited me to look down his 'well'. Sure enough—there it was. He dipped his quart-pot lid and offered me a drink. The water was so cold that it cooled the metal of the cup. I looked up and along that desolately dry creek bed, and then back at my friend. He just nodded his wise old head and gave me that sunshine smile, then quite humbly asked, 'OK Brian?'

'Charlie,' I said as I had another sip, 'you're the best!'

He put his quart pot itself down the hole and, when completely immersed, he slipped the lid on, so that there would be more than a full quart.* He filled my quart pot in a similar fashion by way of simple courtesy, and sat them on the sand beside him.

---

* That was a system we used to take water to the dinner camp. The quart-pot lid was tight fitting and so designed that the meniscus of the water doesn't break. Back at camp, having carried the quart pot vertically, sometimes for a considerable distance, we'd drop our hat onto the ground, dip the crown and, as the lid was removed, allow the excess water to flow into the hollow. While the quart pot came to the boil, we'd enjoy a drink of cold water from the hat.

Then Charlie went back to watching the wet sand. Pretty soon, a European bee landed. He watched it move about and steady up to take on water. The bee had his proboscis down and going for it when Charlie deftly fastened onto his wings with his thumb and forefinger, and held the kicking bee firmly but kindly in his grasp.

Talking all the while in a gentle tone to the bee, Charlie trudged across the sand to a river gum and began looking about. With his left hand he drew a long length of spider web that was hanging in the tree. Then he spun a cocoon about the bee's legs with the web. When he was satisfied, he gathered his reins and stepped onto his horse so carefully, saying, 'When you see 'im go, pass me quart and keep up.'

With that, he let the bee go. After a big dipping swoop the bee managed to get going, and I watched him as I too mounted up. I could follow the bee's flight, as Charlie had left a straggly length of web to trail. I lost sight for an instant, picked it up again as the web caught the sunlight, and from then on it was quite easy to follow. As we went I handed Charlie his quart pot, and he never took his eyes off the bee's progress.

Together we followed quite some distance until the bee went into the tree where the hive was. From down on the ground it was easy to identify that there was quite a big hive up there. Charlie took one look at me, and knew that his time had not been wasted. As we turned to ride back to the cattle and dinner camp he said, 'Yakai Bungee, good bush tucker. We been get 'im by and by.'

We'd walked the cattle the five miles into the yards later in the afternoon, when it cooled a little. With the sun behind us, the cattle would yard quietly and water well. Resting my head up against an ironbark tree and watching my hobbled horse grazing contentedly nearby, I was glad to be rid of the saddle for a while, and enjoyed my quart of tea, damper and corned beef crib. I slid my boots off, drew my trouser legs up and was enjoying the coolness of the shade. I went back over the muster in my mind.

My memory was jolted back to the Mount Bluey tableland earlier in the day. I had been scanning for cattle on a high rocky knob, noting the positions of the smoke billowing high from fires lit by ringers as they moved about, mustering and bringing the main mob around to the west, where I would join them again. There was a lone scraggly tree and nothing much else growing there. It was a place of absolute solitude.

Suddenly there was a rush of air, and the next thing a huge wedge-tailed eagle landed on a dead branch of that scraggly tree, almost on top of my head. The eagle drew his wings and nodded his magnificent head, then gave me the 'eagle gawk'. Everything about him was threatening. The talons on his feathered legs were the biggest set of shredding machines I have ever seen, and his curved and hooked beak was from here to there long; but I think it was the eyes that got me.

When I got over his surprise arrival I admired his plumage, but once he fixed those yellow eyes on me

206

I felt truly ill at ease. I turned my horse, and both of us were glad to leave the eagle to his own magnificent company.

~

It was always a great feeling to yard the mob towards evening and finally shut the gate at the out-station yards. We had other yards with open camps we mustered to, but the out-station was home. We all pitched in and helped the horse tailer unload the packs and carry the bags and swags across the yard to the camp. This was a good solid wooden building up on huge poles, and built on a rise so it caught any breeze about. It had a wide covered verandah all the way around, and the rooms were well ventilated. From up there you could see forever across the plains to the timber. We always kept it tidy, and I had scythed the thistles and weeds that grew about the yard after the rains before we went bush the week before.

We bushed all the horses into the horse paddock and they went sedately to the waters of the anabranch, where they walked out up to their bellies and drank great long draughts through trembling lips, nodding their heads and wetting their nostrils. Then they thrashed their heads about and threw water everywhere in their exaltation. It was always a great joy to me to watch this ritual and the subsequent heading for the bank, then their rolling the roll of freedom in the dirt.

The men behaved pretty much the same—the difference being that we had only one shower. It was under a large round corrugated-iron tank, which was perched high on top of four wooden poles and a platform. Under this was a rough concrete slab, with three sides surrounded by corrugated iron. There was a tap, and a big shower rose in the middle. On full bore, water came out of there in such a flood that you needed to take a deep breath before you turned on the tap, or risk drowning.

Clothes off and boots off—towel, soap and razor, down the stairs and away along the pathway to the shower tank. I could not wait to feel that water all over my body and wash away the dust, grime and horse sweat from all those days of riding. As I threw the towel over the rail a voice from the verandah called, 'Don't use all the water, mate!'

I spun the tap and shut my eyes. Holy Cow! What happened next was the worst! I was hit by a multitude of wasps, which had made their nest all over the shower rose in our absence. I headed out the doorway, grabbed my towel, tried to defend myself, and headed straight for the stairway to the verandah. That was a bad decision. I should have stuck to the pathway, but in my haste headed straight across my scythed thistles, all lying thick, brittle and prickly. I have never been so top-and-tailed in my whole life!

Meanwhile, Charlie was down at the anabranch in the creek, having the time of his life with the other Aboriginal stockmen.

The next morning I was too sore to do anything useful in the yards, and spent the day in the camp. That evening Freddie and Charlie were making preparation to go fencing and were organising their material, packhorse plant, tools and tucker. They had been given instructions to go past Smith's well corner and repair the tailend of the fence going up onto the Mount Bluey tableland.

The following evening before supper there was a call from upstairs: 'Two riders coming in, Greasy, better put another gallon of water in the stew.' It was Charlie and Freddie, at least two days early. What the hell had gone wrong?

They both looked OK and all the horses seemed sound. We all went out to the wagon shed, where they would drop their packs, to meet them. They sat their horses in an attitude almost of shamefulness, as may a young scolded child.

'What you fellas doin' back here? You gone down crook or somethin'?' asked the head stockman.

The cheeks of their usually jovial faces were hanging like sack drapes in a 'dunny' doorway. Their eyes were sunken and full of remorse. It was as if their spirit had gone deep within and they weren't even there any more. For all intents and purposes they had become invisible.

I sensed that this must be some terrible Aboriginal business, as I knew all these men were tribal and initiated. I had seen the great welted scars on their shoulders, across and under their collar bones, on their bellies and upper arms, when at odd times we had shared a waterhole to have a bogie. I needed to know why they had become so terrified as grown men.

'You sure you ain't crook, Charlie? You look like you've taken a dog bait.'

With no eye contact, they hung their heads, their bodies pleading to be understood and forgiven for their failure. As they sat their horses, I noticed that they had slipped their boots from the stirrup irons and their feet hung loosely.

Finally Charlie lifted his head and looked at Freddie, then turned to us and said in a low and hesitant voice, 'No birds up in that country boss. It's bad for us there. Old man eagle told us to stay away, go straight away and keep goin' all the way, little bit long way, an' all the way 'ome!'

That night as I sat on the verandah there was hardly a breeze to disturb the gentle white flame of the carbide light. There were no hobbled horses handy, but I could hear the bells of the mustering horses, which were enjoying the freedom to graze all through the night in the horse paddock.

I was recovering from the hiding the wasps had given me and I had removed most of the thistles from my feet. I was pondering on the happenings of the day. The two Aboriginals, the reluctant travellers of Mount Bluey, commanded my thoughts. Over time I had noticed peculiarities of Aboriginal behaviour and had come to accept them, just little things like not sleeping openly out in the moonlight. And fish caught were always hidden away from the moonlight. But today, those two blokes had been traumatised by a deep spiritual experience. Me too; for I also had seen that eagle.

I had known Charlie for a long time and I owed him so much. He'd taught me how to stretch a green hide on the ground or on an old wagon-wheel tyre; how to cut the strands from the hide, starting from the outside, take the shoulders off and shave the hair down; how to twist all the strands and splice the hobble ring on, keeping it stretched; then, bye and bye, how to rub it down with fat and drag it along the motor road, and then rub it down again. We made great ropes for yard work. He had also been my main tutor in cold-shoeing the horses.

Once we had been mustering up out of ironbark country. In that country I noticed that Charlie always had his dinner camp by a special tree. On this particular day I carried my quart over to where he was sitting and just sat and had my dinner. There was no conversation, but I was aware that he was up to something. Every now and then he would look down to his side and pick something up and put it in his mouth. He was sitting cross-legged and his crib was in front of him.

'What you doin' old man? Don't ya like the corned beef I cooked ya?'

'Oh no, Brine, 'es good. I didn't usen't to eat my crib, not just yet—I got me nice an' quiet sugarbag 'ere.' And he held up a plump little black native bee, chock full of honey, and he popped it in his mouth, and gave a smile and an all-over shaking laugh: 'Come an' see.'

So around the tree I went, and watched. Every now and again one gallant worker of the hive would arrive loaded, and just as it was about to enter the hole at the base of the tree—grab, gobble and it was over, except for the lip-licking. Those little fellows have no sting at all, and I can vouch that the sugarbag honey is the liquor of all honeys.

At the conclusion of the dinner camp, Charlie announced, 'We been see Trump later on.'

The manager, Jim, was on this muster, and his father was the travelling manager for the cattle company. During the afternoon, as the cattle were walking free, I told young Jim McConnachie what Charlie had said. He replied, 'There's no way, mate, Dad would be here—I spoke to him yesterday morning on the phone and he's up in the Gulf on Van Rook.'

We yarded the cattle at Ironbark yards, unsaddled our horses, hung the saddlecloths over a rail and were sitting in a circle waiting for our quarts to boil when there was a cloud of dust on the other side of the yards. A four-wheel drive had just pulled up, and out got Jim's father, the Trump. There was nobody more surprised than Jim.

Old Charlie just sat cross-legged on the ground at his fire with all the other Aboriginal stockmen. I watched him for a reaction. There wasn't any. He had already read that page!

～

The bullocks had been accumulating in the holding paddocks. They were as fat as fools, coming off the early burnt feed following the rain. The ones not quite up to scratch had been camp-drafted out on the flat on horseback, and now we had a mob of cattle that we were really proud of.

I was sitting on my horse out on the wing when they came up out of the riverbed sand. All those months of work; now here they come. Up close the noise, the energy that a thousand bullocks on the move generate is quite amazing. They were gleaming in the early morning sunshine, which had leapt over the hills, right on time. They were roly-poly fat, and seemed to move as one. The landscape disappeared as they passed.

Out in front was the familiar riding posture of that grand old Aboriginal stockman. He looked like a beacon in his brand-new blue bushman shirt and his old, wide, curled-brim Akubra hat, with a Gulf bash up the front. He was a proud man, and yet displayed only a humble dignity. He was confident and reliable and he knew every stone and every tree and was part of the country ahead, because he belonged. Instinctively he would know the changing mood of the mob in behind him, and he was the man who would steady the lead all the way eastward, across the ranges and down to Townsville.

Charlie would be missed down at the Aboriginals' camp above the river while he was away. His infectious laughter and good humour was always in the air. On the nights when they were roasting beef rib-bones on the campfire coals, his laughter drifted on the smoke and rattled around the river gums. It would be well into the small hours, when all was quiet enough to hear the squeak and churn of the windmill, before those people were lulled into a sleep of peacefulness and full-belly contentment. How humble were those who slept on the ground. How close were they to reality.

Still the mob was coming, and up rode yet other Palm Island men. Freddie Toomba and Jimmy Percy, the granddaddy of them all, and Jackie, who could ring a mob of cattle and, bye and bye, unwind them and lead them away like no other.

Charlie's offsider, Freddie Toomba, had not forgotten that he was on show to all the ladies of the Aboriginals' camp. He was well decked out and carried his whip in the crook of his elbow. He turned his horse and rode towards the tail of the mob, encouraging the bullocks in their stride—'Urendangi hey! Urendangi hey!' I saw him fumble at his saddle bag and then turn about and ride forward. He's done it again! Freddie had no teeth, but for special occasions he had a magnificent set wrapped in a colourful spare neckerchief he carried in his saddlebag. He was now prepared for the ride past! The bullocks were the only ones who did not applaud as the true blue, laughing cavalier rode by.

Charlie, well, he just took Freddie for granted; after all, they were two of a kind. Their Aboriginal names had been taken away, but the tribal scars of initiation left no

214

doubt as to who they were—these tall, dark men of the saddle. They were spiritual people within themselves, and I am grateful that they had taken me there.

WHAT A DAY!

There were eight of us, well mounted, who rode towards the sunrise to muster the eighty square mile horse-spelling paddock. We rode almost in silence for three miles before we hit the fence, then we split up at the ANZAC mill, three following the fence and the others covering the inside country. Horses were few and far between. There was plenty of feed, an amazing abundance of wildflowers, and the country looked great.

Then the action began. In no time flat we had eighty head in hand. I was in the lead while my two cobbers were scouting out. As pre-arranged, all the men came together at the Wild Horse mill for a dinner camp. We set our quarts to boil and sat on a long log and enjoyed looking over the horses we'd gathered in our morning's work—around two hundred head in hand.

When we moved off camp into the sun and headed towards the Five Mile mill, it was a magnificent sight as the horses trotted across a great expanse of grey, drying grass, then through sparse timber onto a plain of two to three thousand acres. Horses were coming in at regular intervals, some rather reluctantly, in little family-like groups of up to twenty at a time. The ground was flat and there were men and horses going everywhere.

Kevin, the head stockman, gave the signal and we rung around to pull them up and steady for a while. That number of horses, full of running, can create enormous pressure, and they need to be slowed down for their own good and to remain manageable. We were holding the mob up against some timbered country, and men whose horses had done a lot of the running needed to be remounted on fresh horses.

The horses were a mixture; mostly stockhorses that had seen service in the mustering camps. There were young ones only a short season after being broken-in and turned out to grow, and there were a number of heavier horses from the packhorse plants and for bronco branding.

The experienced head stockman had gone among them at a crouch. Talking all the time and mentioning horses by name as he came upon ones he knew, he stopped now and then to pat them on the pastern and run a kind and knowing hand up to the shoulder. He moved with commanding stealth and his voice cast such a spell that they all succumbed to believing that indeed they had been hobbled, and stood motionless on that spot.

He beckoned one of the ringers to ride up close and hand him a few leads. Before much time had elapsed, the pick were caught properly, led out and saddled. Then the spent horses were set free to have a roll and run with the main mob, which had started to mill and become a little restless. They were itching to run out across this extensive flat plain.

One of the fresh remounts tried desperately to establish a point of view and unseat Ray Crane. It was a magnificent display all round—one would need to be a little more than a bush mug to ride her.

Then we turned westward, heading towards the lowering sun. We had a large mob in hand now, and they began to run. All the horses wanted to be in front as we headed for the station. The wing got too wide, we couldn't hold them, and away they went.

No doubt they knew that the great billowing dark bank of storm clouds was seemingly jumping out of its skin and bearing down on us from over the ranges behind. We closed the wings in and then let them run, coming in behind the two riders on point in the lead. Hooves thundered, manes and tails flew, and those magnificent animals squealed with delight, running before the storm in the greatest of spirits, moving effortlessly across the great treeless expanse of the grassy plain.

They steadied themselves up nearer home. What a terrific sight, seeing them coming down the basalt wall and into Station Creek. The track down was strewn with timber and hard, rounded basalt boulders. Then it swung around pure white column terraces, overhanging water holes in which floated blue-flowering water lilies. Out in front the leaders lengthened stride from the creek and then, under the setting sun, through the gate and into the station paddock went three hundred and seventy-four horses.

When our saddle-horses had been attended to, it was back to the ringers' quarters—and there was only one thing on our minds. Boots and leggings off, moleskins in a heap and stripped to our hides, we headed to the creek as fast as we could go.

There had been a recent fresh in the creek and a good run of water was going over the waterfall and down into our swimming hole, which was volcanic, crater-like and very deep. Up the side on the pathway was anchored a lengthy springy plank we used as a diving board, positioned so that you could take it on the run.

Well, I was first there. It was not until in mid-air, and a long way to the water, that I heard the giggling—too late mate. The station Aboriginal women had scampered from their picnic when they heard us coming and had hidden in the undergrowth. When I resurfaced, the audience responded with yells of delight and a round of applause—'Yakai' and cooees.

What a day!

THE MOONLIGHT STALLION

We had decided to buy this hard-case, rock-strewn, rough-and-ready piece of timbered country near the Great Dividing Range, above the Darling Downs. There were no fences, no buildings and no access to electricity.

There would be water underground—that was my hunch—as to have country and no water was to have no country at all. We sank a bore to 360 feet, and Bingo! The best water in Australia. 'Camp where the cattle camp' is a bushman's philosophy—so our daughter Tania and I pegged out our house plan on top of a flat-top hill with dried cattle pats, and there were views to spare.

Reg Williams had brought his chainsaw and together we cut down the dead ring-barked trees to clear the site. One large ironbark log was left intact and hauled to the western end of the flat. 'Don't you ever cut that log up for firewood, Brian—that's going to be our conference

221

log,' determined Reg. It remains so today. It has become a special place to watch the sunset on the close of day, to reminisce and share with friends.

Together we hauled massive sandstone flag rocks to stone pave the courtyard, some of them weighing up to half a ton. I still don't know why we two always had to do things so big. The overhead ironbark beams, 10 × 4 inches, were 20 feet long. The view to the westwards through massive glass doors and windows, in all seasons, day and night, is awe-inspiring.

We hadn't long moved in when one night I awoke with a feeling of unease, a sensation not new to me. Having spent a lot of time in the bush, signals like this are not to be taken lightly. Our property was isolated in those days, so just in case, I went for a walk about the house. Everything was dark and immersed in silence.

I was sitting on a lounge sofa to enjoy the solitude when I noticed a shadow appear on the floor. I spun around. It was becoming light outside, and I hurried to the other side of the building just in time to see a full moon sliding out from under a cloudbank in the east.

The moon appeared like a white-hot branding iron thrust into the black bucket of the night. The stars in the west, which had sparkled in anticipation, now paled into non-existence. It was such a beautiful night. Captivated, I stayed up and watched through the night, as the shadows in the bushland ran away from the moon's brilliance.

Many hours later I hunkered over the back of a lounge chair and watched as this great moon, now orb-like and of substance, seemed to be drawing nearer as it waned and then threatened to set between me and the distant hills. It drew nearer to acknowledge my exaltation.

Suddenly, the white stallion came into view, measuring his tread so purposefully on the massive flagstones of the courtyard. Each step was a gesture of grandeur. Once his majestic stance was framed by the glass windows, and his silhouette satisfied his vanity, he pounded a front hoof to the stone. The noise echoed through the building, punctuating his challenging stance of virility, as much to say 'Here I am!'

I could not see the moon—he completely blotted that out—but the room itself, where I was crouched behind and peering over a lounge chair, was lit as by day from its white brilliance. In the crisp, clear air of early pre-dawn, every sound was audible. I could feel my own pulse belting. Nothing prepared me for what followed.

Slowly the stallion turned his lowered head to the side—presenting, as it were, yet another magnificent profile to be considered, and almost rolling his shoulder in the process. 'Enough of that!' his vanity spoke. Arrogance and majesty seemed to travel along his spine and arch his neck, forcing him to lower his head onto his chest.

Even though I was looking into the light, his eyes appeared to redden as he glared unblinkingly at the ground. His legs were on the stonework, spaced like four Corinthian columns. He stood statuesque and motionless for a minute or two, then the breath he had been compressing erupted. His nostrils flared as the hot air belted out like steam. A scream from deep within his belly rattled the glass and he shook his head violently, as though he had been exhausted by the sudden release of emotion.

Lifting his head a little, he tugged in a few deep breaths, shuffled his stance a little and then became more composed. Almost relaxed, he admired his reflection in the glass with the moon full square behind him.

Bowing and nodding his magnificent head, he struck his tail high at the dock into an arch over his rump, and began scything it this way and that. Maintaining his body posture, he slowly moved his head to present yet another profile to the stallion in the glass's reflection—or was he communicating with his spiritual ancestors?

The moon was sinking fast and was now below his girth, just above the horizon, away out there beyond the distant hills, which were pink in the dawning light.

~

Moana Omah, the white stallion, had presented himself as no other horse we had ever owned. On that mystic morning, it was as though he communicated with his ancestors in the Arabian deserts, for his stud-book breeding was Silver Moonlight.*

---

* Moana Omah's performance as a saddle-horse, and his progeny, were loyal to their trust. In the 1980 Tom Quilty Gold Cup Endurance Ride, Carene rode him in the R.M. Williams winning team and he was the first stallion to finish.

MARGARET AND THE KILLERS

We were walking a big mob of sheep south off the Barcoo and were approaching Tambo in good time on our way to the Neave River country and the Augathella scrub. It had been a dry season up till now, but a few points of rain had gone through just in time to keep the herbage going and provide a pick for these hungry wethers, to keep them walking and growing wool. After a long day in the saddle I was looking forward to a good pull up. Ahead in the darkness I could pick out a campfire glowing through the mimosa scrub. Home at last.

Although it was exhilarating riding in the moonlight, with the freshness of the night air, it was real good riding into the camp after slogging it out through the heat of the day. I had a saddle-horse and three spare horses and we all were tired, cold and hungry.

Just as I came into the firelight a female voice called through the darkness, 'Is that you, Bungee?'

'Yeah,' I said, 'I'll be over in a while, as soon as I rug and feed my horses.' Funny, I thought, no one down here knows my North Queensland nickname. I wonder who that can be. I didn't recognise the voice, but it had a familiar ring about it. When I'd had a wash, I sat down on a log with a good plate of camp-oven stew and a pannikin of tea.

Bush women are mostly all the same, straight up and down. 'G'day Bungee,' she says, 'my name's Margaret. I'm at the Main Roads camp out past Pelican Lagoons. Walkin' a few are we? Got any killers?'

I liked her from the start. Everything she said was to the point. As I ate my food, I looked at her across the top of the fire. No one else in the camp said a word in answer to her question. I noticed that the glowing embers and the odd flicker of flame made her weather-hardened face take on a commanding appearance against the black back-drop of the night sky, and the fire illumined the stunted mimosa bushes at her back. She wore a ringer's hat at a jaunty angle on the back of her head, and the brim was held curled with a leather thong from the crown.

This lady, Margaret somebody, sat on the log with her knees drawn up to support an elbow, and in the fingers of her cupped hand was a roly smoke of flake-cut tobacco. Every now and again she would take a drag on the smoke, seemingly to punctuate the conversation. All the while she held the other palm outstretched a little to shield her face from the heat of the fire, as the intermittent night breeze lifted to fan the glowing coals. I thought to myself that I would need a poultice on the back of my neck to draw a 'durry' as big as that—and keep it going.

'No,' I said, 'they are not my sheep. I am shifting them for the Chandler family of Delta Station.'

'Oh, come on now Bungee, you must 'ave picked a few up on the way? Don't tell me you ain't!'

In a condescending manner I replied, 'Well; there might be *one* in the mob.'

'We killed early on this evenin' boss, so she could have half, if she's stuck.'

'Okay Loosewire, give her half a mutton. And Margaret, what's the deal?'

'Well, I'll tell you what,' Lady Margaret replied, as she squared her hat up a couple of times. 'How about if I take all your drovers' dirty clothes from their swags back to our camp and wash 'em, and bring 'em onto camp tomorrow arvo? I'll find you easy. You'll only be six or eight miles along the route by tomorrow evenin'.'

'That's a deal mate, bloody good idea. Fine.'

The next evening, as the sheep came into the break for the night camp, there she was, and another woman as well. The clothes were all washed and folded. They even smelled nice. All we had to do was sort them out. The men thanked the ladies most profusely. They were happy as Larry about the arrangement, and could not wait to jump into the billabong and then change into their clean clothes.

'Tell you what,' says Margaret, 'if you get in early tomorrow, do another killer up for us and bring it over to the Main Roads camp, about ten miles in towards the Augathella road. We'll cook you men up a bloody big feed. Yez can 'ave a hot shower, and we'll put a few cold ones in the fridge for ya. What do ya reckon, Boss Drover?'

I had only to take a glance at the men to know that if I refused I would be first into the billabong, clothes and all! So we agreed.

The next evening went as planned. We finished the day and headed off early to the Main Roads camp, anticipating hospitality as promised. We were far from being disappointed. As it turned out, I had met her husband in the late 1950s when he was shifting a mob down to Boulia from Winton.

It was a great success all round. I had never seen such great tucker come out of a camp oven. We all went to our swags, clean as whistles and full as ticks. That, when you are droving, is a rare experience.

A couple of days later Jim, one of the men, said, 'What about we do another mutton up for Margaret? She does a bloody good thing for us all. If we don't do it tomorrow, we'll be too far away to cut back to the Main Roads camp. There's a couple of strays come into the mob today, just before we ran into them goats on the anabranch. There is a nice young wether with horns. I seen 'im in the break this evenin'. He's got two red brand dots on his back. I can spot him easy. Okay by you Brian?'

'Yeah mate, sure, I'm easy. Go for your life!'

On this particular section of the stock route, there was quite an officious stock-route inspector, and he had already caused me a lot of concern. As I had a permit for droving wethers only, he had made me yard the sheep and he drafted off all the good-sized sucker lambs that had been born as we moved along. This was disappointing for us all, as they had been nurtured by my men; some bottle-fed at night when they were younger, to keep them going strong. The small ones were even shifted to the next camp by Loosewire, the fencer and cook, so they never had to walk. Yeh, we reckoned he was a bit over the fence all round, this bloke!

Jim killed the young horny wether the following late afternoon, close to the camp, which was laid out in a clearing of a patch of mimosa scrub, sheltered from the cold evening breeze. He was standing over the newly slaughtered sheep, casually stropping a skinning knife on the steel, when the stock-route inspector and his offsider roared into camp in their four-wheel drive.

Nobody moved; but all eyes were on Jim. He was one tough looking bloke whichever way you looked at him. He'd fought against the Japanese in the Pacific and he would never take one backward step. He just stood his ground, and kept stropping that skinning knife, slow and purposeful, with his jaw set and his steely eyes on the Toyota and its two occupants.

The inspector held his ground, and kept the engine running. The offsider jumped out and ran around to where Jim was. He glared at Jim and hesitantly turned the sheep over to observe the paint brand. As our brand was two blue dots, he knew instantly that we were in the wrong.

Still bent over the sheep, he looked up into Jim's face. Jim was still slowly stropping the Green River knife and holding that steely stare. The offsider, thinking better of it, and taking the right option under the circumstances, looked across at his boss and gave him a nod and thumbs up. He got back into the Toyota as fast as he could, and they left in the same manner as they had arrived.

Jim cracked the biggest grin and received whoops of support from all us bystanders. His was a classic performance, quite spontaneous, and he sure as hell got me off the hook. Not a word had been said.

'Margaret will enjoy this one, boys,' Jim said. 'Maybe we'll only give her half. I reckon we earned a few chops! What do ya say, Boss?'

BUNYAS

The Bunya Mountains form a high point on the Great Dividing Range, north-west of Brisbane. The rich red volcanic soil supports fine rain forest, and the most magnificent specimen, among many, is the bunya pine. The base of the tree looks like an elephant's foot and the trunks are tremendous steeples of towering timber. Periodically they shed a bunya cone, which contains up to a hundred walnut-sized seeds—a great attraction for the Aboriginal people. The Bunya Mountains have forever, according to their story, been a social meeting place and one of tremendous significance for ceremony and cultural exchange.

White men, too, have visited the Bunyas in time of need. Reg McCullen, grandson of the first packhorse mailman out of Ipswich to the South Burnett, told me that as a lad in the Depression years he used to ride to the Bunyas with a packhorse and collect bunya seeds. They have a rich food value, and would supplement his family's meagre diet of whatever they could afford or grow in those hard years.

It has been my experience that if one has an affiliation with country, given a chance that country will grow on you, as have the Bunyas on me.

~

Years ago I was up in that country and standing up against the trunk of a bunya tree among a bed of nettles, peering into the drifting, dripping fog to observe anything of interest. There was a shift of air and a moan came from the bowers above, then the fog thinned a little …

There it was, a scrub wallaby a little distance away, squat, with his back arched and his tail laid out flat along the ground behind, like a downpipe to drain the water from his rain-saturated back. He shook his ears violently to rid himself of water and then, with new focus, acknowledged my presence with a blinking stare of disbelief.

I dragged my coat up around my neck and agreed that we were both a couple of mugs for being out in this weather. Then the breeze changed again and swirled the other way. The fog lifted, as if by a thermal current, partially revealed a grotesque form adjacent to the forest.

I left my shelter, and walked towards it. The ghost-like apparition was a set of timbered cattle yards in need of repair and a shave—for lichen and fungus drooped thickly from the timber, as a tribute to its age. The yards appeared kindly, in a way, and complemented the scene.

Having been engrossed I had not noticed the cattle that had come to encircle me, to snort, nod and, like the wallaby, shake their heads in disbelief. They were magnificent cattle, Angus, fat and so sleek that the water never hung on their hide but ran directly off, and they were standing up to their knees in lush kikuyu grass. They had a sweetness about them, as do all healthy animals. I walked back to the humble homestead in the mist with my obedient entourage close behind.

'What do you think?' asked Frank Unwin.

'Everything you say is true, Frank. What's the plan?'

'Well you've seen something of the country; now here's what we're gonna do. Susie and I are going to get married and together we are going to turn this place into a monumental environmental place of discovery for people from all over the world to enjoy our Australian heritage, and especially Australians.'

That was twenty-five years ago, and they did. I am so proud of them, and Australians all must be grateful that among us there are dreamers who help us to believe in the dream. The cattle yards have long gone, with the cattle, but the wallabies remain.

One day I was at The Bunyas soon after a school group had left, and there was endless laundry to be hung on the line. At a loose end, I volunteered with the peg basket. A lady offered to assist, and together we got stuck in. As we went about the job at hand, she began to talk. 'We had some dramas last night, did you hear? An elderly English lady was lost out in the forest, and they had to get the Search and Rescue squad up. They finally found her early this morning with a spotlight from the rescue helicopter, so they say. She was OK, a bit cold, but otherwise OK.'

The story intrigued me, so I followed it up. I went to Frank's office, got the lady's name, the family she was with, their address and telephone number. Much to my dismay, I eventually discovered that the lady concerned had finished her sojourn and had flown back to England. I expressed an interest in her story, the family kindly gave me her address, and a correspondence developed between us.

The lady was a most stable, intellectual and educated person, a schoolteacher all her life, specialising in chemistry and science. She must have got something right, as she was a granny and had seventeen grandchildren. This was her seventh visit to Australia. She had never met an Aboriginal person, nor did she know anything, as she said, about their very interesting culture. Anything she may have sensed up the mountain for seven to eight hours 'could not have come from inside my head', she had written.

In her letters she talked me through her journey, wandering at leisure the pathways through the magnificent rainforest; total solitude. 'It is so peaceful, and to even think was to disturb the silence. There was a ferny grove off to the side of the pathway, which was catching the sun's beams, reaching down and shafting through the near total canopy.'

On sitting down most comfortably, huddled up among those ferns, she felt almost embraced by their welcome. Soon she had the most surprising sensation of spiritual expansion, and became as one with the environment. Too spellbound to move, she remained motionless until the stars came out. This is what she wrote.

'After a short space of time I noticed that the stars were fainter and seemed to be covered by a fine net curtain; could it be phosphorescent spider's web? I don't remember seeing many spiders. The curtain faded and there were the stars once more.

'The apparition kept appearing, although it was slightly changed and became more opaque, more like a cream curtain, and this did obscure the stars. Later on the picture changed again, and it seemed that cottonwool was rolling in between the trees. Could it be just mist rolling down the hills? [I was later told there was no mist that night.] Next, the cottonwool settled into shapes, two of them, one on each side. On my left was a lozenge-like figure, with what looked like a very small head. I thought of it as a dinosaur. On the right was a small tubby figure, which I could only describe as a very small dumpy pony with horns! Neither of these explanations would seem to fit the marsupial animals of Australia.

'These figures stayed with me until I was "rescued", although they were not permanent and they came and vanished as did the various curtains. In the central dark area where the trees overlapped was a different type of figure, smaller and not so clear. These figures were somehow shiny.

'Next, the figures seemed to advance towards me. I waved my stick and the central ones swayed then backed away, like hanging lianas. Then I thought they were not to harm me, so I lowered my stick and they advanced once more. I now came to the realisation that perhaps they were to care for me, to the point that someone, something was trying to say something to me, in a more pressing manner each time. Much later, as I heard men approaching, I noticed that the back cloth seemed to be solid like a tent, enclosing various figures and blotting out the background trees.'

With the lady's full story under my belt, I went to visit Frank at The Bunyas, to share it with him.

'Remember that elderly English lady who was lost in the Bunya forest, Frank?'

'Yes, I do quite vividly', and he reclined a little further into his green upholstered armchair, anticipating an epistle.

I told him of my searching out and contacting the lady, then related her whole story, describing the sketches she made and the maps she sent me. When I was finished, Frank was not overly impressed, which was a disappointment to me.

'So, what do you reckon, mate?'

'Of course I believe everything you say, Brian. You know why? Because I've heard it all before!'

236

'How did you manage that, mate, because I am the only person that she has divulged her experience to.'

'Well, I'll tell you. An old Aboriginal man, years ago, told me the same story. Now you figure that out!'

THE SCRUBBER BULL

I did not recognise the ringer hobbling towards me from the horse yards. It was right on dusk and his silhouette against the fading glow in the sky was quite indistinguishable. As he drew nearer I saw that he was not in good shape at all, He limped and hobbled his way towards me, holding one arm akimbo as though clutching his ribs, and his thigh with the other. I paused and watched him come in. Then I recognised the hat. 'Is that you Harpo?' I called.

'Yeah mate, that's me, sore and bloody sorry.' Then I noticed that he had no boots on and he walked laboriously in stockinged feet, and they too looked worse for wear.

'What's with the no boots mate?'

'Hang on, I gotta sit down. Bugger the boots. Take a look at this 'ere!' He turned on the log and I could not believe it. His riding trousers were torn from above his leggings to his belt. 'Not bad eh? Lost about half a pound o' steak off me rump as well, mate, and jeez it's bitin'.'

'You blokes, of the Black Springs camp, went out to do the brander scrub today didn't ya?'

'Yeah we sure did. We had a great day. I didn't pull up too well, mate, but the boys had a lot of fun.'

'I've got a spare pair of boots you can 'ave,' I offered.

'No mate. I'll be right till mornin', an' I'll get some from the station store. I got some dancin' pumps at the quarters, meantime.'

After supper, when all was quiet and peaceful and the day's rough edges had been forgotten, Harpo told me the saga of the Brander Scrub.

'We got into them scrubbers early in the piece. We'd 'ad a go at 'em earlier on in the moonlight but they were too bloody quick. They split as they hit the scrub and we lost 'em.

'Today we struck 'em right. I got onto a big horned cleanskin bull, and stayed with 'im. He was too big for me to step off and toss. I just hoped someone'd hear me and back me up. I was fair up 'im, and jeez we were liftin'. Mate I was packin' 'em, but I stayed with 'im. Then that new ringer, ya know, you might 'ave seen 'im about. 'e wears them R.M. Williams shirts with the gussets in the back and them double pockets. Well, he's good mate. He came in behind me and yelled. "Stay with 'im!"

'Just then a piece of timber hits me above the leggings and ripped me pants, arse and all, nearly throws me out of the saddle. I lost me stirrup iron but stayed on, and we were as flat as a strap. This new bloke, he grabs him by the tail as he came in on the other side, and rolled him like you wouldn't believe. He was off his horse and had the tail round his hind leg, and we had a couple of bull straps on 'im in no time flat.

'It wasn't long before the rest turned up, and they couldn't believe we had the big bludger tied up. They weren't too sympathetic about me trousers, or me leg for that matter. They said, "You get paid for chasing cattle not climbing trees Harpo."

'Anyway, one of the ringers said he had a camera in his saddlebag, and he wanted to take a photo of this bloody great cleanskin. By now he was buggered and layin' flat out, and still blowin' like buggery. Every now and then he'd give a heave and a bellow, a snort and a fart—he'd never been tied up before—and he lets everyone know that he was not a happy chappy!

'Just for fun, they reckoned they should put a pair of boots on his horns, just for the photograph, before we sawed them off. I was wearing a pair of elastic sides so, being a mug, slipped them off and put one on each of his horns. We all stood around for the photo. The other blokes were hangin' around talkin' about their run on the other cattle, and just havin' a smoke, and sayin' that the brander scrubbers might be a little bit more easy by 'n by to wheel, now that the ring leader had been quietened down—well, he would be directly.

'One of the ringers, Ginge I think it was, was takin' 'is 'orn saw from its saddle pouch and was just sayin' as he turned, "We're gonna lighten your load top 'n tail, ol' fella."

'The next thing, the great bludger gives a groan and a bellow, he busts the tongues on the bull straps, leaps to his feet and goes for 'is scrapers, boltin' for the scrub. An' he's wearin' my boots as 'e went! We couldn't head 'im. We were all dismounted and 'e caught us by surprise. Strike a bloody light mate, we never even cut 'im or ear-marked 'im, let alone cut 'is 'orns off. After all that, I haven't got much to show for it.

'Funny side is, the boots must've fitted 'im, 'cause they never came off. We looked, but we couldn't find 'em. He'd be the only bloody bull in Australia that went bush in a pair of R.M. Williams boots!'

DANGEROUS DAN SMITH

Dan was shanghaied by the scruff of his neck from the south-west of Queensland to a private school in Brisbane. His parents made a great sacrifice to educate their son, but Dan was like an old gidgee tree; he didn't transplant at all well. He did become adept at using the English language, and that never left him. A love of the bush and its people stayed with him all his life. He grew to be a hardened man, but those few who really got to know the inner man stayed with him until the end. Through my close association with his wife Beverley and their children, I came to know something about Dan.

One day an old Aboriginal man called Wally Peglar came to the saddlery where I was doing a bit of stitching. He had worked for Dan's father down in the Bulloo area, and was an honourable and likeable person, He just sat there for a while, and I happened to glance up while we were talking and noticed his old hat. The crown had nearly walked right off the top of it.

'Hang on, mate,' I said, as he was about to go. 'Give us that hat. I can't have you walking around like that. A man's gotta have a decent hat, and if he can't afford a new one, you gotta have at least a fixed-up second-hand sort of one!'

I got a piece of off-cut kangaroo hide, ran the blade around and cut off a nice piece and stitched it in by hand, all the way around. Wally ran his fingers around and around and eventually it was to his liking. He put it on his head and said, 'Thank you very much, Brian. I do appreciate that. How much do I owe old R.M. for the job?'

'Job's right mate. He'd kick my backside if I charged you anyway!'

'That young lady—that blonde girl up at the office—is that Dan Smith's daughter?'

'Yeh, mate, sure is—name's Ali. How did you pick her?'

'Her old man, I know him real well. Dan; we called him Dangerous. I used to work for his old man down on the Bulloo River. Well, I tell you what, they reckon Dangerous can do almost anything, but I'll tell you what he can do. I seen it—he can row a boat faster than anybody I ever seen! Him and his old man were havin' a blue at the house. Dangerous is comin' out on top, so the old fella goes to get the rifle and Dan heads for the creek where they had a small rowboat upside down. Dangerous flips her and jumps in and was goin' for 'is coit, and the old fella's up on the verandah rail takin' pot shots at 'im with the pea rifle. Dan was rowin' 'is 'eart out, and there's bullets landin' all round 'im. Yeh, 'e come up tough, ol' Dan!'

I guess those early tough years helped to shape the man I came to know, a man who used few words in conversation and displayed even less emotion.

When his wife told him she was pregnant, he never said a word. He just went out, caught a horse, saddled up and came back to get a pair of fencing pliers. Beverley asked him, 'Where are you going? Haven't you got anything to say?' Dan's reply was 'Kids cost more money, don't they!' And he mounted his horse and rode off.

~

As a young stockman, Dan entered the bulldogging at a rodeo held at Ailerron in the Territory. This was a fledgling sport, and there were a number of vocal opposers in attendance. Dan asked his hazer to take the beast to the rails as best he could, at a gallop. He had lined up one of the 'vocals', and when he was set he left his horse and dived clean across the neck of the horned steer he was supposed to toss, and took out his quarry on the other side of the spectator safety rails.

As his children were growing up, Dan changed tack and took up being a windmill expert. Having grown up and worked with Aboriginal people most of his life, he had acquired much of their sense of humour. The story goes that Dan was in his mill-rig truck and heading out across the Barkly Tableland from Camooweal. It was hot in the cab and two young Aboriginals he was giving a lift to pretty soon dozed off. At the appointed turnoff to the station, Dan stops the truck. 'Right, you young fellas—out!'

'Oh c'mon, Mr Dan—you know us—it's only four mile into the station. Give us a ride in!'

'No,' said Dan, 'I just ain't got the time. Anyway, it's only four mile and there's two of you. That's only two mile each.'

The young fellas looked at each other, and one said, ''E's right ya know; two and two makes four. See ya Mr Dan!' They piled out as happy as Larry.

Dan did put his education to good use, and he had an extensive vocabulary. He wrote some great bush poetry and many will remember him for that talent. As do many of his kind who work in isolation out in the bush, Dan probably enjoyed a drink, and a few more than was good for his health. Sadly it affected his life and his relationships—and the older he got, the more like Dangerous Dan his countenance became.

My memories of Dan are mostly of chance encounters, for he was usually away in the bush some place else. I remember him as a strong, solid, direct sort of a bloke, almost confrontational in his astuteness. He seemed to place all his weight on his own judgement, which is characteristic of the lone bushman, who has to be self-reliant and back himself in any situation.

~

A few years back I was by the open fire in Reg Williams' lounge room one cold winter's evening. Reg was laid back and comfortable, reading as always. I was doing repairs on a saddle. There was nothing like this humble farmhouse. It had a huge open fireplace and the mantel, crowded with equestrian trophies, was a piece of timber good enough to plank a frigate.

The hearth always held another log for the fire, and on the wall were tiers of books on any subject from the Kosciuszko high country to philosophy, poetry and politicians' speeches. On the wall hung a lifeless chiming clock. I once asked Reg why he didn't wind it up. 'I like to look at it,' he said, 'but I do not like to sit here watching the pendulum swing to and fro—ticking my life away—so I took the works out and threw them away!' On the floor was a huge Persian rug, and when Reg went bush the rug went too, into his tent camp in the style of the Afghan camel gentlemen he'd known years ago.

There was a knock on the front door, and into the warm room came Dan. He was cold, and he had been on the road for a long time. The two men just nodded a greeting. It was as though Reg had anticipated his arrival. Dan went to the hearth and backed up to the fire. When he was comfortable Reg asked, 'How are ya travellin'?'

'Not so bad, old mate.'

'We're havin' a drink of tea. Help y'self.'

A little while later Dan asked, 'And how you goin' mate?'

'Never better!' was the short answer, until Reg had finished what he was reading. Then he put his book down, took his glasses off, picked up his tea and made some amazing statements about the condition of the waters on the stock routes in Queensland, where the feed was, who had had rain and who had big mobs on the road. 'Have you just come down from the Territory?'

'Yeh!' said Dan as he turned and put his mug of tea on the mantelpiece and then spread his well-toiled hands to the coals.

'Did you see any big mobs on the road down the Barcoo to Tambo? I've got a little mate walkin' a mob through there. Was there any travelling the Barkly?' On and on ran Reg's questions about the pastoral industry in those parts of the north-west, and especially any news of old mates.

'Did you camp at The Weal?'

'Yeh, mate, then I came right through yesterday,' said Dan.

My ears pricked up, and as I continued waxing my thread and then running another line of stitches I remembered when I first went to Camooweal in the late 1950s. I had landed there in a mail truck from The Isa and we'd called in on a few stations on the way up. I was interested to note that the kegs of beer on the truck going to Camooweal had tarps over them, and the tea-chests of bread for delivery were practically uncovered in the dust and heat. Barkly Tableland people clearly had a distinctive set of priorities.

I soon discovered that The Weal was a pretty small town, considering its strategic importance over the last hundred years. All that was left was a store and two pubs, The Top and The Bottom. They were large single-storey buildings with wide shady verandahs opening out onto the roadway. Both seemed to squat and hug the ground, like native brown frogs waiting for the rain. This country is as old as the hills—and they had long since worn away.

The main street was part of the main road to the Northern Territory, and it was wide enough, I reckoned, for turning a team of yoked bullocks and a wagon. Hundreds of thousands of head of store bullocks had passed this way, having walked the Murranji and other northern stock-routes and passed over the Barkly on their way south to be fattened in the Channel country of Queensland. Many, many teams of drovers had wet their whistle, and many had measured their length on the bare boards of the bar-room floor, in these two grand old pubs.

I was looking for a ride across to Tennant Creek at the time, and there was little if any traffic. It was hot as hell and I didn't bother unrolling my swag; I just lay on the old splintered boards of the wooden verandah. I was woken by the sound of bells, and they weren't horse bells. To my amazement they were goats—a great string of them right along the main street, marching through town behind the proudest biggest billy I had ever seen. He was so majestic that I practically sat up and saluted his royal highness as he went past with his entourage.

The drovers of old would have made short work of a couple of those young ones, a leg of mutton making a good change from their staple diet of salt beef. Those drovers of history are well documented, but my favourites, if my memory serves me correctly, were the Nolans, round about the time of the First World War. They took a mob all the way down to Adelaide. They left their plant there, caught the train to Melbourne and had a few beers with Chloe at Young and Jackson's (or the Princes Bridge Hotel as it was called in those days), and then back to Adelaide, picked up the droving plant and walked them all the way back to Camooweal. A horse in the droving plant won the Camooweal Cup that year!

~

I was so engrossed in my own thoughts that I had drifted away from the two old bushmen who were still drinking their tea. I hadn't even started on mine. 'Yeh, mate,' said Dan, 'nothin' much has changed about the old place. They reckon there's still a few thousand walking down through there every year, but of course the trucks are shiftin' most of 'em now. Tell you what hasn't changed. I was in The Top pub a couple of nights back. We'd had tea, and me and me mate were just havin' a few quiet ones and these three young fellas pulled up in a ute—top boots, big buckles and black hats.'

Reg just nodded into his cup as he looked into the fire. He knew what was coming next, because Dan never backs down.

'Well,' said Dan, 'I'm buggered if I know why, old fella, but they must've reckoned they could wheel us, 'cause they picked us for a scrap straight off.'

Me mate said, 'What d'ya reckon, Dan—we'll go for broke and job the lot of 'em?'

'Na,' I said, 'I'll handle 'em.'

'And how did ya go with them, mate?' Reg asked, as he lowered his mug of tea.

'Well,' said Dan, 'I must be getting' slow, old mate, 'cause I'll tell ya what—that last one took some puttin' down!'

THE SILVER STAR

We were a few horses down in numbers after the big muster. The Company's bull drover said that he was shy of a few as well. So on the weekend, when there wasn't much else offering, I caught a horse and went for a ride. I had decided to go into country where I had not been before, on the off-chance that no one else had for a while either.

Having no luck at all, I headed for higher ground later in the day, to have a look around. I came out onto a bank, which was part of a gigantic concave wave-like structure of basalt rock, like a long boundary wall. I saw one like this years later, further south on Emu Plains. Down in the floor of the adjacent valley was a flat that stretched for miles and seemed never ending. In the horizon's haze I could just make out some hills in the distance. At their foot was a mirage that looked like a terrific waterway.

The sun was beating down on the white-barked gums growing in the rock, and the contrast with the blackness of the iron-bark trees and the blueness of their foliage was captivating. The heat radiating up off that basalt wall was nearly enough to lift my hat off.

Then I saw them: twenty or thirty brood mares and their foals, just along the ridge. They were not what I had been looking for, but what a magnificent sight. Usually while mustering, everything happens at such a pace there is no time like this, simply to enjoy the country.

But there were missing horses to find and I had to get down into the valley, to satisfy my curiosity. There must be another way in. There was—tricky, but possible. There was little sign of any horse tracks, and cattle tracks were few and far between. The prospects for success were not good, but even so, I was drawn onwards. I found my way down, and some time later I was heading back through that magnificent valley and approaching its lower end. In front of me a sea of grass bent away, with the warm breeze behind it.

All of a sudden, there was a change. The grass became sparse and the groundcover stunted, weedy and barren. Rocky ground reared up in front of me—too rough to ride through. So I dismounted and began to lead my horse and to pick my way through this minefield of basalt pinnacles and rough, boulder-strewn terrain. The further I went the tougher it got. Perhaps I had made a bad decision, and on higher ground the going might get better. Where I was, my horse could easily lose a shoe or two, or some injury might leave me a long walk home.

Just ahead of me was something out of place amongst the rubble on the ground. It was a large piece of rusty

254

iron. In fact the ground all about me was strewn with rough and rusty steel pieces and old bits of wood. I took my horse to a spindly tree, hobbled and tied it up.

I spent quite a while walking around and piecing together what I could see. There were steel wagon tyres lying out flat in the dry grass and partly buried in the loose soil, and the remains of wooden axle hubs. The spokes were all gone. There were some remnants of timber, but all the steel was there, off what I reckoned was a fair-sized wagon. It must have been there for many, many years.

When I had shifted a bit of the gear around, and worked a few things out, I went to the front of the wagon and scratched around in the dry grass and unforgiving soil for any further clues. I was realising that this was quite an amazing find.

It was then that I found the remains of harness as well. It had been baked by the relentless sun and the numerous grass fires that would have gone through over the years. The worst of my deductions was that the harness was in line. Yes, the horses had all perished in harness, chained to the wagon, unable to escape. This wagon had been hauled into this terribly rough piece of country and could go no further. What a horrific way for magnificent animals to have died. What of the teamster? Who was he, and what had happened to him? Where had he come from and where was he going?

I found bones, and more harness pieces—buckles, hames and 'S' hooks, swingle-tree couplings—and all manner of chains almost buried in the rubble. The ground was very uneven, so I could only hazard a guess as to how many horses there had been in the team.

This was rough country, so what was a wagon and a team doing here in the first place? Looking around, I could not contemplate taking this on with a light wagonette, let alone something this size. Maybe the team had a horrendous fright and bolted. The possibilities were many. I looked all about this wretched place. This was a valley of indescribable agony and death.

The worst discovery of all lay right out in the front—a shiny, six-pointed silver star on a cardboard-like remnant of leather. This must have been the forehead-band of the leader; the proud leader of the team.

I rode on back to the station and came in late. 'No luck at all,' I told my mates, 'No luck at all.' I kept my discovery to myself. I was not selfish. I just had trouble coping with such a tragedy. I have kept that star as a memento. Whenever times have got tough through the years, I need only to hold that star in my hand and remember that poor old fellow in the lead.

TING-A-LING

From the air, cattle stations in the north-west were a glint in the distance. On closer inspection they became a cluster of corrugated-iron buildings, with the station name painted boldly in black on the homestead roof for identification by the bush pilots and Flying Doctor.

On the ground, there was usually a good accessible layout. The station ringers' quarters were as far as practical from the big house, and a wide dusty roadway ran through the middle, with a wagon and buggy shed, harness shed, engineer shed and a couple of houses for senior and permanent staff. There was a dairy, an office, a blacksmith shop, a meat house and a cook-house, all laid out in an orderly fashion and mostly kept pretty tidy. Aboriginal quarters were away to the side, near the creek.

Communication up until the mid-1960s was through manual telephone—to the out-station of the property and indeed to anywhere at all. There were the bush mailmen, who were an entity unto themselves; the recent advent of the bush pilot, Bob Norman of Cairns; and, of course, the Royal Flying Doctor Service.

The job at hand was to erect a new line to an out-station. A pathway was to be cut through the timber, clear felled with axes, and poles had to be cut, barked and sunk by hand. There were slings to be made for hanging insulators from angle trees, and the new wire had to be run. Sounds like fun! In fact it was tremendously hard yakka, but well rewarded by the knowledge that communication with the people was established. There were two of us to do the job, an off-season drover's cook, who had done his trade with the PMG, and myself.

The blacksmith shop was straight across the dusty roadway from the station office. All the station traffic, people coming and going, went past the open side of the smithy shop. There always seemed to be something of interest going on for me to observe while doing my work.

Shoeing of horses for stock work was a constant demand. Every man was responsible for the shoeing of horses in his care, and most became proficient in the job, with most shoes being worked cold.

In my new position I relished the opportunity to work on the forge again. I had been schooled as a blacksmith, so to get back into a smithy shop and enjoy the smell of burning charcoal in the furnace was as good as a holiday. The working of steel and the tap-tapping, clang-banging rhythmic sound of the hammer on steel and the anvil was most enjoyable. It had been part of my life from as long ago as I could remember.

As very young boys, my brother Norman and I had taken our horses and spring cart seven miles along the gravel road into town, to get new tyres fitted on. At the end of the day, when the tyres had been cut and shut, sand-welded and fitted back on the spoked wheels, we headed home, the proudest young fellows about.

I came out of the smithy's shop one day for a blow, to get a breath of fresh air and have a good tug at the canvas waterbag that was hanging on a wire in the shade on the corner of the building. It wasn't quite smoko time, but I already had twenty-five sling spears made up and stacked in an old army steel ammunition box, ready for the insulators to go on.

The station manager came down out of his unpainted corrugated-iron office, stood on the long, well-worn, wooden bottom step in his moccasin boots, and looked all about. I was quietly amused. You would reckon he was about to cross a busy city street. He was looking right, looking left, looking right, before he crossed the road. There was no traffic, so I guessed he was looking for a victim. Maybe it would be me, so I hung up the pannikin and went to work again.

A young ringer appeared out of the saddlery and harness shed as the bell went for smoko, and he was heading towards the cook-house.

'Neville,' calls out the boss, 'got a job for you mate. After smoko, could you take a horse and ride the Bluff

Downs telephone line for me. I have been trying to catch Jim Boileau all day. The line must be down. See what you can do. Good lad. Oh, by the way, you'll be going out to the breeder camp tomorrow, so could you organise a packhorse early. There's a bit of gear, some tucker and mail to take out. See me after breakfast. Good luck.'

A pretty daunting task all round for such a young bloke, as it was a long way across to the Bluff. He would have been flat out being fifteen years old; but that's how young men became responsible, by accepting responsibility. Young Neville didn't need the encouragement. I understood that his father had left his mother with a bunch of kids, and Neville, being the oldest, had to get out to work and support his family, which he did in a grand style. I had been in a mustering cattle camp with him, where he was always allotted older camp horses that knew their job. They were educating him. He was an inspired young fellow, and you would bet that he would always do his best.

Late that afternoon the young ringer rode up to the office and sat his horse until the manager came out to get his report. 'All fixed up boss. Fixed him up meself.' He then turned his horse and rode away. A few minutes later the boss is out again, and he spoke to the mechanic who had turned up from nowhere. 'Dix, would you take the Rover and check the Bluff line for me? A ringer rode it, but it's still dead.'

He looked across at me, as I was tidying up and damping the furnace down for the day. 'Strike a light Brian, if you get any blacker you'll look like Bronco Johnston (a good-looking Aboriginal folk hero who could fight anything and ride anything).' Then he headed back up the steps into the office.

Just on dark, the Rover pulled up at the mechanics' shed and Dix called out, 'Try her now boss.' I never waited around. I was off to get cleaned up for supper. The bell had not gone yet so I joined young Neville for a yarn on the verandah steps. It was always a good place to shed all the ups and downs of the day and put everything to rest. It was another day tomorrow.

'How did you go on the Bluff line mate?'

'Oh pretty well. I found where the wire was broke, across a gully, and I had me time cut out getting both ends together.'

'Yeah,' I said, 'I understand your problem if you never had any spare wire. So what did you do?'

'Well, I tied me 'orse up and I wish I had taken some hobbles, because if he had taken off I would 'ave 'ad a bloody long walk home. Anyway, when I couldn't get both ends together, I slipped one of the reins off me bridle (I got good long split red-hide reins with the gulf-knot hitch, ya know). I put the reins through a loop in one wire and pulled the gulf hitch up. Then I slipped through a loop on the other one and used the rein as a windlass. I pulled that bloody wire up tight and tied a good knot in the rein, and let her go. There she was slinging high over the gully as good as gold!'

We heard the cook-house bell go, so we sloped off for supper. Thank goodness. With a bit of luck, we would be in and gone before the mechanic turned up!

Jumping the Rattler

A while ago, when there was no hand-out from the government for people down on their luck and needing to move on to seek work, jumping the rattler was a good option if you were game enough. Hitch hiking was equally dodgy, as traffic in the outback was pretty scarce.

The first train I ever rode in Queensland I had to jump, and that was back in the 1950s. Over the years I have come to appreciate that the state's tracks had been laid over and through the toughest terrain you'd encounter anywhere on the planet, except snow and ice, and I have nothing but admiration for those workers, their skills, the humble tools they used and the mates they lost. I have made a fair study of the old tracks. Many hundreds of miles of the old lines are no more, and only the track beds, timber and some brick-arched bridges can be seen.

Like most Australians at the time, I had come from somewhere else. A family story from the mining fields, told by mates of my Dad, tells how their grandmother was confronted on the porch of her miner's shack in Western Australia by an Aboriginal man carrying a spear and a woomera. She stood her ground and demanded, with her feet rattling in her boots, 'Where did you come from?'

'Me no come from—you come from,' he answered.

If I ever need reminding, that story has always kept me in perspective.

I grew up in New Zealand, but my father was an Australian and fortunately I grew up with an Australian vocabulary. When I was quite young and reckoned I could ride a bit, I asked my Dad about the possibility of working on an Australian cattle property when I grew up. 'No trouble', my Dad said, 'I heard that King George owns some country over there—maybe he'd give you a job one day.'

So, having arrived in Townsville, my New Zealand cobber, John Holmes, had gone ahead to make a transport connection to Bluff Downs from Charters Towers. I was waiting to get my train out to Mingela. I had the right time of departure but unknowingly was standing at the wrong platform, with my new swag and port and a heart full of hope and anticipation.

A huge train had just pulled in, and people flew out in great haste from doorways and windows, like rats out of a hole in a chaff sack. I had never seen anything like that before. I shouldered my swag and small port and was enthusiastically heading towards a carriage.

A porter stopped me and said, 'You still here? You don't go on this train; this 'ere is the Sunlander and she goes to

Cairns. Your train leaves from around the corner, if it ain't already gone, so you better get!' I galloped 'around the corner' and I could see some nondescript carriages give a lurch, so I jumped up on the deck of the tailender.

A little way out of town, as we began to make haste, I noticed that all the men in the carriage were looking at me. I wasn't any different; I was just ordinary and carried a swag. I noticed that they were all dressed pretty much the same as each other, but they had no luggage, except small crib ports or a dilly bag.

Then one kindly fellow sidled up to me and says, 'Where ya goin' mate?'

'Mingela.'

He said, 'Well ya better pile off here young fella. This 'ere's the workers' train to the Stuart Cement works, and you'd better be doin' it pretty quick and lively, 'cause in about a hundred yards,' he said, out of the side of his mouth as he peered through the open window, 'we leave the main line and go into the works.'

He ensured that my swag left first, which was good, as I quickly learned which way I should land in order to survive. When I hit the side of the track, I thought that was the worst horse I had ever tried to ride. I walked as best I could back along the track, picked up my swag and port and headed up to the roadside nearby.

There were two women and a child standing on the other side of the road, maybe waiting for a bus. They took one look at me, and then both looked the other way, as though they were at a tennis match and were avidly watching the ball that someone had clouted clear out of the court. They had seen a hobo thrown off a workers' train, and any such person was not to be looked upon by ladies.

~

Three years after this event, I was in the company of half a dozen stockmen who had just come into Pentland on the Western line and headed for the hotel. We'd been out bush for quite some time and, as was the way then, there was no alcohol at all on the station properties. We were ready to wet our whistle.

To square things up with the local policeman, I walked the considerable distance across the line to the police station and paid my respects on behalf of his brother-in-law, with whom I had been working in the north. In so doing, I advised him of who we were and not to pay too much attention to the noise that would be coming from the pub. There'd be nothing too much to worry about!

As I walked out, thinking I had done the right thing, I was about to put my hat on when I looked across the street and saw two ringers from the brigalow scrub riding this bucking horse bareback down the main street, which was the main road westward to The Isa. 'Well, there goes my speech to the copper,' I thought.

And so the day progressed. After a while it was decided it was beard-shaving time, and 'Who were these mysterious faces behind all the fungus?' The publican obliged, and out came the razors, scissors, soap and brushes. Ringers are not necessarily the best barbers, and the results spoke for themselves. 'Nick, nack' comes to mind, but there was very little nack in the nicking, and there was a fair amount of bloodletting, but all in good humour. After months of thirsting for a cold one had been well and truly satisfied, a big bottle of OP Bundy rum was placed on the bar. 'OK!' says Carmody. 'We'll cut 'er out.'

Well, maybe they did, but I wasn't there at the end. My next recollection was lying on a railway platform with my head resting on my swag roll. I could hardly recognise myself—my beard was gone, and as I ran my hand over my face I found crusty blotches. A few clumpy bits where the razor had missed resembled ring-barked scrub. There was a fair amount of the long hair missing as well.

Oh dear, where was I? I rolled over, and was so stiff from lying on that unyielding platform for God knows how long. A porter walked past and I said 'G'day' in a voice I hardly recognised. He didn't return the greeting. By the time he'd done his business and came back towards the station office, I was standing up. 'G'day,' I said again, as I tried to straighten my hat out a bit.

'Oh, g'day—you looked a bloody mess when your mates dropped you off this morning early. They said that you choked down in Pentland, but at least they brought you down this far to Charters Towers. Yez had all jumped the stock train, and they went on through. Didn't look too flash either, none of them. They just piled you off and laid you out nice and tidy and said to keep an eye on ya, and that when you've done your business in The Towers, catch the rattler this arvo and they'll meet you in Townsville.

'I remember one of them said to go to Stan Pollard's and get a new hat. Another one, the dark fella, said to make sure he gets a decent haircut. He better turn up tidy, 'cause we're goin' to Rocky on the Sunlander, and you're gonna ride in the Rocky Roundup, so they reckon. I think I got all that straight. You can 'ave a shower and work on that shave along there in the navvies' shack. See ya!'

He turned around to assure himself that I was standing up and erect, and gave me a wave of his papers as he went. He had that short, positive stride, so I reckoned that he himself had worn the riding boots for longer than a short while in his youth.

~

A few years later I dumped a married man's swag alongside the railway line at Hughenden, a short way from the station on a level piece of ground. I flattened out the long grass and said to my wife, 'This will do for a couple of hours camp till the train leaves on the branch line to Winton.'

It looked a pretty good camp place to me, but my wife was a bit touchy at the prospect. Just as I was assuring her that it was safe, no snakes, and the bull ants only come out at night, a likely looking sort of fellow came striding along from the station. He didn't look like a railway man—he wore moleskin pants and a low-crowned, wide-brimmed bushman's hat.

'What d'ya reckon you're up to mate? Who are ya, and what are ya doin'?'

I said, 'Well, this is my wife Carene, we're on our honeymoon and we were just gonna have a bit of a camp before we catch the rattler down to Winton.'

He stood there looking sideways at the pair of us. 'Winton—honeymoon—well ol' son, the bad news is that the rattler down to Winton through Oondooroo has been re-scheduled and won't be going for another three or four days at the inside. What d'ya wanna go down there for anyway?'

'Well,' I said, 'I used to work down there, and there's a couple of blokes I'd like to see—a couple of Murranji drovers, Bruce and Jeff Simpson. Who are you?'

'Joe Napier,' he said. 'I gotta place just out of town. Yez can camp there with me and Gloria till the rattler goes down to Winton.'

'Joe Napier? You're a rodeo man. I saw you at Rocky in 1959. That was the year Bonnie Young rode in the bull ride with his arm in plaster, and Peter Poole, the Pommie, was the chute boss.'

'You've got a memory. Now you best twist your bluey and chuck your gear in the ute over there, and I'll be with you directly.'

That was the prelude to a hectic three or four days of waiting for the train to go. At Joe's selection we rolled our swag out on a double wire-wove base propped up on four

4–gallon drums, out in the dust under the thinly thatched bough shed, with the pot plants. The first day we three went boundary riding on a sheep property. While on the job we ran down a few pigs, which we caught and put in his sty. The second day Joe and I took turns down a well, and desilted it with shovels, buckets and pulleys, while Carene went shooting. The third day we went mustering sheep and shore a few, my first in an open-air shed.

That evening at supper Joe told me of his plan. 'Every now and then they have a bang-tail muster on the town common. Everyone who's got cattle, horses or goats on the common has to pay so much a head rent. Well I got the whisper a few days ago, and went to the Shire Office to put a few quid down on a few extra stock I had running out there. I thought we may be able to pick up a few extra, like. Tomorrow at daylight they're gonna run everything on the common into the saleyards. You and I are goin' over to pick ours up!'

The next morning, Joe and the council stock overseer were wandering up and down the laneways inspecting the stock. The stockee had a notebook and Joe's got a good eye for a good horse. 'That's my cleanskin colt,' Joe said, pointing with his whip handle. 'He's out of that bay mare of mine we saw in the earlier pen; the one that's got a filly foal. And that baldy filly is out of the chestnut mare that's got a cancer foot. I'll have to shoot her. The brown colt with the white sock is out of the old brood mare of mine. We missed him last muster'—etc. etc. etc.

270

'Right Joe, that about comes up to the tally on the books. We'll cut 'em out for ya pretty soon.'

In no time at all we had a fair mob of horses in the main laneway. Joe said, 'Get on your horse. We'll put 'em straight into the sandy river bed and bulge 'em right along to the bridge. You take the lead up onto the road and then wheel 'em through the gate when we get 'ome. That's my best mare you're riding; you'll handle 'em easy.' And away we went on the most exciting run with horses I had had in years. Joe was cracking his whip and the hooves and sand were flying. The horses enjoyed the run. Perhaps they thought they were going home—little did they know!

As Joe wheeled the tail of the mob in through the home gate I heard him yell to my wife as we cantered past the house, 'Bring the ropes and brands, flunky!' First time Carene had been called a flunky—though competent, she had yet to learn the outback vocabulary.

The last one we branded had just got to its feet, stood prop-legged and shook the dust, when a ute pulled up almost panting, with its door left open for a breather. The stockee came striding over, pointing a finger at Joe and with a look on his face as though he had just swallowed a plum stone. 'You Napier! You've pulled one on me, and you b----y scoundrel are not going to get away with it this time. I thought you were fair dinkum; but you'll go for a row, mark my words!'

I seized the moment. 'Hang on mate, it's been a long day. Let's go over to the house and have a drink of tea and I'll knock up a batch of scones. What d'ya say, and we'll talk her through.' And that's what we did. After all, it was fair and square—far as we were concerned!

The train down to Winton was Queensland Rail at its best—boxcars and no through passageways for the guard. Passengers paid at one end, and the tickets were punched at the turnstile at the other end of the journey. The boxcars were old, stately and beautifully nostalgic. They had been built of the best timbers by craftsmen and had wrought-iron work of the highest quality.

We slid into an empty carriage, without tickets, and the train pulled up at a navvies' camp. There were huge timber water tanks that had been drawn on by steam engines in days past. Now they were a roosting place and a guzzle for the thousands of birds that thrived on the western grasslands of Flinders and Mitchell grass.

A parrot was sitting on a railway jigger on the side of the track, just outside our window. Carene slid the carriage window down and said 'Hello, you lovely cocky. Pretty cocky!' The cocky sidled along the steel-brace handle bar, thrust his crest in the air and with eyes wide open announced, 'I'll cut your bloody throat!'

As the train was nearing Winton, I briefed Carene on the strategy. 'Just before we reach the shunt-line, you'll see a train curving away on another line. The swag goes out first—then us!'

'Why that far out from the station?'

'Because', I said, 'the Inlander will be in and we won't be seen from the station.'

The swag hit the side of the track with a thump and Carene and I had an end-over-end experience, but no harm came to us, as the train was slowing down and we were alighting from the last of the passenger carriages. We picked up the swag, marched into town and never went near the station turnstile.

The first bloke we met was an old friend who worked for the railways. 'Where's ya stayin' in town? We'll leave one of the sleepers of the Inlander open for you and yer missus. Keep it quiet, and the job's right!'

We had a great day in town renewing old acquaintances, then off we went to our Railway Hotel. Sure enough, the boys had serviced the train and left one sleeper unlocked, so we piled in. We slept like a log in a bog in the wonderfully cool and starched railway linen sheets.

The next thing I remember was a bump and a lurch. 'Wake up, Carene, we're on the move!' Before either of us was dressed, all our gear went out the window and we went after it. We quickly gathered up our belongings and bolted. Seems the so-called mates had shunted the train and pulled her up so that the carriage we were in was right outside the station master's office. Good joke!

We knew there was not a chance we'd get near that train without a ticket, so a little later on we fronted up to the ticket office: 'Two for Oonderoo, mate.'

'C'mon Brian, you're not going to Oonderoo.'

'Yes I am mate, me and the missus—Oonderoo.' (Oonderoo was only twenty-two miles out—a PMG camp and a handful of fettlers.)

Way north of Oonderoo, I was enjoying a crib with Carene as we rocked along through the well-grassed countryside, laughing at the kangaroos and the odd fox that came belting out from under the line as we passed. They'd been sheltering from the sun in the water culverts. Then it occurred to me that Joe, who was offsiding for the train guard back in the van, had no tucker.

We were carrying the railway safe, which was loaded with wages for all the railway gangs on the Mt Isa line and all the way back to The Towers. The guard was well armed, and Joe Napier would be a force to reckon with even if he only had a pick handle.

I wrapped a spare bun with a lumpy salad filling and stuffed it inside my shirt, pushed up the window glass and climbed out backwards until I stood on the footboard. These were like running boards, at about the same height as the top of the wheels. We were rolling along at a good rate, so it was important to keep my body hugging the carriage. My grip on the rounded window ledge wasn't good enough to support too much weight, so there was a lot of concentration and balance required. One glance down at the track whizzing past was sufficient encouragement!

The last carriage now. What I had to do was attract Joe's attention in the guard's van. I could not reach the door handle, and the trouble was that the door opened the wrong way for me, in that it was hinged from the back to the front. Joe and the guard were playing cards on a tin trunk of some kind; well they were until the guard looked up and saw me peeping around the corner of the door glass. He jumped to his feet, knocked over the card game and, in a frenzy, made a lurch for a firearm. He lost his balance and went down on the floor. Joe had a grin from ear to ear as he helped the old fellow up to his feet. I guess he'd never been in a robbery before!

'Well,' said Joe, 'what's all that about?'

Out of my shirtfront I pulled the humble crib and offered it to him. 'Good man—I was getting bloody hungry and I was tonguin' for a feed. You didn't do much for this old bloke. He reckoned you were gonna rob the train, and he nearly had a full-blown heart attack. You'd betta square off with 'im. Look at his bloody revolver. I don't reckon he could hit a bull in the backside with a bucket of wheat on a good day, and he was shakin' that much I don't reckon he could've cocked the bloody thing.'

Carene and I left Hughenden on the next train through to The Isa. I can remember that it was evening and I heard her going through the carriages handy, calling my name. As she came out of one carriage onto the deck I answered, 'Up here, mate,' from my perch on top of the carriage.

'What are you doing up there?'

'The only place to travel this hour of the day,' I answered down. 'It's cool and you can see both sides of the track and the way ahead. It's a great sunset. I just sit up here and take it all in—she's my very own train. Come up here and join me and together we'll rocket into the sunset!'

~

A few years earlier I'd been on the Ghan, going south to Adelaide on the old line through Oodnadatta. The train pulled up and I enthusiastically opened one eye and peered out across the desert. You never knew what you'd see in the desert.

One evening on sunset I'd spotted the only creamy white dingo I had ever seen standing majestically on the crest of a sand hill, and he never moved as the Ghan passed him by. This trip, I saw an old Aboriginal with a camel cow and a baby camel, almost as white as snow and maybe only a couple of days old.

I was travelling second class at the end of the train with two old Aboriginal couples. They were lovely dignified people, dressed as best they could be. The men were huntsmen, warriors and guardians of their kind, falsely gowned in cotton hand-me-downs and battered hats. Under these were visible at the brow and temple the long twisted strands of plaited hair that encircled their heads. They had the marks of initiation, and one incisor tooth had been removed. They sat upright on the bench seat, hands clasped together in their laps, with fingers entwined like tree roots searching for moisture in the arid soil of their homeland, and they were contented.

I pointed out the camels to them—too late, they would already have had the entire story in their minds. One thing you can't do is to teach desert Aboriginals to be observant!

I said, 'Keep an eye on my swag, Bungee—I'm gonna go and say g'day to that old fella and take a photo of his camels.' They respectfully nodded, and turned away. There were a few men busy up near the loco, so I took a chance and ran off across the sand. It was about a hundred and fifty yards to go.

He was a tall, fine old man; he never spoke, and he had one of those wide, rolled-brim Stetson hats with a big high crown and a Gulf bash up the middle. He was proud for me to take a photo of his camels, but he turned his face so that the camera never saw him.

I bid the lonely cameleer good day, and as I turned to head back for the train, to my amazement everyone was on board and she was underway. Summing up the situation, I took to my scrapers and headed for the flat-tops—the long flat-deck wagons used to transport loaded trucks from the south to The Alice, to save them doing the Birdsville Track.

I came alongside, and the only way I was going to make it was to take one on the fly—no second chance here. It must have been the elastic in my riding boots—I went high enough and landed on the rough, hard wooden deck. As I stood up and got my balance I realised there was a cheer squad at the front of the first-class carriage.

I kept running and jumping across onto the next flat-top as it came to bear, until I finally got to safety, to the shade and another tug on that waterbag. It was 122 degrees Fahrenheit at the Oodnadatta railway station that day, in the shade.

The following morning, short of Port Augusta, I put on a clean shirt (that I had washed and hung out of the side of the train to dry), dusted my boots off and went to the head of the train, to the first-class sleeper carriage. It was my first time into South Australia, and a lovely morning.

A well-attired steward came past me with a loaded tray. 'Good morning, Sir. Tea? Black or white? How many sugars? Yes Sir. Biscuits Sir?'

Much later the same steward walked the length of the train looking for a passenger who seemed to have disappeared. He poked his Brylcreem head and his bow tie into the spartan second-class carriage and recognised the stockman lying full-length on a bench seat. Looking at me disdainfully, he announced, 'Why Sir—you are an impostor!'

The head steward, however, later paid me a compliment. He sought me out, gave me some money and said, 'When we pull up at Port Augusta, go for ya scrapers across to the pub and get me a bottle. You'd be the only bloke on the Ghan who could do it and get back before we pull out!' I did, just, and my reward was a huge hamper of sandwiches and chops.

We of the second class sat serenely at a banquet, and enjoyed unspoken fellowship in our dusty castle. By journey's end our shared waterbag hung lifelessly in its bracket outside the carriage.

～

Carene and I travelled on the old Ghan some years later. We'd had a snack, and just before I dozed off

I made mention of a cairn of stones out across the desert. I woke later as the carriage gave a lurch, and on looking out I spotted another stone cairn, another memorial to some lonely battling soul in the wilderness.

'That's the same one you pointed out to me before you went to sleep,' said Carene. 'We've been stopped here for quite a while. Someone said they'd heard perhaps the sand goannas had undermined the tracks up ahead.'

I closed my eyes and thought, 'At this pace, the old Ghan would be dead easy to take on the fly. I don't know about jumping the rattler—it may be quicker to jump off and walk!'

ON THE SLATE

Some friends and I were going into the Northern Rivers of New South Wales a few years back, intending to ride the length of the Guy Fawkes River. We planned to come out the top end of the New England escarpment just short of the Ebor Falls, onto the tableland, and cross to the Ebor pub.

It was going to be a good leisurely horse ride through great sweeping river bends and magnificent scenery, with the added attraction of numerous mobs of brumbies. We would enjoy each other's company and explore this silent and seldom visited wilderness—and maybe do a bit of fishing. We had a couple of packhorses for the camp gear, swags and tucker.

Calling into a small roadside general store on the way down into that river country, I wandered around to pick up a few extra odds and ends that I would need for the seven-day trip. This place was so insignificant, I don't believe it even had a name. However, the store was essential, as it was the only one for miles in this wet

281

scrubby country to supply all the locals' needs, though they were few. Most, as I understood it, were semi-feral, and botanists by nature!

I put the items I wished to purchase on the store counter and waited to be told how much they would cost. The bloke behind the counter was having a real good look at me, from my bush hat down to my leggings and riding boots, and back up again. He did not look happy. 'You gonna pay for this stuff?' was a question I found hard to fathom.

''Course I am,' I replied, 'I need them. That's why we pulled the truck up here, so that I could get 'em. Why do you ask?'

'Well most people living around here put it all on the slate till pension day.'

'Well that doesn't apply to me mate. Now if you don't mind, let's get on with it.'

'Ya know what,' the storekeeper said, and he goes on in a quieter tone of confidentiality as he packed my things into a box. 'This bloke, new in the area, never seen 'im before in me life; 'e comes in 'ere, piles a stack of tucker on the counter, and up and tells me to put it on the slate!

'I says, "No fear. No way mate! Stone the crows, I can't carry that much; I don't know ya!" Well what do ya reckon, he says. He says, "Leave 'er all on the counter, I'll be back directly."

'Ya know, 'e was only gone about twenty minutes and 'e was back. Did 'e 'ave any money? No chance! Ya know what 'e's got? Well I'll tell ya. A Polaroid photograph—and he stuffs that under me nose and says, "How's that for collateral?" It was a brand spankin' new photograph of a marijuana crop in full flight.'

'What dya reckon?' the storekeeper exclaimed, as he eye-balled me for a response and slammed his hand down on the counter.

'Did you give him a go?' I responded.

'Yeah, I gave 'im a go!'

GONE FISHIN'

We had been mustering cattle all day since a pre-dawn start, and everybody was looking forward to a good pull up on dinner camp. 'We'll yard the mob down along the Clarke,' Ray said. 'There's a good wire yard there, and we'll be able to keep an eye on 'em.'

'Better watch 'em good' said old Munday, an Aboriginal stockman. 'I seen ten dingoes on the way down; mob, big fellas, black. Maybe thems the ones got 'em poddy yes'day.'

We put the cattle through the gate and while a couple of men rode off to check the fence I rode over to get a look at the Clarke River. I had never been there before and waterholes always held a fascination for me. The river was down, but the whole scene was one of peacefulness.

There were large, gleaming white boulders and golden sand, fringed with silver-trunked gums. The sky was as blue as blue can get and there wasn't a puff of cloud to be seen. On the edge of the shallows, standing mute, was a jabiru. Aboriginals came to call this bird 'bullaman', from their name for mounted troopers. The association was with their uniform—the blue/blackness of the body colour, the whiteness across the shoulders from the neck, like their amulets, and the ever so long red legs, like the stripes down their trousers. He was a big bird and his large pointed beak gave him a no-nonsense appearance. Standing so still, he might well have been admiring his magnificent plumage and stature—one of the outback's great birds—in that jacaranda-blue waterhole.

Jim rode up alongside and said, 'Watch out, look out! Old Bullaman get you! We'll come here for a couple of days fishin' when we've cleared up all the cattle on this side.' I could see turtle heads like floating corks. Plop, and they were gone again. Yeh, we could have fun down here.

Later, as I walked from the fire carrying my quart pot, to have my dinner, I passed old Munday sitting cross-legged, chewing on a piece of corned brisket fat, 'You better watch that bullaman, he bin get you, but 'e not bin get me, ha! ha! Hey look out!'

Back at the out-station the gear had been made ready, and early the next morning the cattle were all drafted, dipped for ticks and sprayed for buffalo fly. Then we had to brand all the cleanskins. As a rule, if there were not too many and they were not too big, we would scruff them. Working as a team in a smaller yard, one man took the head, his mate took the tail and flank, and they upended him and put him down flat on the ground. The head was turned back to hold fast and expose both ears for marking. The ringer on the back end placed the arch of his foot above the hock to force that bottom leg forward, and with both hands held the top leg backwards and bent at the hoof to prevent kicking. The animal was then earmarked, branded and castrated if necessary. It takes fit men and good teamwork to do this.

However, if it was a big yarding, we'd use bronco horses. The style of bronco branding was not as in the Territory, where they used a bronco horse and a ramp, and the roped animal was snug onto the railed ramp. We worked two bronco horses outside the yard, and the ropes were inside the yard with the cattle.

The procedure was simple. All the cattle to be branded were in the high-railed branding yard. Any big troublesome ones we did straight away and turned them out with the other cattle. They were all roped with twisted greenhide ropes and handled quite methodically. Ray roped a hind leg and called 'Up horse'. Neville, whose horse had the other end of that rope attached to its harness, rode away and pulled the calf to the rails. At the same time, Munday roped the calf's front leg and called 'Up horse', and Jim rode away. The calf was dragged to the rails in a stretched position and was operated on, then a call to signify all was done. Both men released the ropes as they called 'Back horse', and the tension was taken off. The calf was released and returned gratefully to the mob. This whole procedure took one or two minutes.

Roping is a skill, and once mastered is a great attribute; but for the sheer hell of it, Jim and I were a great team at scruffing and we'd take on practically anything!

Calving percentages were down in the country we'd been mustering, largely due to the population of dingoes. They were taking a huge toll. We had stock in the yards with signs of mauling, and although many healed some never had enough ear left to carry the station ear-mark. They just had little stumpy cauliflowers. So the hatred of dingoes grew in us.

The branding yard was a cauldron, especially when there'd been a big yarding. Our bodies became a collage of sand, dust, blood and sweat. The heat from the branding fire and the red-hot brands, as well as from the sandy yards themselves, became immense. The stench of burning hair and seared hide was repugnant.

It was always good to start as early as possible—and to get to the end of a necessary job, done well, with little or no injury. Bumps and bruises, bits of skin off here and there and the odd rope burn merely punctuated the day's work. Tallies were important to us all. They were the measure of our efficiency as stockmen, and the way we handled the cattle was the measure of the pride we had in our ability.

Things happen fast in the yards with station stock. I saw a young heifer, maybe eighteen months old, walking away from the pressure in the yards. A cranky bull, with no other reason than just being bad, put his head down and crushed her against the rails, one of his horns buried to his poll in her chest. He shook his head and she was dead in a heap, and the cattle walked over her body. Needless to say, that bull was on a short ticket to nowhere!

288

Crows gathered on handy dead trees to roost and gawk, and those that were game perched on the extremity rails, carking and cawing and doing their little crow yodels as encores. They were delighted by the sight of a dead animal, besides all the other titbits that were discarded at branding time. Crows are fascinating birds because of their intelligence, but they thrive on death.

Their rituals are fascinating if you can ignore the terrible sounds of their overtures to feasting—the jerking of the neck, stiffening of one wing in a downward jerk and flicking of the tail feathers. Now and again, aside from the raucous cawing, they had a private muttered conversation. Their sense of humour is outmatched by the sombre look in their dark and emotionless eyes, that seek death in order to survive as scavengers.

Few of us stayed in the camp for the weekend. Ray and Munday loaded up Lion the packhorse, and away they went straight after breakfast to do some boundary riding in the Clarke Hills. Ray looked a dangerous man as he rode away, well mounted as always and well turned out. Other than his usual saddle (which he had built himself) his saddle gear of quart pot, saddlebag, horn saw, and fishing line in a beautifully rounded hand-stitched pouch, there were the customary bull straps about his waist and a saddle rifle in a handy scabbard. He also had a bright new red-hide ammunition belt around his middle and a 'stand out loud' neckerchief about his throat.

Ray was a great mate, a great tutor and had a sense of fun. He was dependable, never smoked, seldom swore and stayed sober in town. If it was a dull day the sun shone in his face, so if he was going boundary riding on his weekend off after a tough muster, that kind of says it all.

Jim, Neville and I had promised ourselves a weekend fishing down at the Devil's Elbow section of the Broken River. The Clarke was a little too far for a jaunt. It was a quiet two and a half hour ride over to the river. Not having to be concerned about any cattle we saw, we just jogged along at a leisurely pace behind the packhorse, which seemed to know exactly where he was going. We threw down a few matches to burn off the tall dry and rank spear grass as we went, and let the two weeks of torrid mustering drift away.

The bush is silent when there aren't any mobs of cattle bawling, stockwhips cracking, horses whinnying or men shouting. Once down at the wire horse-holding paddock we watered our horses, washed them down, hobbled them and let them go. You could just tell by their attitude that they were going to enjoy a change as well. They liked the river water and the fresh pick in the paddock.

We made a brew of tea and then put our heavy canvas camp fly over a ridge pole held up by two forked poles at one end and the fork of a tree at the other. There were two angle poles each side at each end, and a running pole on each side to fasten the canvas onto. The weight of these slid downwards on the angle pole, and we had a camp. We put the pack bags and our saddlery at one end and our swags at the other—home again!

We had a bit of a blow, and then went down to have a good look at the river. The sight of so much good-looking water after a hot day was pretty tempting, but no hurry. This was going to be our place for the next couple of days. There were ominous signs of an impending storm, and as we wended our way back to the camp we felt a few drops of rain. This is a big country; we were witness to the storm, but the rain was a long way off.

As the late night campfire burned down, thunder was rolling and echoing in the distance, like an empty drum cascading down a steep slope. There was a hollowness in the sky that echoed the mellow, rattling thunder—which was punctuated by thrusting and flashing sheets of lightning that lit the ground, blinked into darkness with a rumble, and were gone.

I tried to read for a while by the carbide light, but the storm (not to mention my two mates) was so persistent I couldn't concentrate. Neville was sawing wood as he snored and Jim, who usually refrains from using long words, was getting his tongue around a few hairy and curly ones in his sleep.

I was up early, and stirred the coals to get the fire going and the billy on, wondering if we were going to catch any fish in that beautiful big hole. I roused the boys and we had a quick breakfast of corned meat and damper and the luxury of some tinned fruit, then down the cliff face to the river. It was a steep track, and once at the bottom we had a sharp climb around and up onto the rock proper. The waterhole was deep, so we wouldn't be using our short spears there just yet, but it certainly was a wonderful place. We got settled around the rock and cast our baited lines out into the river. We had a few nibbles, but there was not a seriously hungry fish anywhere about.

'I think we'll give 'em a try a little later on boys; there's nothing doin' just yet,' said Jim, as he rolled his line up. He climbed around the eastern face, downwards and then out onto the extensive gravelly river bed. He undressed and proceeded to wash his clothes, as they were the ones he rode out in yesterday. He gave everything a good doing and then laid them out on the dry gravel.

Some time later, something made me look upstream, into the gorge where the river came through between sheer walls. I heard the rush of eagle wings, and an almost indescribable sound. It was like a bunch of trains all coming in at the same platform. Then, around the bend in the gorge at the Devil's Elbow came a head of stout that all Ireland would have been proud of. It was 'the head' of the flood that followed.

'River's rising, Jim!' I yelled.

The next instant the river came through that gorge like an express train. Jim was rushing in and out of the still shallow water below the fresh, grasping as though catching a turtle. He had seconds to clear, then he gave a yell as the flood came towards him. The rock face was mighty steep and I went around it as fast as I dared. We had no idea how high the water would go.

As he reached me, Jim said between puffs, 'Bloody river came up before I saw what was happening. It grabbed me washing and they were off, but I got 'em all back except for one of me camp tennis shoes. Bejeezus, these rocks are rough on me feet!'

The river was still on the rise, and due to the shape of the high rock walls around this large eddy area it was now a swirling muddy turmoil. I took a couple of snaps of the river rushing over the newly formed rapids, then ventured a little closer as the water level seemed to have stabilised.

'Hey, catch that tennis shoe!' yelled Jim. I looked up ahead, and there it was floating towards me. It had been washed into the swirling eddy of the back water and then away into the mainstream, taking all of five minutes to do the round trip. When I retrieved it, Jim hollered above the roar of the water, 'Ever seen a shoe swim upstream, turn around and come down again—well that's what that tricky hunk of footwear's been doin'!'

On the riverbank we calculated that sudden runoff after overnight rain to the west had lifted the river level four to five feet, and we stood at the edge marvelling at the power of the water.[*]

Hearing something scratching behind us, Jim told me softly to turn around. We turned in unison, and there was a dingo on the high reaches of the gravelly riverbed,

---

[*] The catchment areas of most waterways in North Queensland are immense, and all that runoff channelled into a gorge can have catastrophic consequences.

scratching at our discarded clothes. I could not believe my eyes. A dingo that close! I was petrified, as I had seen many examples of what they can do to cattle.

The dingo paid us little heed. We had no sweaty clothes on and we were down wind—as if that mattered to him at this distance. To him, who had probably never seen man before, we may have looked like big kangaroos. I'd say he was about one year old, in great condition, and he was a big dog. He began to parade about us, at about nine to twelve feet away, sniffing, puffing and scenting the air and the ground alternately.

I ventured to whisper to Jim, 'He's quiet!'

'Nuts! Look at those bristles stickin' up all the way down to the point of his shoulders. Are you blind, or too bloody scared to notice? One thing is for sure, he ain't scared of us!'

The dingo looked away as though listening, so I leant down and picked up my camera, set it in a great hurry and snap! When he turned and went over to the riverbank, I eased away and fairly ran up the cliff face, sixty feet of almost sheer rock.

Once at the top I looked back down, and there was Jim, snarl for snarl with yet another dingo. This was a much bigger dog and he was even closer to Jim. His crouching and stalking posture indicated that he was more in earnest in his aggression. Jim was backed up against the flooded dirty brown swirl, and it did not look good. He had plenty of stones, but maybe he knew better than to return the aggression.

Barefoot and naked I raced to the camp and grabbed the rifle and a handful of bullets. Neville sat on his swag roll with his mouth open and never said a word. Back at the cliff top I could see that both the dingoes had gone. I tried to pick up their tracks, but I was unsuccessful.

'That big bugger was fair dinkum,' said Jim. 'He was goin' to take hunks out of me, snortin' and gettin' his hackles up, so I gave him a few goolies and he took off like the dingo bastard he is. Bejeezus, you made tracks up that wall when you went! Well I reckon you must have suckers on ya feet like an old green tree frog. Where's Neville, 'e OK?'

'Well I reckon he's still up at the camp gettin' over the shock.'

'To hell with the fishin',' says Jim, 'and bugger the dingoes—let's enjoy the river.' So we went for a swim.

The river was moving slowly now, but maintaining its high level. The bank on one side was sheer smooth basalt, mosaic in colour and all of fifty feet high. On the other, a more gentle slope consisted of gigantic crumbling boulders, the fossilised remains of an ancient coral reef, shaped like huge hand-grenades. Some were solid and smooth, like rolled-out two-storey buildings. We sat down to watch the river and reminisce over the events of the day.

That evening, the dingoes were calling everywhere about us, probably going to feast on a dead calf we had come across before the sun went down. If we saw them in the morning we would surely shoot them. In the morning early we saw that the river had gone down—the dogs were silent and the bush was back to normal.

We arrived back at the out-station about the same time as Ray and Munday. As Ray stepped off his horse, dropped the packhorse lead and rolled his split reins around a rail of the bough shed he asked, 'How'd you fellas go—get a wet arse and no fish?'

'Well, you could say that,' said Jim, 'you could say that!'

THE MIN MIN LIGHT

This was big country, good horses, big mobs of cattle and hard tucker. There was always the unknown, but expectations were high. We were preparing to go bush again as modern-day cavaliers, with the greatest job of all.

The horses for our mustering camp had been checked out. Stockmen knew their own horses and were systematically shoeing them, one after the other. Young horses, up for their second season, had to be coached up a bit and re-ridden to be reminded of their schooling. We didn't need any buck-jumpers out on the muster, but there were always a few that would have a go. That was the spirit of this animal we loved and admired.

Out in the yards an Aboriginal stockman had mounted a horse that he knew well, and then it started to buck pretty severely. She threw the rider after about six good ones. The poor old fellow had just got the plaster off a broken arm, and he bruised it rather badly again. He lay on his back in that dusty yard. He wasn't worried about his arm, it was his pride, and there were tears in his eyes as he staggered to a rail and cradled his head in his arms. I felt sad for my old friend. Even though we had all been there at odd times, it was a bugger of a place to be—beaten by a good horse in front of your mates.

The new men in the camp had horses allocated, and it was up to them to prepare their stock the way they saw fit. Men on top wages handled what they were drafted; usually they would take ones that had been together and ridden as a team by someone who had moved on.

The shifting of an entire camp is quite an undertaking, and a lot of gear has to be prepared for the season ahead. Everything had to be checked and maintained in good order, from veterinary equipment and spaying gear to cooking gear, from horse hobbles to Bex powders. Harness was a big item. Everyone was responsible for their own. There was general equipment also, like pack saddles, bronco gear, billies, camp ovens and water canteens for the packs. All the branding irons had to be checked and packed, and all the newly made twisted green-hide roping ropes had to be greased and dragged.

Some men were better than others at saddlery. Counter-lining of worn saddles was an essential, and sufficient horsehair from tails had been accumulated. In order to curl the hair for padding and counter-lining a saddle, it has to be spun into a long rope. One bloke has a carpenter's hand brace with a hook fitted into the bit chuck, and he keeps twisting while the other helper adds horse hair, little by little. The finished article is like a thick woollen twisted yarn. When there is enough, it is boiled to hold the curl, then when it's dried out it's undone, fluffed and teased out. The curl in the hair prevents impaction, because when it is pushed tightly into the saddle padding by a stuffing iron, it does not set hard and, most importantly, is kinder to the horse's back.

Ray Crane, who had made his own saddle from scratch, had left it on a rail, the seat soaking under wet corn sacks. 'Tomorrow,' he said, 'I will ride it dry, and then it will fit my backside forever more. Amen!'

I was greasing an endless pile of harness when there was a cooee from the cook-house. 'Hey Brian! You want to get some practice ropin', holdin' and tyin'? Well get in here quick.' I jumped to the call. A bag of rice had split on hitting the hard wood floor and was going everywhere at a gallop. What fun—when the cook-house is happy, it's a happy camp.

Clouds of dust came from the horse yards, and out on the flat a ringer was taking it quietly on a young one. Anvils clanged and rang. One of the popular anvils was a large wagon axle supported at each end by a solid stump of wood. Two or three men could be shaping horseshoes at one time. Then all would be quiet for a time as they went into the bough sheds to continue shoeing. Two of us went into the wagon shed, and came out in a hurry as we were confronted by a large brown snake. 'Bugger him,' said Jim. 'I think I was going to cut some whip falls anyway!'

And so the day went on, until dusk. We were all sitting around playing cards and recapturing the highlights of the day when Ray got up and said, 'I think I'll go and turn the beef.' He left with a carbide light in his hand, and I could hear him singing as he walked across the yard.

The meat house was out across the flat a short distance. It was wooden, with a witch's hat roof and gauze in the walls at about head height to allow good ventilation. We had killed a spayed cow a few days ago, and all the meat hooks were hanging empty now, as we had eaten a lot of the fresh meat—chuck steak and rump.

The slabs of meat that were left were on the sloping wooden platform boards that formed a table, a bit above waist height. They had been sliced a little, and copious amounts of coarse salt and quick cure had been rubbed in by hand, methodically and enthusiastically, for days. As the juices of the meat took up the salt, the meat needed to drain, and more salt was added as it became a little drier. Tomorrow it would be hung up on the vacant beef hooks to dry as much as possible. By the time we were ready to go bush, it would be dry enough to roll into jute corn sacks, to stow in the pack bags. Two or three good lumps would be left on hand in the meat house for when we returned in a few weeks' time.

Salted beef had to be soaked overnight in the beef billy to reduce the salt prior to cooking, and then slowly cooked in fresh water. The cook always packed pre-cooked meat on the road for the first day out.

Now the words of a song that was sung at night around the cattle comes to mind:

> The billy I boil me beef in
> Must carry me water too
> For they would think me gettin' flash
> If I should ask for two.
> There's a broken-handled pint pot
> And a rusty old tin cup.
> That's all that's on the table
> In me old Bark Hut!

And so the card evening continued. Later, the screen door opened and shut with a bang and I looked up at Ray as he put his light down and went to wash the salt and brine from his hands. 'Any of you blokes know about anyone expected here from Pandanus?' he enquired. 'Anyone heard a vehicle coming?'

There was no answer for a while, then the cards were tabled and the matches taken from the long bar of kerosene soap we had been using as a crib board. Someone said, 'No, but maybe the fencers are moving camp, or maybe Alec and his yard-building mob are on the way through from the station out to Dosey.'

'Well come outside and take a look for yourselves. There's a vehicle all right.' His voice was challenging, and we could not all get through the door at once, but we tried.

'Well, what?' asked somebody.

'Well, that!' said Ray, most emphatically, pointing up towards the airstrip.

'I dunno,' said Carmody, 'looks bloody well like a set of headlights to me, but they are pretty close together. Maybe only one headlight, but they are pretty pale lookin', almost like a carbide light. But it couldn't be; that's too far away.'

'Hang on,' says another, 'it's moving off the roadway by the strip and it's going through the trees. There's no bloody road there! I'll tell you what, that's only three hundred yards away, and I can't hear any engine noise.'

'Bugger yez,' said Neville, 'I'm getting' the gun. I don't like spooky bastards, specially ones that go sneakin' about the camp. Dinkum!'

'Hang on,' said Jim, 'See that? It's dancin' up and down, and look about, it's going backwards. There it goes again, through the timber. Well bugger me. I know what that is. Well slap ya watery blinkers on that, cats. What yez are lookin' at is what is known to the Aboriginals as a Min Min light. I'll tell ya what, young Neville, you'll never catch him, and what's more, you won't be able to put a bullet through him either. I seen him once before. They are pretty rare, but they pop up now and again. Tell you what! We'll have trouble if they seen it over at the Aboriginals' camp.'

The head stockman came back into camp a little while later and announced, 'They're gone. All gone. Only bloke left in the quarters is old Jack, the gold prospector. He said he never heard them Murris go, but his old red cattle dog was hiding under his bunk and he thought that was pretty unusual. He never saw the Min Min.'

Having accepted the Min Min light, everything settled back to normal. I pulled on a pair of boots and away I went into the night by myself to get a good look at this phenomenon. It was still about, away out there in the timber country, about two hundred yards away. It was like a mirror reflection dancing on a wall. It was not static at all. I could not get close to it, as it seemed to move away as though it was sensitive to my presence.

It was not an illusion, but almost magical, the way it seemed to go right through the trees. It was pretty hard to get a handle on it. There was no way I could understand or comprehend it, other than that it was visible and fair dinkum.

I turned and came back to camp, which was well lit, and the shaft of white light from the carbides was beaming out from the windows of the out-station. Perhaps none of the ringers were ready to turn their burners down just yet!

By comparison, the Aboriginal quarters—a sizeable wooden structure with broad verandahs and, Queensland style, on stumps—was a decidedly dark silhouette on the skyline on this moonless night.

'They won't be back for a couple of days,' said Jim, 'you can bet on that.' And he was right.

HECTOR

Beth Kelly, a great grandniece of my childhood hero Ned, was a fine looking woman, and she sat across the table and looked me straight in the eye. 'There's a nice old man and his wife living in a retirement village in Masterton. I think it would be good if you were to visit them,' she said.

Hector Rope had come from England in the mid-1930s, and went bush. He did what every unsupported bloke did at that time, and got jobs where he could, in shearing sheds or humping wheat. He never got far enough north to do cane cutting, as war was declared. With a spring in his step, the young colonial enlisted for service.

Toughened, tanned, and as hard as nails from manual work, with a slouch hat to protect him, he landed at Tobruk. The enemy tried to blow them out of the ground as they dug in to protect the port on the Mediterranean coast, and then dive-bombers did everything they could to send them to smithereens.

'You know, Brian,' old Hector said with wavering voice as he tapped my arm with his weather-worn hand, 'sometimes those Stuka bombers missed!'

I stayed for some hours, and that was the only time he wavered in his speech. He was a strong, kind, lovely old man. He showed me with pride photos he had kept of his fox-holes in Tobruk, the mates he defended them with, and those who died in the attempt. I thought, what motivated those young men, who will be known forever as the Rats of Tobruk, to fight like threshing machines?

When the Japanese invasion of Australia was imminent, Hector and many more were shipped back to North Queensland to be trained in jungle warfare. Their training camp was out of Ravenshoe on the Mount Garnet road, at a place called Green Swamps, later renamed Wallabadah.

Hector spoke of a young man whose passion for Australia had consumed him. The fellowship of his mates had sustained him and he had put his life on the line at Tobruk. No ungracious oriental gentlemen were going to sneak in the back door of his new country if he had anything to do with it!

He began to tell me of New Guinea and the horrors of that campaign. He told of the sound of death as the enemy's mortar shells and the .50 calibre machine guns rattled the ridges. The struggle—the jungle—the terrain—the filth—the fight. Then he went silent, as he read pages of his memory that were too saddening to repeat.

Even though these stories have been told by others for sixty-odd years, I sense that none of the telling has come near to the reality of being a soldier like Hector and living through those conflicts. Not being an Australian citizen, he gained no assistance under the government's soldier settlement scheme to acquire land at war's end. He just got back to doing what he did best, worked hard and put yesterday behind him.

Hector sat nodding his head for a while, eyes partly closed, and I thought perhaps he had nodded off. Then he held his head up and continued:

'I scraped up enough money to buy a piece of vine scrub land out of Calliope, near the catfish scrub and witchy-proof, north of Many Peaks.' The homestead had been the bush nurse's cottage when this area was a hive of mining and timber-getting activity in the late 1880s, and the cottage was made of the customary split slabs, with an earth and antbed floor.

'Then I got a bit cashed up and went for a trip, and blow me if I didn't run head into one of those shipboard romances!' He and his bride of sixty years exchanged admiring glances across the plush lounge room in their city retirement home. I could tell the trappings were not essential to this pair of pioneers.

'Ya know, that vine scrub country,' he continued, 'in a good year you could grow anything. In a dry one you could flog a flea across most of it and you wouldn't lose sight of him. So, we just grew what we could on our new place at Ubobo, and I worked where I could and that kept us going along all right, didn't it Mum?'

The only reply was a half smile and a nod of contentment from his wife, Marjory, who was sitting so demurely with hands clasped in her lap and tiny feet tucked under the chair. It was easy to see why old Hector had been chopping wood for her for sixty years!

As we talked along through his life I began to shift my attention from his grand old face to his hands. They were broad, brown and knobbly, and the fingers curled to a half fist. I could see that they had been fashioned on the peg of a cross-cut saw, and they would have fitted around a maul handle that drove the wedges into those big logs. They could easily have snarled a stranglehold on a crowbar and driven it down through the tough going and rock in a strainer post hole, then milked a cow with ease. And yet they could so gently have caressed a child's head.

I sat pondering on these impressions and, when Hector presented me with a bridle he had made, I was left in no doubt at all. He could plait like Trumby, and as he ran those old hands over the Turk's head knots and then out along those silky, flat plaited reins my admiration stepped up another peg. He also showed me miniature horse-drawn wagons he had made, wheels, spokes, steel tyres and hubs, the lot; every one was a work of art.

The afternoon passed swiftly as I shared with this 96-year-old man memories of friends and places we both knew. The coincidences were quite uncanny. This 'Pom' had laid his life on the line for Australia; he had fought every yard and earned every breath he had taken since. He is an Australian, in my reckoning.

The afternoon drew on, and I reluctantly closed his door behind me. I had, in fancy, been living a book I had read many years ago.

CHINAMAN MILL STORIES

O ur camp was on a knoll overlooking Chinaman
Creek, and a stone's throw from the windmill. The
waterhole in the gravelly bed of the creek had a clay bank
where I had fashioned ledges to hold my scrub brush,
toothbrush and kerosene bar soap, and a long branch to
hang my towel on. Lying in that waterhole after a good
bogie at the end of the day, watching the sun going down
through the timber and thinking about a roast in the
camp oven, was about as close to heaven as a working
man can get.

It was always rewarding then to sit on a log in the
camp, dry off near the fire and watch that big golden
currant bun dive down through the timber. The tea-
trees down along the creek stood dark in contrast to the
final glow of the sun. In the twilight, birds began their
evening song. Crows in jerky flight were wending their
way in solitude to the community roosting places. Dollar

birds hovered, screeched and cawed over their haven in a tall dead gum tree. Lousy Jacks (apostle birds), high in a sandalwood tree, fussed over their young in a precarious nest the community had made from mud. Butcher birds made their characteristic crystal clear call and nodded and bowed their heads, and peewits added their final chirp of the day in alternating duets, with wings extended. Finally, the infectious laughter of kookaburras rattled then echoed over the bushland, and soon all became hushed for a while—except for the willy wagtail, who would give intermittent chirps as the night progressed.

The camp's flickering carbide light sent forth shimmering elongated shadows that merged into the blackness of the bush, and everything became silent. That silence seemed to welcome and herald the arrival of mosquitoes, the croaking of frogs at the tanks and along the creek, and the insects of the night. The sky was black now and the stars began to shine as if through holes in a tin roof. Over in the south I could see the Southern Cross and all the other star groups that had become my friends over the years on nights such as this.

I sat and watched the flickering firelight playing on the silver gum trees. Now and again a sudden shift of air fanned the fire and it illuminated a complete tree trunk. The effect was like a flash of lightning striking downwards and outwards along the reaching boughs and branches, as they too caught the firelight. The insects, in a long drone of whistles, whirrs and clicks, added their eerie noises as they seemingly tried to out-do one another. They would cease instantaneously, then continue again, as if instructed: 'Hey, take a deep breath fellas, and here we go again!'

I had taken a brownie fruitcake from the camp oven and it was resting on a clean piece of sacking, cooling off atop a flour drum. It was beautifully browned and hadn't sunk in the middle or cracked at all. We would eat a wedge with a pannikin of tea before we hit our swags. That was always a good way to mark the end of another good day.

Looking at that brownie cake reminded me of a most unusual happening when we had come back to the mill for dinner camp in the middle of the day. I was giving my axe a rub with the sharpening stone while the billy boiled when a car came along the dusty road and pulled up below the tanks. I watched the strangers go about their business as I honed the axe.

First a bloke got a billy out of the boot, and quick and lively lit a fire at the side of the roadway. In a busy fashion he strode across to the tanks, filled the billy, had a swig, then set the billy to boil. Meanwhile, the missus, with the help of a screwdriver, took off a steel hubcap and was busy mixing a damper in it, having added a pannikin of water from the billy. When she was satisfied that the dough and the fire were right, she laid the hubcap down on top of a small nest of coals.

Well, it all happened very matter-of-factly, without any conversation. In no time at all they were done with the tea and damper, had a smoke, scattered and covered their dying fire, emptied the billy on the mound, jammed the hubcap back on, and away they went in a cloud of dust. They never said 'G'day!' and they never said 'Hooray!'

I had turned to my mate and asked, 'What did you make of all that, Bob?'

'Well, yes and no, but out here I reckon his name'd be Smith for sure!'

Bob walked over to the fire and pulled a pair of stumpy fencing pliers from the pouch on his belt to lift the billy and make a drink of tea. He wore those pliers everywhere, for he was an old PMG man, and did everything by sevens. I guess that came from tying insulators on the main telephone wire—seven twists was standard. He put the billy down handy, and from the camp oven he speared the last crisp baked potato, left over from dinner, with the honed-down blade of his old IXL pocket-knife.

As Bob sat on his flour drum and admired the spud, perched on the blade like a toffee apple, he said, 'Did I ever tell you about the old Chow greengrocer in Brisbane? Well, back in 1912 we gave a young roo to a fella in Brisbane and he grew to be about four to five feet high. When the Chinaman came on his regular rounds he used to give the roo a lettuce leaf, regular as clockwork. Well, one day he turned up and he didn't have any lettuces. So as the old Chinaman passed the roo on his way up the pathway, the roo up and kicks 'im flat as a bicky.

'The family, having heard the gate latch fall and then all hell breaking loose, ran to the front gate, and there's the Chow down on the ground. Every time he goes to get up, the roo floors 'im again.

'Struth! You should've seen it. They reckon there's vegetables getting thrown all hell west and crooked around the yard. The roo's as angry as all blue blitherin' blazes. The Chow hits his scrapers, gets booted in the arse, and goes flat on his dial again, "Wha'for? Wha'for?" he's yellin', and his old straw hat gets pummelled and his cane baskets went for a row. The only thing intact after the blue was his shoulder pole.'

It took old Bob quite a while to get over reliving the episode before he could gather his spud off the ground, dust it down, settle enough to eat it, and continue.

'I went up the Gulf pretty early in the piece. Normanton was still frontier country in those times, after the gold rushes down Croydon and Georgetown. I remember me and me mates used to get an old hammer gun and go duck shooting. One day I knocked a couple down and me mate, who could swim a bit, went out into the lagoon about forty yards through the lily pads to retrieve them, see. Well he's just lifting his arm to get the first duck, and a bloody crocodile grabs the bastard and drags it under. The duck like. Then you should have seen me mate. There's a hell of a shocked look on his face, a flurry of arms and legs while he gets his little arse into gear, and boy did he go for broke. He's flat like a lizard drinkin'. He looked like a Southern Cross mill in a cyclone. Brave bastard me, I'm givin' him heaps from my possy on the bank. By Christ, I was glad when he flew outa that waterhole. We gave duck huntin' away after that.'

Words failed Bob. He just sat there rocking on his precarious perch on the flour drum, with tears of laughter running down his cheeks, and shaking his bowed head. Then, 'Old Ginger made a bow wave on the way out of the lagoon that would have drowned a bullock!'—and that set the old fellow going again.

~

There was a noise out in the bush somewhere; it wasn't a bird call or a dog noise, a cow in the distance or the old mill creaking as she turned. It was a strange noise, so I let out a cooee in case it was somebody poking about. To my amazement, it was answered.

Someone was coming in out of the night, so I immediately emptied the billy and put her on again fresh. I heard a horse nickering and a stick snap, some spurs jingling and then a curse. Only Jim Doolan curses in that manner, with a tilt towards the Irish.

'Is that you Jim?' I called.

'Who else would be stupid enough to ride all this way in the dark to see some slab-sided bugger like yourself?'

I could see the outlines of more than one rider as they hobbled and tethered their horses at the troughing by the mill tanks. Into the firelight walked Jim. It was sure good to see him, and we shook hands and I took a good look at him. He looked more like Doolan every time I saw him. He was always well dressed: Santa Fe boots, moleskin trousers, corduroy jacket, red neckerchief, and always a blue shirt. He was now sporting a Colonel Custer moustache, not to mention the long fair hair that curled well below the nape of his neck. He was a handsome piece of gear, and by far the best ringer on the property. I guess he would rate on any property, in any company. Then the other rider came into the flickering firelight.

'This here is the Cuba Kid,' said Jim, by way of introduction, and I made him welcome.

To me he looked the part: thin build, drawn features, lantern jaw, high cheekbones and no top teeth. He also was wearing Santa Fe boots, white moleskin trousers clean but a little feathery around the edges, cream shirt and a leather jacket, a flat crowned hat and big batwing leather chaps.

So this was the Cuba Kid I'd heard so much about. He was the celebrated bull drover for the cattle company Queensland Stations. He was called Cuba because, by accounts, he had been fostered during the war by the folks at Cuba Plains, down near Pentland.

Bob had had enough for the day so he said 'Hooroo' and turned in. The other three of us pulled up a flour drum each to the fire and enjoyed a mug of tea and a wedge of the brownie cake.

It wasn't long indeed before the boys were warmed up and ready to talk. They talked about episodes in the bush, throwing and tying wild scrub cattle, drinking sprees; about bastards they had met; about top cattlemen, good horses and horsemen; about good saddles and good saddlers like Tim Carr and his Tim Carr Poley of The Towers; about ropes and rope makers, whips and whip handlers. Then, as the night wore on and the stack of embers under the fire got bigger and brighter, the yarns got longer.

With yet another billy of tea to go round, Jim said, 'Funniest thing I ever heard at night time in the bush was this jackeroo bloke. One night he reckoned he could drink a bit. Well two good tugs of OP from a demijohn and down he went. The other ringers bent him around like a bull ring, and did his top fly button up to the top hole in his shirt. When he comes to, out on the dusty flat, you could hear him cryin' out in the dark, "I'm paralysed, I'm paralysed! Help me! Help me! I can't straighten out!" He never mentioned drink again.

'Remember that time on the road Brian, when we were drovin' that mob down from Montgomery. We took on that young fellow, reckoned he could play cards. Well, Cuba, we were using tins of Log Cabin for chips. We took all his tobacco, and trying to win it back he gambled everything he had—swag, watch, wedding ring his missus gave him. We even took his toothbrush and his boots. We left him go to sleep on the ground under a saddlecloth by the packs. Before I ran the horses in the morning I dropped the lot on him and said, "Ginge, don't you ever gamble no more, or I'll set on you. Is that understood?"'

I well remember the next night round the fire. Ginge was sitting next to Jim. We'd had a good day and all was forgiven. Ginge had changed from being a competent yet reckless ringer into a calmed and responsible person. And I know in his heart that he would now and forever fight to the death for Jim Doolan, who taught him the lesson and gave him the chance of his life.

'Well young Ginge,' Jim had said, 'we had a tough night last night, didn't we?' And he slapped me on the knee. 'But tonight's a good'un, and I'll tell you why.' With that, he stretched a leg out in front of him to undo the horseshoe buckle, and slide his pocket-watch pouch off the belt. He laid the watch on the palm of his hand, reverently unlooped the plaited lead from the watch-ring, then passed it to me. 'Stick that in your kick young Brian, and remember me, and if you ever, ever get an inclination to gamble, take a look at it and maybe you'll change your mind.'

When I examined the watch, I discovered that on the end of that beautiful kangaroo-lace plait was a semi-flattened silver dice. To this day, I have never gambled. Such were the lessons learnt from great taskmasters in the bush.

'I never had much to do with them jackeroo types of fellas Jim,' said Cuba. 'I mostly work by meself. But tell ya what, the last trip down to The Towers I goes into old Stan Pollard's for a walk-about. I spots them short arse, red nylon scanty britches. I says to Stan "How much?" and he tells me, and I says "How do they come?" and he says in a box, one gross. I says "How big is a gross?" and he says twelve dozen, and I says, "I'll take 'em."'

'What in the hell were you gonna do with that many of them what d'ya call'ems, young Cuba?' asks Jim.

'Well, I'll tell ya,' says Cuba. He shifted his backside to get a little more comfortable on the rim of the flour drum and rolled his cigarette to the other side of his mouth with his tongue, had a short pull, then continued.

'You know as well as I do Jim that the lubras out in the Gulf down the Einsleigh and along the Gilbert River, they don't wear any underpants. So when I got back up to the Einsleigh, all the station gins gathered when I'm unloadin' the packs off the plant horses—to see what I've brought home for them. Well, I dish out these red and blue knickers by the handful. 'Course they'd never seen 'em before, an' because they were as bright as all hell, they all straight off thought they were like them R.M. Williams satin rodeo shirts with the bullock-horned pockets.

'So here was all the station lubras out on the flat for all to see, bare breasted and struttin', with their arms thrustin' skywards like a bunch of angry redclaw yabbies! One arm was through this hole, one arm through that hole—and nowhere for their head to go. Oh bugger, I just gave up! Oh Jeez, Jim, you could 'ave drowned a frog in the tears that was rollin' down my face. I had to lean up against a yard post, I was that bloody sore from laughin'.

'Ya know, I told the lot of 'em, "You bloody Gulf gins ain't got any dress sense at all!" It was good fun, Jim old mate, bloody good fun.'

'You meet some funny buggers,' said Jim. 'I remember on Rockhampton Station, in the Gulf, there's this long

320

lairy Aboriginal stockman, fella called Nightingale. He comes out of the yard on this big rangy horse, and it's fairly liftin'. Old Nightingale is wearin' one of them flash satin bullock-horned shirts. He's hangin' up pretty good, with a pair of long goose-neck spurs, and he's got 'em strapped to his long, horny bare feet, and his big toes are clutchin' like buggery to those four-bar irons!

'Just when the horse was winding up to give another big root, a gin screams out from the rails, "You can ride 'im Nightingale!" Nightingale gives a big toothy grin right around his face and belts the horse with his lairy plum-coloured hat, right on the arse. The horse pulls to the side an' dug in a big one, a real beaudy, came down hard and shanghaied old Nightingale, arse over 'ead, and 'e sails away in glorious fashion and lands in a screamin' heap, face down in the dusty yard.

'The boss gives him a tin of paint and sends 'im off to paint a gate, to quieten him down. Then came knock-off time. Down I go to get him. There he is sitting on top of the cap rail, practising with his spurs, jabbing them into the post. Biggest pair of spurs I ever seen on bare feet. He's probably crooked for lettin' that gin down, and he'd be shamed, for sure.'

'Yeah,' said Cuba, 'you run into 'im on the road drovin'. When I was just a kid I can remember a story an old fella told me about these two old drovers. They'd had a set on each other for years. Well one time they finally came in from opposite directions with a mob each, and met at a set of tanks on a bore. After supper, when the two camps were settled, she was on. Everyone knew that it was gonna be on. One old fella took out his false teeth and put them on a stump. The other bloke took out a glass eye and placed that alongside the set of teeth. Then he had words. He says, "You look after them, that they don't sneak up and bite me, while I have a go at jobbin' this old codger!" And then they shaped up. I don't know who won the scrap, but they was fair dinkum.'

'Well, Jim,' I asked, 'what do you reckon is fair dinkum anyway?'

'Well, that's a loaded question.'

'Fair dinkum, I'll tell you what's fair dinkum,' says Jim. 'Women! They can pull on a pair of ridin' pants and a pair of R.M.'s boots, and not go ridin'. They can put on a swimsuit and not go swimmin'. But, hey look out, when they put on them weddin' dresses they mean business, and that's fair dinkum. Tell you what though, I was over at Cairns, over Christmas last year, and there's half a dozen sheilas at the pub invites us to go and have a beach party. Well you never seen anything like it. We got a big fire going and I thought they were going to cook some tucker, 'cause I was as hungry as hell. But no, they just up and pulled their clothes off and headed for the water, and all they was wearin' was them Cuba-style scanty britches things, and brisket straps—you know them what d'ya call'ems! And that's fair dinkum!'

I told the boys about the car that had come through today, and Jim's retorted, 'Cars, I gave them up good. I hate 'em. Cars, you can dice 'em far as I'm concerned. I once cranked an old T Model Ford till it boiled, but she never started and she never moved an inch!'

'I'm gettin' cold 'round the ears mate,' says Cuba. 'Better stoke the fire up a bit.'

'Yeah,' says Jim, 'we're easy two thousand feet above sea level here. It'll start getting' cooler in the evenin's from now on. Did I tell you old Dick the camp cook had a heart attack and fell in the bloody fire, Brian? Jeez it was bad. We had to get him all the way to the station. Wasn't too flash. He's comin' good though, they heard. His burns are healin' well too by all accounts.'

'Cooks,' says Jim. 'Cooks, cookoos and wilful murderers. There's one bloke comes to mind. Cross-eyed he was, not a bad cook, but oh mother was he cross-eyed. They reckon they seen him peelin' onions in the camp and the tears were runnin' down his back! God he was a case. But there was this real ugly bugger, good bloke, don't get me wrong, but he had buck teeth. I swear he could eat an apple through a tennis racquet.

'Talkin' about teeth, Brian, how's your mouth where the flyin' doctor took that one out? Mine's been givin' me heaps. I'm gettin' bits of tooth and rubbish out. It was infected for a while but I kept suckin' on a piece of that pink rock-salt we've got for the horses. That sorted her out.

'I heard that flyin' doctor only came out in a hurry to deliver that baby,' says Jim, 'and he didn't have any dentist gear on him. Never again mate. Too tough for me. It was a bloody long ride that, into the station. All night it took us. When we got in, Cuba, Brian said his toothache was that bad he'd take anything to get rid of the pain. So I says give us a look, and I planted a right-cross on his jaw and laid him out on the verandah of the ringers' quarters. When he came to, he says, "I don't know where that came from, but it's a bit better!" Then I says, "Your turn mate," and he got up and laid one on me, but he couldn't put me down, all he did was give me a worse headache! Yeah, bugger of a turn out, but the flyin' doctor did the best he could.'

~

The moon was creeping up higher now, and I could see the tethered horses over by the tanks, standing hip shod and face to face with their heads bowed down. I guess they were sharing each other's warm breath and gaining comfort from the company.

Horses are amazing social animals, and I often noticed that horses which belonged to particular stockmen always grouped up together. Aboriginal stockmen's horses, likewise, were most always apart from the others. What determined their social structure, I'm not quite sure.

'Well we better hit that billy again, Brian,' says Cuba, 'I'm getting' bloody cold round the ears. Tell ya what, I could go another slab of that brownie.'

'Cuba, you run into that Dougy Campbell lately? Strike a light he's a larrikin. I heard this story about Dougy on the road with a travelling mob. There was a bush race meeting going on, so Doug decided to go to the bush dance. Well, the story all hinges round the brand spankin' new set of long-drop dunnies. Everybody at the dance is all dressed up, except Doug. He's straight off the road, so 'is chances are pretty slim, he thinks. So he heads off to the dunny anyway, just for starters.

'He's never seen anything like it, and they're all lit up with generator power. Great long row of them, men's and women's, all joined together but partitioned. Being a bloody larrikin, he wonders what it would be like puttin' his head down through the seat at one end and looking along at all them white bums. So he took off that bloody great hat 'e always wears. So he did. And right along the other end there was a sheila with exactly the same curiosity! They looked at each other in shock. Then, straight off the cuff, Dougy pops the question, "May I have the pleasure of the next dance?"'

'Don't do that to me, Jim,' says Cuba. 'It's not at all good for me 'elf all this laughin'!'

'Well me old mate,' Jim said, 'we better light a shuck and clear out.' They rolled a smoke in the firelight, drained their pannikins, said hooroo, and went to their horses. I followed them out of the firelight and watched as they put their hobbles around their horses' necks, checked their girth cinch, mounted up, turned and raised a hand in farewell and rode off into the night. I could hear Jim singing as he went, his own adaptation to a Jim Reeves song, 'Don't Ever Take Those Rib Bones From Your Hair'.

Jim was heading back to camp to run horses for the day's muster. Cuba, well, he was going to gather his plant horses up and head a hundred miles north-west to the Einsleigh. I never thought to ask him what he had in his pack-bags, but you could bet that they weren't empty!

TED

The windmill expert on the property was affectionately known as the Basalt Spider. I guess he was called that because he was small, dark, hairy and wiry. He could scale to the head of any mill on the property, and was the best in his trade. He was employed to maintain all the mills on this 1400 square mile property. Ted was his offsider.

I had met Ted at the station when he was in for a blow. He may well have been classed in those days as a 'yella fella'. Blackened from the sun, and always a touch of grease, he was part Afghan, part Chinese or Malay, part European—a product of the melting pot of Normanton's population in those early days.

Even on 'off days' Ted would have his little fire going out on the flat in front of the station ringers' quarters, and have a billy turning over shortly after the morning star got up and away, as though keen to get going early. There he would sit on a stumpy log in the firelight and drifting smoke, and drink his tea. Ted's brew was as thick as tar. You could almost kick it.

On a Sunday, after breakfast at the cook-house, he would lie on his swag in his room and read westerns. This would continue after he had responded to the smoko bell, and onwards to dinner-time, and through the afternoon.

The men's quarters were old but well constructed—a great long building of solid unpainted wood and corrugated iron, up on stumps, with a wide verandah. Open doors led to double-bunked rooms that were unlined, and hot as hell most of the time. Still, it was cooler than outside, and a dry place to sleep when it rained. There were no glass windows, only corrugated-iron flaps propped open with a forky stick or some such.

The verandah was a place of great character. Men of the bush had walked those dry, splintered boards over the years, and had satisfied their thirst from the canvas waterbags that hung on wires, plump with water so cold they had condensation dripping off them. When the men came in from the out-stations and bush camps, mustering or droving plants, this was home.

Ted would lie there, as quiet as a mouse in the semi-darkness, smoke, and read his westerns. From time to time there was a splott, as he flick-speared a soggy dumper onto the ceiling, where it stuck like a limpet, swung a couple of times, and then settled like a contented flying fox. Over time they would go brown and fossilise.

Sometimes I would pause by his open doorway, say g'day, and observe him sitting on the edge of his bunk, laboriously working some flake-cut tobacco in the heel and palm of his old black and calloused but finely made hands. Had those hands never been tortured by grime, grind and toil, they could have been those of a concert pianist.

As he rocked and ground that black tobacco in a slow, purposeful motion he always seemed deep in thought and far away. He would nod in acknowledgement of my greeting, and then drift back to his foggy thoughtfulness, contemplating the unfathomable. Ted was a kindly sort of person, but I never knew how to be his friend. There was always a protected distance or barrier between us.

On this particular day, I paused a little longer and watched him roll his cigarette. A Tally-Ho paper was at full stretch to go around the tobacco he had prepared. He licked the paper and then, with one hand, twisted it in his mouth to form a conical-shaped durry.

'What ya doin', old mate? Havin' a quiet day? I see the new platform you and your mate are building for the drilling rig. Got a flash new gantry for the gin pole for handling the windmill heads I see.'

'Yep mate, we're ready to go this evenin'.'

'What's the book you're readin'? Larry and Stretch western?'

'Yeh.'

'How's it goin'?'

'Not too sure yet, I'm still figurin' it out.'

Later, as the cook-house bell went for supper, I poked my head in. 'Comin'? They've probably got fresh beef. They killed yesterday evening.'

Ted was lying against his unfurled swag—and staring at the cover of the unopened paperback western. His durry was hanging at the corner of his half-opened mouth, and he ran his tongue along his tea–and–tobacco stained teeth. He slowly put the book down, swivelled onto the edge of his bed, and slid his feet into his work-worn, lace-up Blucher boots.

He nodded his head, struck a match, and got his smoke going again. Then he let out a slow puff of smoke and admired its blueness as it lifted towards the window, as though the smoke itself had unravelled the secret.

I asked him again, 'How did it go mate?'

'Oh good, good. I just got it all figured.'

'How?' I said. 'You weren't even reading it.'

'No—no,' says Ted. 'Ya see mate, I can't read at all. I just study the pictures on the cover and kind of work it all out from there.'

I looked around the room at the stacked shelves of westerns. 'You mean Ted, that you have figured all them out?'

'Yeh mate, had to. Nothin' much else to do on the days off.'

'Ted,' I said, 'you are a bloody genius!' and we went off together along the dusty track towards the cook-house, in a silent, friendly walk.

TED

Other stockmen with less on their minds walked past with their short, jerky strides, absorbed in light-hearted conversation. We two were miles away, Ted probably going over in his mind the happy conclusion to his laborious deduction, and I marvelling at this illiterate man who was such a skilled tradesman in his own field. I was humbled.

THE BUSH BROTHER

Countless people have ventured into the outback to take the Christian message and give pastoral care to those living in isolation. The first time I met Father Peter Mayhew, of St Barnabas at Ravenshoe, was at the christening of our son, Glenn. A short while later, on another lovely day after church, the congregation headed out to Con's Pool for a picnic with all the kids, country style.

I was standing on the banks of the waterhole. The grass was green and the sky was as blue as a Queensland topaz. The women of the congregation had left their formality on the pews of the church and were now sitting around comfortably on the ground with billowing summer dresses about their knees, enjoying happy conversation. Hardly could they hear each other for the noise of the children, who were having the time of their lives nearby. They were, in succession, swinging out on a rope and cartwheeling into this fabulous rainforest swimming hole.

Peter and I had turned our backs to the water and the children's glee, in order to hear each other speak. 'Brian, how would you like to give St Barnabas one day of your time a week? We need someone like you to give them some bush skills and encouragement along the way. They are all good boys, from Aurukun, Thursday Island and Papua New Guinea, and of course there are quite a number from the Australian bush as well.'

Before he began the next sentence, he turned abruptly and dived fully clothed into the waterhole. I too turned in haste, to investigate this strange behaviour. There he was, treading water and supporting a desperately ill child, holding him out to me to drag up the bank.

'I should be grateful, Brian,' he spluttered as he bobbed above the water again. He looked ridiculous—like a waterlogged frill-necked lizard—with his balding head, sharpish features, and clerical collar and black bib floating above his neck on the surface of the water.

When everyone bounced into gear and got the young child going again, Peter—waterweeds, dripping daks and all—returned to our conversation.

'What happened, mate? How did you know that kid was going down?'

'I just heard a sound that I heard years ago. One's ears become tuned to these things on occasions such as this. Oh yes—some time Brian, I'll come out to your property and we shall discuss the matter I mentioned earlier. But I must go now; there is the serious need of a change of clothes!'

The ladies stood as one and clapped their appreciation on Peter's departure, and all the kids in the waterhole gave this lovely man a good old bush cheer. Bush kids know a champ when they see one, and they were looking at one, squelching away in his town shoes and waterlogged clothes.

Peter did come to the property for smoko, on his rounds. He had with him a youngish bush kid who never spoke much, had bare feet, khaki shorts and shirt, and a haircut to match his bush-kid face. That unsmiling face needed only a nudge and it would shine—I could just tell that there was a spirit in there.

'Mr Taylor, can I go and say g'day to the filly in the orchard?'

'Sure thing, Rastas—don't go too near to her hind legs. She's just being broken in and we've got her handy to drive in the long reins later this arvo.'

Peter was doing his best to convince me that my time away from the property would be well compensated. He would pay me well, and besides, the boys would benefit immeasurably. I was still undecided when I heard a horse cantering. It couldn't be. I looked out the lounge-room window and there, sure enough, the chestnut filly was going around the sizeable orange orchard at a fast clip. And there was a rider.

I bolted to the orchard. Little Eve, who was not a big horse at fourteen hands, had a frightened look on her face, as she should have had. Young Rastas somehow had mounted her bareback—and with no bridle. She had taken off with him. Not to be put down, he must have leaned forward and put his arms around the horse's neck. The next time he went past, I was horrified to see that he had his hands behind the horse's ears and his bare feet were clasped at the ankles around the base of her neck. He was swinging under her neck, in front of the pounding hooves—and he was not going to let go at any price!

I pulled the filly up and steadied her down. Rastas did his best to apologise, and stood to take a kindly disciplinary broadside from Peter, who had placed a knowing hand on the boy's shoulder.

'He's OK Peter, no harm done, but if you've got bush kids like this here Rastas, I would be pleased to give them some of my time.'

~

On my first day in the school classroom I introduced myself. 'My name is Brian, and I'm not here for the good of my soul. How we go is pretty much up to you blokes. Now for starters, I would appreciate it if the boy in the seventh row would take his hat off while he is inside, please.'

'Can't, sir', and the look of insolence he gave me would have pulled a plough!

'Why not?'

''Cause I keep my pet snake under it, and my head keeps it warm.'

'Well I am sorry mate, but this will be his last class. And one other thing before we begin. Would the dark boy in row four take his army greatcoat off in the class for me please.'

'Can't sir, 'cause I keep my pet ringtail possum in the pocket. It's bloody cold over in the dormitories in wintertime. He doesn't get out; he'll stay put, trust me.'

'What's your name lad?'

'Haynes, sir, from Papua New Guinea.'

Haynes from Papua New Guinea and I became lifelong friends.

~

To get the ball rolling I had organised a field trip out to a mate's place, where they had been clearing land from scrub (rainforest) with huge machines. They were clearing stumps, stick-raking and ripping—in general, preparing virgin land to go into potato cropping.

Geoff Keough and his brother Max were the third generation of hard workers on this property of high-yielding cropping and cattle. The old people had done it the hard way, all the way to North Queensland in wagons from New South Wales. Kindly Geoff was enthusiastic to teach the young ones about the job on hand: blowing stumps and stubborn great trees.

Geoff was down a hole under the last tree standing in a cleared rubbly paddock of bush fell. It was still rough, ups and downs, stump holes and cloddy. He had carefully placed Nitroprill and diesel down under the tree base in several places and was getting ready to lay the charge when Peter Mayhew, who had arrived unannounced, looked over Geoff's shoulder and, pointing, asked, 'Did you catch him, Geoff?'

Geoff jerked his head around in surprise. 'Catch what?'

'The rat.'

'That's not a rat tail, Father. That's a fuse, and I've just lit it, so you'd better take to your scrapers as fast as you can and get to hell out of here, if you don't mind me saying—QUICK!'

With that, Geoff stood up and went round the other side of the tree, as fuse smoke started curling up from the holes he had dug under the root system. Then he trotted unhurriedly across the rugged ground for about eighty yards. He turned to face the blue smoke (from the fuse) that was enveloping the base of that huge tree, so big that the crawler tractors had not been able to shift it. Then she blew—woompft!

The blast sent a shock wave of air across the ground, which shook as if the earth was going to cave in. The tree got such a fright, seemingly, that it left home in a hurry. Most of it landed intact and prostrate on the ground. Pieces as big as fence posts chased clods of dirt and smaller pieces of timber all around the sky. When the fun was over and the debris had come down again through the clouds of airborne dust, all was quiet once more.

Geoff turned triumphantly to the students, who were all lying flat on the ground with their fingers in their ears. 'That's how you do it, but don't any of you blokes even think about touching explosives unless you're with somebody who knows what they are doing!'

Everyone was standing in awe, reviewing the results, when a faint, almost inaudible plea came from behind: 'Please help me Geoff, please help me!'

We all turned as one—oh no! It was Father Peter Mayhew, thoroughly snagged in the barbed-wire fence. He'd gone straight back the way he had come in one hell of a hurry. And there he was, hanging like a frizzled flying fox on a high electric wire.

'Strike a bloody light, Father,' said Geoff, shocked. 'You could have been killed! I'm real sorry.'

'You mean to say Geoff that I am not dead after all. I almost feel that way.'

All the students stood about in a most concerned manner while we released Peter from his bondage. It was not the fact that he had been pummelled—it was that he had gone to so much trouble to come out in the bush so as to be there with the boys. He went to the top of the ladder, and to my knowledge he never came down.

Father Peter Mayhew had been a prisoner of war on the Burma Railway. He had survived, probably due more to providence than any other reason. He was as English as marmalade, and no more gentle, kind man ever wore the clerical collar. Even so—he was tough. He went to the top of the ladder, and I miss the man who had a single phrase for all occasions: 'Goodness gracious me!'

～

A young brother of the Order filled in for Peter at one stage. He too was a great bloke. He called at home one day, right on dinnertime. (Can't blame him for that, as they mostly lived on very little. Probably had more dinner times than dinners.)

'How ya travellin' mate?'

'Not so bad, been goin' good; had a few ups and downs, but Peter has got helluva big feet. His shoes take some fillin'.'

'How are ya handling the wet season?'

'Not so bad really, but I had a bit of a problem last week. I had to go out to Mount Surprise to do a christening on a property. I am not at all experienced with creeks across the road, so I just put the Landrover in 4-wheel drive and engaged the hubs, and then in I went. We went right through the creek, but coming out the other side, up the dirt roadway, she stopped. It would not start. Oh dear me—all the people were gathering at the station for a special lunch. They would have come from miles around. Here am I, my first time out bush, and I'm stuck at the creek. Another useless Pom!

'I dried the distributor, the spark-plug leads and the coil lead. Nothing—it would not start! So there I was, sitting at the wheel with my head in my hands, when I thought of Father John Flynn, the Catholic priest from Herberton. I know he was a legend out in the bush. What would he do?

'I concluded that he would just sit there, say three Hail Marys—and away he'd go. So, I did just that. Put my mind in neutral, my gears in neutral, foot off everything and feet flat on the floor, and said three Hail Marys. I turned the key on, and pushed the starter button down with the palm of my hand, and away she went. Makes you wonder, Brian, makes you wonder!'

CHEERS!

Cooktown is where James Cook beached HM barque *Endeavour* in 1770, and the river that slowly snakes its way across the Cape York Peninsula is named after her. Just over a hundred years later a trading port was established there. Twenty-five thousand men passed through to the goldfields, and another ten thousand worked and lived at Cooktown—many were Chinese.

When I rode into town in 1977 time had mellowed that metropolis with sixty-three licensed hotels, and only three of the originals remained. Talk about history! Just down the street was the stump of the very tree that the *Endeavour* was tied to when she was beached for repairs. Up on Grassy Hill, which separates the sea coast on the eastern side from the town, had lived the aristocracy of one hundred years ago. In the main street was the old convent, which is proud that its kerbside stone fence is exactly the same length as the *Endeavour*.

I tied my horse up to a verandah post and walked into the bar of the West Coast Hotel. It had been a while for me, but nothing had changed in this grand old lady. It had two storeys and was built in the old times on colonial lines, with wide verandahs, all solid timber and mortised joints in the carpentry.

Standing spellbound, I looked at the paintings by Junior Baines—there always seemed to be something new in them that I hadn't noticed before. The murals were on the walls right up to the ceiling, perhaps eighteen feet high. They depicted the Palmer River gold rush, when this country was in its heyday. The whole work was quite exquisite.

The barman was busy, but I didn't mind waiting for service. Yes, it was so good just being there again. I wondered about those who had stood at that bar over all those years. What were they wearing? How long since they had wet their whistle? Had they been teamsters to the Palmer miners from the west coast of New Zealand (after whom the pub was named), or tin scratchers like the popular writer Jack (Ion) Idriess. Did he have a couple here before he went to fight the Turks in Palestine, and fronted up like the rest of his mates at Gallipoli?

I thought too about Bill and his brother Barry Crump, two New Zealand mountain bushmen who, not so long ago, were famous crocodile hunters and hell raisers from here to the Cape, across the Gulf, and all rivers in between. Their exploits were legendary. There was a time when they came down to Cooktown for a spell and were camped in the old boat shed down on the river. They struck up a great friendship with a kindred soul, Junior Baines, who was doing a painting of Captain Cook in the Sovereign Hotel along the street—for the princely sum of four beers and a meat pie. Imagine that!

The story goes that everything was fine until some tourists arrived. They must have been lost to get north this far by road, which was worse than atrocious at that time. I had come up myself a few years back to pick up a couple of horses. When I got to Cooktown and over to Leffi Bowman's, all I had on the back was a stack of steel pipes tied in a heap along the deck. The road was so bad it had broken every weld on my stock crate! Leffi and I cobb-and-co'd all the pipes back together with no. 8 wire, in the semblance of a stock crate, and I trucked the horses south to Millaa Millaa, unloaded the horses and pushed the crate over the side in a heap. Yep, I reckoned those tourists must have been lost to get to Cooktown at that time.

The licensee's missus was engrossed in conversation with the well-heeled tourists and the cultural exchange they had to offer, not to mention the prestige, and Bill and Barry were getting a bit tired of all the carry-on. Being crocodile hunters they may have looked a little out of the ordinary, but they had plenty of money from their lucrative trade, and they certainly had a thirst. Service was lacking.

A young lad from about town walked to the doorway and inquisitively peeped in. Barry beckoned him. 'How would you like to earn ten bob?' This to the lad was a fortune, and his eyes opened wider than his ears. 'Well, all you have to do is go across the road to the post office and send a telegram,' said Barry, as the lad nods his head and runs his tongue along his lip. 'Here's another ten bob to cover it. Hang on while I write her out for you. Right, now you got that?'

'Yes Mister!' The lad jammed his hat down until it folded his ears, and he took off.

'Good lad,' called Barry after him.

The neglected, thirsty drinkers leant on the bar, smoked and waited patiently for developments. Junior Baines carried on with his painting of Captain Cook, up the ladder.

The young lad sprinted to the post office to send the telegram, and was about to head for the door in great haste to spend his ten bob when the post master called, 'Hey! Hang on, young fellow. You may as well deliver it for me.'

'Right.' The boy takes the telegram and pockets the shilling and asks, 'Where do I have to go to? I hope it's not too far, 'cause I ain't got me bike.'

'Straight across the road to the publican's missus, at the Sovereign,' said the post master.

The boy, revelling in his new-found fame and fortune, announced with a flurry to all and sundry from the hotel doorway, 'Telegram for the missus!' He gave the crocodile shooters a knowing wink from under his battered hat, and he tossed the shilling. All heads turned to the doorway.

'Come, come, young man,' and with a flourish the missus adjusted her glasses, then opened the telegram with a gesture of aristocratic flare. Imagining it was of some immeasurable importance, she began to read aloud, 'Dear Madam, What about some service'—her voice trailed to a whisper—'for the bastards along the other end of the bar!'

I was still gazing in wonderment at the murals when the proprietor approached and put both hands flat on the bar in front of me. 'Well now, you look like you're going somewhere. What'll it be?'

'Yeah,' I replied, 'bit of a jaunt. Riding down to see Vernon Atkinson and his wife Anne at Minnamoolka.'

'You are joking? That's way in behind Ingham somewhere ain't it? How far is that?'

'About four hundred mile.'

With that, he poured me the biggest glass in the bar. 'Here,' he said, 'that's on me. Stirrup cup if ya like.'

I took my time drinking the beer, and was remembering my friends and other times, and contemplating the adventure I was about to undertake. The proprietor came back and said, 'Is that your horse tied up outside?'

'Yeh,' I said, 'That's my mare. Pretty ain't she?' The mare stood patiently with a light swag rolled behind the cantle and two light panniers on the shoulder. She was a magnificent animal; fit, well-shod and ready for the journey.

'Well, you better get going mate. You've a long ride ahead.'

'Can't go yet,' I said.

'Why not? What's holdin' ya up?'

'Well,' I said, with a cheeky grin, 'That's a bloody long way to ride on one stirrup!'

I downed the second beer, said goodbye to those shadows on the wall, gathered my reins and rode out of Cooktown, heading south to the Lion's Den.

THE WAKE

Loosewire Lloyd and I pulled up at the edge of the road near the pub in Almaden in North Queensland. Looking all about at the desolation, we reckoned the early settlers must have had some fun around here, but they left in a hurry a hundred years ago.

There was an aged, traditional railway building out on the flat, and there were hunks and heaps of old iron everywhere. Old railway bogies and equally rusty lengths of pipe twisted and clawed, like tentacles from some underground monster, at the blue sky and the hovering molly hawks,.

Oh God, it was hot and the grass was dry as chips. Everything I touched or walked on went crunch. Over a way, some contented mixed-coloured Brahman cattle lay on their bellies, forelegs back and heads held high, chewing their cuds like bovine pharaohs, such was their dignity. Every now and again one would flap an ear to shift the flies.

There was not a sound anywhere. We walked about and there was nobody to be seen. All we needed was some fuel, and we had parked at the only bowser in town, which looked like it had grown out of the hard dry ground. The bowser station must have run away in the wind or been eaten by white ants.

'What an amazing place! Where is anybody?' asked Lloyd.

Then a voice called, 'G'day! G'day ya bastard! G'day!'

We looked all around; still nobody. The voice repeated the greeting, and we spotted the culprit. A sulphur-crested cockatoo slowly edged his way down a tree and sat handy on a low branch, about head high. He spoke to himself in some incoherent sentences which seemed to give him pleasure. Then he leant out of his hideaway amongst the leaves, had a sideways gawk at the pair of us, and repeated his greeting.

I said to Lloyd, 'You keep him amused and I'll go and find somebody.'

I walked to the pub, along what hardly qualified to be called a street. When I stepped inside the doorway, away from the heat and glare, all I could see was black. When my eyes became a little more adjusted, I saw half a dozen working men along the bar. They were standing about six feet apart with a big glass of beer in front of each one, and they were all staring at me as though I had reneged on my last shout.

'I would like to buy some petrol. I'm going to Wrotham Park and I'll be calling in to top her up on the way out tomorrow.'

The barman just nodded, dropped the keys on the bar and gave one of the drinkers a sideways nod in the direction of the petrol pump. I never heard a single word spoken all the time I was in there.

As we went through the doorway and out onto the road my reluctant petrol attendant said, 'He died, ya know. He just bloody died!'

'Did 'e?' I said. 'That's bloody sad news.'

As he trudged towards the pump, with more of a shuffle than a shift, I thought he must have lead in his boots. He kept shaking his head from side to side, and his grey bush hat, sitting high and loose on his head, had trouble keeping up with the nodding motion. Going by the wide, dark sweat stain around the band on the crown, it had had plenty of practice over the years.

'Hey, Lloyd,— 'e died ya know.' Lloyd took one look at my companion and got the drift in one.

'Well that's bloody tough goin'. Died ya reckon? Stone the bloody crows—makes ya wonder.'

'How much d'ya want?' asks the nodding hat.

'Fill 'er up' says Lloyd, 'fill 'er up. Bugger me—died ya reckon, beggared if I know mate. Ya never know, do ya?' Just when we had solved all the problems of the unknown—'G'day you bastard' screeches the cockatoo from the tree.

'Square up at the bar, mate.' So we all went to the bar and I paid for the fuel. Lloyd looked at me and we looked at everybody else looking at us in the most unwelcoming fashion. 'Better get,' said Lloyd. 'It's a long trot down the

351

Mitchell.' So we walked out, greeted by the heat, the haze and the molly hawks.

'Ya can kinda tell 'e died, can't ya,' said Lloyd with a grin, and lifted his hat and gave his crown a scratch.

As we got to the ute one of the drinkers from the pub, who must have been on his way as we left, stood in the dusty roadway to have a chat.

'Bloody up and died, they reckon,' said Lloyd, in a most concerned manner. 'It's a bloody shame. What did they call 'im out 'ere?' he asked, trying to get a clue. He had leaned over with his elbow on the bonnet and his chin cradled in the cup of his hand. He stamped a foot to shift some flies while waiting for an answer.

'Blue, mate. Just Blue.'

There was a pause, and then he added, "E was the station master's dog, old Blue dog. Never gonna be another one like 'im.' And he sloped off along the street with his head on his chest, studying his boots, while his arms hung loosely at his side. He stopped, slowly turned around to say 'Never!' then continued on his way.

'Struth!' I said, 'Fancy that mate—'e's a bloody goner!'

'Well bugger me,' said Lloyd. 'Poor old bloody Blue dog, eh! 'e bloody died. Ya never would've picked it!'

'G'day ya bastard!' came the voice from the tree.

And so we went on our way with a full tank and the memory of a dog we never knew.

LIST OF WORDS

anabranch An alternative route, usually dry, for water during floods; or a billabong (water hole) remaining when the river returns to its normal course after flooding.

antbed (or **anthill**) An earthen conglomerate constructed by an ant colony, becoming larger over time.

antpad A well-worn arterial track from an antbed or anthill, made and used by the ants going to and fro in food gathering.

baldy Cattle or horses with a blaze of white hair down the face.

ballpeen hammer A double-headed hammer—one side for striking, the other rounded for burring rivets.

bang–tail muster All stock have the end of the tail hair cut off square, as positive identification.

basalt Porous volcanic rock.

battlers Hardworking honest toilers, often poor.

big house The main homestead residence on a property.

billy lids Small children.

blow (**it of a blow**) Time for resting.

blowing horses Horses gasping for breath under exertion.

blue A bit of a fight (scrap).

bogie A bath.

boil up To boil the billy or quart pot on fire to make tea.

bore casing (or **macaroni**) Steel-pipe casing for a drilled water borehole.

bough shed A pole-constructed shed with wire netting and green leafy branches for a roof, making a cool shady place to work, or put plants.

break (pen break) A netting-wire fence built to contain sheep on a droving route each night.

breaker A young horse being handled and trained (broken in) for stock work.

brisket The chest.

bronco branding A method of securing cattle for branding by the use of bronco horses and ropes.

bronco horse A sturdy horse used to haul the ropes when bronco branding.

brood mare Female horse of breeding age.

brownie A fruit cake cooked in a camp oven.

brumby An untamed horse running in the wild.

bull drover A specialist drover who can handle mobs of bulls as they are driven from one station's breeding property to another.

bull straps Heavy leather straps, usually carried by stockmen around the waist, for tying up thrown cattle by the hocks.

bundy Bundaberg rum (OP = over proof).

bungee A friend (Aboriginal origin).

bushed Turned out to spell (as with horses); lost.

camp-drafting A system of drafting cattle in the bush on horse-back. A horse with this exceptional skill is known as a 'camp horse'.

capped rail A rail fastened across the top of two gateway posts to hold them firm.

carbide light When water is added to a piece of rock carbide held in a specially designed canister, a clean burning gas is produced—which, when lit, gives off a white light.

carpet snake A non-venomous Australian python.

cattle pad A well-defined cattle track.

Chinaman, Chow A man of Chinese origin.

clay pan A dry, desolate, eroded place with no topsoil or vegetation.

cleanskin mickey A large unbranded male calf.

clumper A horse with heavy-horse genes (such as Clydesdale, Shire or Percheron), suited to light harness, or as a pack horse or bronco horse, for branding work.

Cobb and Co. twitch A double strand of no. 8 fencing wire twisted tightly with a pritchel around a post and rail, or any such construction that requires a firm hold; from the name of the famous coach company.

cockerbullies Tadpoles.

cocky's joy Golden Syrup.

cogged (of horseshoes) With the heels bent down at right angles to provide better grip for the horse.

coit Backside.

concertina leggings A very old style of legging used by Australian stockmen. The central concertina section is made of pliable, oily kip leather, and is reinforced with solid hide, top and bottom.

Condamine bell A horse bell, traditionally made from the blade steel of an old cross-cut saw, with a metal striker. Used by stockmen and drovers, it was hung from a leather strap or greenhide thong around a horse's neck. As no two bells sounded the same, the horse could be located, day or night, by the sound of its bell.

cooee A traditional call in the bush (Aboriginal origin).

coogee A nondescript milking cow.

to corduroy To lay timber sticks and trash across sand, bog or mud at right angles to the travel direction, so as to provide traction.

corned beef Beef cured by rubbing coarse salt and quick cure into it, then dried.

crib A cut lunch.

crickle grease Golden syrup.

crook Unwell.

crow-bar A steel bar about 6 feet long and with a wedge-shaped end used for digging in hard ground or as a lever for heavy timber work etc. Sometimes referred to as a brown snake.

currant bun The sun.

damper A basic bush food, like a scone, cooked on the embers of a campfire or in a camp oven.

Dee billy A D-shaped billy, a collection of which forms a 'nest', with each billy fitting inside the next. The biggest is the beef billy. They were packed inside a leather pouch on top of the camp cook's packhorse load.

demijohn An earthenware half-gallon jar encased in a wickerwork basket.

dinkum, fair dinkum Honest, true.

the Dividing Range The Great Dividing Range runs the full length of the eastern side of the Australian continent. It acts as a watershed, with rivers flowing east to the Coral and Tasman seas, south to the South Australian coast, and north to the Gulf of Carpentaria.

djungerie Small, shy, hairy men, feared by children, from the Aboriginal spiritual world, or Dreaming.

dog bait 1080 poison, for dingo eradication.

droving plant A group of horses equipped for droving work.

durry A hand-rolled cigarette.

flunky An offsider or helping hand, usually not well qualified.

fresh A quick rise in the water level of a river.

gibbers Rounded stones.

gin (also **lubra**) Aboriginal woman.

ging A shanghai.

giz-gog sauce A homemade sauce, from gooseberries.

Gladstone bag A rounded, elongated, leather hand-grip bag, gusseted at both ends, with a sliding clasp latch and ribbed leather handle; widely used by doctors.

from go to whoa From beginning to end.

to go bush To head out to places unknown.

good sorts Of good quality.

goolie A stone (Aboriginal origin).

Greasy The cook.

hammer and tack Following as closely as can be.

hands high A horse's height as measured by hands, based on a man's hand being 4 inches (about 10 cm) wide.

hard yakka Hard manual work.

hazer A horseman who controls a beast by riding at a gallop on its far side, to enable the bulldogger to dive off his horse, take the beast by the head and wrestle it to the ground.

head ringer The head stockman in a cattle camp.

Hell, west and crooked In a desperate hurry and total disarray.

hip shod The stance of a horse with the weight off one hind leg.

to hit your straps Of harness animals, to pull hard and go like hell.

hobbles A chain with two short straps used to tie a horse's front legs together. The horse can still walk to graze.

Holy Cow! An exclamation of surprise.

horse collar Leather sheaths stuffed with straw and shaped to fit a horse's neck. Steel hames are fitted to the collar, and on them (at the point of the shoulder) are flat hooks on which to fasten the trace chains, which pull the implement or wagon. I have seen hollow steel collars with hickory hames.

horse tailer A specialist stockman and horseman who tends and is responsible for the horses in a droving plant.

humping wheat Carrying and stacking 3 bushel bags (about 80 kg) of wheat.

humpty doo Unpredictable.

irons Stirrups.

jackaroo A male stockman in training (an apprentice).

to jump the rattler To ride illegally on a train.

kick A trouser pocket.

kooty skeeters and wonga bugs Any living creature that walks, crawls, flies or slithers; most also bite.

Lion's Den A celebrated and still functioning shanty pub of the late 1880s, south of Cooktown on the Bloomfield road.

Loosewire Lloyd A great old bushman, mountain man and specialist fencer who was a Second World War veteran, New Zealand Divisional Cavalry.

Now deceased.

the makings Tobacco and cigarette papers.

maul A heavy wooden mallet for driving steel wedges for splitting logs.

miggles Marbles.

missus A matriarch, head of the household.

mocker Clothes; hence tidy town mocker for 'going to town', as opposed to 'groppy mocker'.

molly hawk (or **black kite hawk**) An Australian bird of prey.

the morning star Venus, which heralds the dawn and is also the first star in the evening.

Murri An Aboriginal person (used in parts of Queensland and New South Wales).

navvies' shack The living quarters of railway fettlers or workers.

night horses One or two very good horses that are kept in—to run in the mustering horses in the early morning, or to use in an emergency. In a droving plant, such horses are usually exceptional in every way and are treated accordingly, as all their skills are depended on, especially in night work with cattle.

off-sider A person who works with and assists the boss.

oily kip Soft, pliable waterproof leather used in the gussets of pack bags. R. M. Williams used it for leggings and some boots.

out-station A humble dwelling for stockmen, usually many miles from the main homestead, from where they mustered cattle from even further out.

over the fence Unreasonable or unfair.

pack bags Two leather bags slung on hooks off the 'tree' of the pack saddle, one each side, and held in place by a leather surcingle (strap); used to carry equipment.

packhorse plant A group of horses harnessed with pack saddles.

pannikin (also **pintpot**) Enamel or metal drinking cup.

pea rifle A .22 calibre rifle.

pen break A fence surround, made of steel posts and heaving netting wire, constructed at the close of each droving day to contain the sheep overnight.

poddy calf An unbranded and orphaned calf that may need to be hand-reared.

poll   The top of the head: 'polled' means without horns.

port   A suitcase (from portmanteau).

pound yard   A small drafting yard with many gates on its perimeter, situated in the cattle yards just before the crush entrance towards the dip.

quart pot   A traditional stockman's oval, flat-sided steel or copper billycan, with a lid shaped as a cup and fitting snugly at one end. It has oval handles and is carried in a leather pouch on the near side (left) of the saddle.

quick cure   An additive to salt to help corn beef and retain its colour.

railway jigger   A manually operated conveyance once used to transport a few workers along a railway line.

rattler   A slow moving train, usually a mail train or rail motor; 'jumping the rattler' was to hitch a ride as a non-paying passenger.

ringer   Stockman. The term probably originated from the traditional Australian technique of controlling a mob of cattle by ringing, or turning, them into a circle, like a Catherine wheel. Quite amazingly, they keep going round and round for a while. To then peel them off, to unwind them as it were, and walk them away in a line as a travelling mob was a sight to see. This work required great horsemanship and cattle sense.

ripple iron Similar to corrugated iron, but stronger and with smaller corrugations; used for external wall construction.

R.M. R.M. Williams, a legendary Australian.

roan As in horses or cattle, a complete blending of red and white hair all over the body (red roan); can also be black and white hair (blue roan).

to root To buck (horses).

to run scrubbers To chase wild cattle on horseback in timbered country in order to throw and tie, or yard them, before branding.

Scobie hitch An intricately plaited leather–lace knob on the handle of a stock whip, named after a family of celebrated whip plaiters.

scrub Thick, nondescript timbered country. In northern parts, the term is used in an uncomplimentary way to describe rainforest.

scrubbers Cattle which tend to be in hard, timbered country and have probably never been yarded.

seat awl A steel spike of six inches or so with a leather turk's head (plaited knot) on the hand-held end, used for teasing the stuffing in a saddle when it has become compacted.

to shanghai To take someone away without their consent.

shy Short of the correct number or tally.

slab house A dwelling with walls constructed of vertical hand-hewn boards, roof trusses of sapling poles held in place by wooden pegs, and thatched with slabs of stringybark.

on the slate To give financial credit.

slip tail A moveable rail used at a gateway. The rail end fits into an elbow cut in the gatepost, and is sometimes held in place with a wooden peg.

smoko Usually tea and damper, scones, brownie cake or similar food eaten at morning or afternoon tea time.

snug up To be dragged to the fire by a strong bronco-branding horse, with the use of a green-hide rope.

to square off To apologise.

to square up To pay one's dues (debts).

spear grass   A grass with vicious barbed spear-shaped seed heads, which render wool useless and can penetrate the carcass.

spring cart   A double shafted, leaf-sprung wagon with two big iron-shod wooden-spoked wheels, drawn by a single horse.

stag bullock   An aged bullock that never fattened and avoided being mustered, and has grown massive horns and become an ever-vigilant leader.

stamper battery   A steam-powered, belt-driven, camshaft operated vertical stamper for crushing gold-bearing ore.

stinker   An old billy (male) goat.

stockee   A stock inspector or overseer.

stone pitched   Paved with flat flag- or cobble-stones to provide an even and solid surface for steel wagon wheels.

sugar-doodle   A somersault.

sulky   A light-weight vehicle with twin wooden shafts and two iron-shod spoked wheels, drawn by a single horse.

swag A blanket, clothes and personal gear rolled neatly inside a canvas swag cover (about 8 feet by 10 feet) and held firmly by a couple of spare stirrup leathers or red-hide reins or other dual-purpose item.

swingle tree or bar An extremely strong hardwood bar to which the trace-chains from the horse collars are connected. They, in turn, are coupled to the wagon by a central 'S' hook.

tail pulling Attention to the tails of unhandled horses which, with time, become long, straggly and matted. They can be teased out with a sharp stock-knife in vertical drag strokes and, once thinned, the tail hair is then greased with fat and left to grow, free flowing and shining.

to take on the fly To jump aboard a train in motion.

talking about The calling out of horses to their friends from whom they have become separated.

teamster Generally a person who drove teams of horses that pulled or hauled heavy wagons, as did bullock drivers (bullockies). There were many women teamsters.

The Alice Alice Springs.

The Isa Mount Isa.

The Towers Charters Towers.

The Weal Camooweal.

trump The overall boss (top card).

waddy A hand-held stick that can be used as a weapon (Aboriginal).

wagonette A light four-wheeled horse-drawn vehicle, often used to cart gear in droving plants on plains country.

wait-a-while Lawyer cane—a forest climbing plant with long, unyielding tendrils of rose-like thorns.

walk-through cow shed A shed with milking machines installed, rather than the stall bails where cows were milked by hand.

wash pool In some places, sheep were washed in natural pools before blade shearing (with hand shears).

watch Riding around the cattle on camp at night.

willy wagtail A small slender-bodied dark bird with light under-belly and a long tail which it habitually wags sideways while chirping incessantly. The wagtail's flight is jerky.

Wrotham Park The home station of celebrated woman pioneer, Evelyn Maunsell, in Hector Holthouse's book, *S'pose I Die.*

Yackai! An Aboriginal exclamation of exhilaration.

yarraman An Aboriginal word for horse, meaning large teeth.

yunk Very young (children or animals, even baby birds in nests).